Extraordinary Sex Therapy

How do we help our clients discover the depth and breadth of sexual healing? *Extraordinary Sex Therapy* offers a range of innovative health-based approaches and models to explore the complexities inherent in sexual pleasure and potential as well as in trauma, pain, and dysfunction. The practitioners whose work is represented here expand the clinical conversation about sex beyond performance goals and tread courageously into unquantifiable realms of sexual and relational desire, health, and transformation.

All of these practitioners describe work that embodies therapeutic collaboration with their clients as they confront sexual concerns that include body image, emotions, meanings, and nuances of partner interactions along with the influence of neurobiology, language, gender, addiction, socioeconomics, and cultural conditioning about pleasure. Their interventions range from education, visualization, and role-play to identifying erotic archetypes, coaching about sensual touch, and using plant spirit medicines to activate imagination and spiritual connection. Their descriptions ring with singular authenticity, depending on their training and the particular clients and issues they address. Each practitioner provides clinical examples and techniques in enough detail so that readers can incorporate elements of these approaches into their own practices.

This book was originally published as a special issue of *Sexual and Relationship Therapy*.

Gina Ogden PhD, LMFT is an award-winning sex therapist, supervisor, researcher, teacher, and author. She is founder of the ISIS Network, an international collaboration of practitioners whose mission is to expand the practice of sex therapy to include the full range of personal and relational issues: physical, emotional, mental, and spiritual.

Extraordinary Sex Therapy

Creative Approaches for Clinicians

Edited by

Gina Ogden

Routledge
Taylor & Francis Group
LONDON AND NEW YORK

First published 2015 by Routledge

2 Park Square, Milton Park, Abingdon, Oxon OX14 4RN
711 Third Avenue, New York, NY 10017, USA

Routledge is an imprint of the Taylor & Francis Group, an informa business

First issued in paperback 2017

British Library Cataloguing in Publication Data
A catalogue record for this book is available from the British Library

ISBN 13: 978-1-138-84296-0 (hbk)
ISBN 13: 978-1-138-05968-9 (pbk)

Typeset in Times New Roman
by RefineCatch Limited, Bungay, Suffolk

Publisher's Note
The publisher accepts responsibility for any inconsistencies that may have arisen during the conversion of this book from journal articles to book chapters, namely the possible inclusion of journal terminology.

Contents

Citation Information

The chapters in this book were originally published in *Sexual and Relationship Therapy*, volume 29, issue 1 (February 2014). When citing this material, please use the original page numbering for each article, as follows:

Chapter 1
Introduction: Are we asking questions that help our clients?
Gina Ogden
Sexual and Relationship Therapy, volume 29, issue 1 (February 2014) pp. 1–7

Chapter 2
Sexotic therapy: embracing the exotic, irrational and paradoxical experience of living and loving
Alireza Tabatabaie
Sexual and Relationship Therapy, volume 29, issue 1 (February 2014) pp. 8–20

Chapter 3
Extraordinary interventions for extraordinary clients: existential sex therapy and open non-monogamy
Michael D. Berry and Meg Barker
Sexual and Relationship Therapy, volume 29, issue 1 (February 2014) pp. 21–30

Chapter 4
In search of Aphrodite: working with archetypes and an inner cast of characters in women with low sexual desire
Chelsea Wakefield
Sexual and Relationship Therapy, volume 29, issue 1 (February 2014) pp. 31–41

Chapter 5
An integrative medicine approach to the treatment of HSDD: introducing the HURT Model™
Keesha Ewers
Sexual and Relationship Therapy, volume 29, issue 1 (February 2014) pp. 42–55

Chapter 6
Compassionate authenticity: a treatment model for working with women with low libido
Lindsay B. Jernigan
Sexual and Relationship Therapy, volume 29, issue 1 (February 2014) pp. 56–67

Chapter 7
Sex addiction – an extraordinarily contentious problem
Paula Hall
Sexual and Relationship Therapy, volume 29, issue 1 (February 2014) pp. 68–75

Chapter 8
Calming the tempest, bridging the gorge: healing in couples ruptured by "sex addiction"
Ruth Cohn
Sexual and Relationship Therapy, volume 29, issue 1 (February 2014) pp. 76–86

Chapter 9
Getting in touch with touch: a use of caressing exercises to enrich sensual connection and evoke ecstatic experience in couples
Linda De Villers
Sexual and Relationship Therapy, volume 29, issue 1 (February 2014) pp. 87–97

Chapter 10
"Extraordinary" sex coaching: an inside look
Patti Britton and Sarah Rose Bright
Sexual and Relationship Therapy, volume 29, issue 1 (February 2014) pp. 98–108

Chapter 11
Sexual healing with Amazonian plant teachers: a heuristic inquiry of women's spiritual–erotic awakenings
Yalila Espinoza
Sexual and Relationship Therapy, volume 29, issue 1 (February 2014) pp. 109–120

Chapter 12
Reclaiming women's sexuality: the intersection of Shamanic practices and sex therapy
Linda E. Savage
Sexual and Relationship Therapy, volume 29, issue 1 (February 2014) pp. 121–131

Chapter 13
Opinion Piece: In praise of "ordinary" sex therapy
Pam Henderson
Sexual and Relationship Therapy, volume 29, issue 1 (February 2014) pp. 132–134

Please direct any queries you may have about the citations to
clsuk.permissions@cengage.com

Notes on Contributors

Gina Ogden is an award-winning sex therapist, supervisor, researcher, teacher, and author of nine books on sexuality and relationships. She is founder of the ISIS Network, an international collaboration of practitioners whose mission is to expand the practice of sex therapy to include the full range of personal and relational issues: physical, emotional, mental, and spiritual.

Alireza Tabatabaie is a medical doctor and COSRT accredited sex & relationship therapist practising in the UK and Iran. He is currently a PhD candidate at the University of Cambridge, UK, investigating the socio-cultural and religious aspects of sexual health and education.

Michael D. Berry is a PhD candidate in research psychology at University College London, UK, and a psychotherapy trainee at McGill University, Montreal, Canada. His research focuses on the psychosexual treatment of sexual dysfunctions.

Meg Barker is a senior lecturer in psychology at the Open University, UK, and a therapist specializing in sexual and relationship therapy. She has previously published books on sexuality and counselling and is co-editor of the journal *Psychology & Sexuality*.

Chelsea Wakefield is a Jungian-oriented sex therapist in private practice near Asheville, NC, USA. She is the creator of *The Luminous Woman® Weekend*, author of *Negotiating the Inner Peace Treaty*, and is working on a book about sexual individuation and working with archetypes in sex therapy. She is a member of the American Association of Sexuality Educators, Counsellors and Therapists and the National Association of Social Workers.

Keesha Ewers is an IFM Board certified functional medicine and ayurvedic practitioner as well as a certified sexologist, clinical hypnotherapist, enneagram coach, EMDR (eye movement desensitization and reprocessing) therapist, and host of *Healthy YOU! Radio*. Her clinic, Fern Life Center, is a fully staffed, nurse practitioner run, integrative medicine primary care clinic that focuses on individualized and personalized medicine.

Lindsay B. Jernigan is a licensed clinical psychologist in private practice in Vermont, USA, where she offers individual and couples therapy, group workshops, and professional supervision. Her practice is in an integrated health care center where she co-founded Eastern View Mental Health: A Center for Authentic Development.

Paula Hall is a sexual and relationship psychotherapist in private practice. She provides individual therapy and group programmes for people with sex addiction and is founder of the Hall Recovery Course which is now available around the UK. She is also the current chair of ATSAC (Association for the Treatment of Sex Addiction & Compulsivity) and trains on their professional certificate programme. Hall is also the author of *Understanding and Treating Sex Addiction* (Routledge, 2012).

Ruth Cohn is a certified sex therapist in private practice in the San Francisco Bay Area, USA. She specializes in work with adults with histories of childhood trauma and neglect and their intimate partners and families. She also practices EEG neuro-feedback. She is the author of *Coming Home to Passion: Restoring Loving Sexuality in Couples with Histories of Childhood Trauma and Neglect* (Praeger, 2011).

Linda De Villers is an adjunct professor at the Graduate School of Education and Psychology, Pepperdine University, Los Angeles, CA, USA. She is also a psychologist who does private practice as an AASECT-certified supervisor and diplomate of sex therapy. She is the author of two books, *Love Skills* (Aphrodite Media, 2001) and *Simple Sexy Food*™ (Aphrodite Media, 2012), and presents nationally and internationally on these and other related sexuality topics.

Patti Britton is a world leader in sexology. She writes books, articles, and curricula, and is a popular professional speaker/presenter/trainer in sex coaching and clinical sexology. She is the author of *The Art of Sex Coaching* (W.W. Norton & Company, 2011) and co-founder, with Robert Dunlap, of the premier global online training/certification organization SexCoachU.

Sarah Rose Bright is a sex and pleasure coach/educator. She is at the leading edge of the development of sex coaching in the UK. She is the first certified professional sex coach and the only certified sexological bodyworker in the UK.

Yalila Espinoza is an intimacy counsellor, who received a PhD in East–West psychology and spiritual counselling training from the California Institute of Integral Studies in San Francisco, USA. She offers individual counselling and group workshops focused on sexual initiations in the USA and Canada. She is committed to holistic and embodied presence that is grounded in a symbolic and sensual co-creation with all living beings.

Linda E. Savage is an AASECT-certified sex educator, MFT and licensed psychologist in private practice. She has specialized in sex therapy for 30 years and trains therapists in the pleasure model. She is the author of *Reclaiming Goddess Sexuality* (Divine Feminine Publications, 2012), which blends ancient wisdom with current clinical knowledge and also the author of *Maiden, Mother, Wise Woman: Reclaiming Our Sexuality*, a companion CD of guided meditations.

Pam Henderson is a psychosexual therapist working in private practice in Cambridge, UK

INTRODUCTION
Are we asking questions that help our clients?

"Out beyond ideas of wrongdoing and rightdoing, there is a field. I'll meet you there."
—Jalal ad-Din Rumi

What questions are we asking our clients?

"How many times do you have intercourse per week/ month/ year?" This was a question considered primary to my sex-therapy training in the mid-1970s. I was coached to follow it closely with: "How often do you achieve orgasm?" These and other performance-focused questions to address with clients were rooted in the then revolutionary concepts that it is possible to quantify sexual response (Kinsey, et al., 1948, 1953) and that the success of sex therapy can therefore be based on behavioral goals and measurable outcomes (Masters & Johnson, 1966, 1970).

Quantifiable approaches to dysfunctions of intercourse and orgasm have proven effective, even launching a booming pharmaceutical industry since 1998 with the advent of Viagra. But effectiveness has been mainly for clients who present with issues that require no attention to emotional and relational complexities that accompany sexual problems. Despite their limitations, performance outcomes remain a fixed idea in much of sex research and sex therapy training today, too often inhibiting what we ask our clients about the depth and breadth of sexual healing, pleasure, and potential, and what we ask ourselves about which approaches and models are most appropriate to use.

To complicate matters, today's focus on performance and goals also discounts advances in neuroscience (e.g., Fisher, 2004; Komisaruk, et. al., 2006) along with the combined wisdom of a spectrum of therapies that indicate sexual experience to be far more complex than outlined by quantitative research; it is rooted in the fabric of our clients' lives, from physiology, mental conditioning, emotional engagement, and spiritual meaning to the influences of socioeconomics and culture (e.g., Bateson, 1972; Britton, 2005; Bass & Davis, 1988; Daniluk, 1998; Ellison, 2000; Herman, 1992; Jung, P., et al., 2001; Klein, 2006; Kleinplatz & Moser, 2006; Maltz, 1987; McCarthy & Metz, 2004; Morin, 1995; Perls, 1969; Savage, 1999; Schnarch, 1991; Zilbergeld, 1992).

The truth is, there is no objective way of defining sex, let alone sex therapy, whether the purpose of sex therapy is to help clients recover from sexual abuse or create optimal conditions for ecstatic union. For solidarity in this belief I am in debt to colleagues who publicly posit the inherent complexities and suggest that the academic and scientific conversation about sex and sex therapy may be in danger of becoming so narrow as to create a kind of dysfunction in itself (Britton, 2005; Eisler, 1995; Kaschak & Tiefer, 2002; Kleinplatz, 2001; Perel, 2006, Whipple, et al., 1992).

Separately and together, many of us have sought to broaden the therapeutic conversation about sex beyond specific performance outcomes, and I am doubly in debt to these colleagues and many more for support in my conducting an independent survey: "Integrating Sexuality and Spirituality" (ISIS) (Ogden, 2002, 2006a), which has evolved into the integrative ISIS approach to further both therapists and clients in exploring the intangibles of sexual experience: feelings, meanings, and relationships, as well as behaviors (Ogden, 2006b, 2008, 2009, 2012, 2013).

It was this collegial spirit that moved me to welcome the invitation to edit this issue of *SRT*—to offer a place for new voices along with established ones. This issue does not pretend to be definitive. The range of sexual concerns is admittedly vast, well beyond the scope of these pages. You will note omissions, including age-related factors, most gender and cultural intricacies, the sequelae of affairs, and more. The intent of this *SRT* issue is to go deep and be thought-provoking and practice-oriented, rather than be broad and inclusive. The practitioners whose work is represented here explore the complexities of sexual and relational health, pleasure, and even the nature of transformation. Their models and approaches are "extraordinary" because they expand their practice of sex therapy beyond specific outcomes to incorporate realms of sexual experience that cannot be counted and measured by methods currently available to sexual science. Transpersonal psychiatrist Carl Jung called such realms the "irrational facts" of experience (1970, p. 505).

What Is Extraordinary Sex Therapy?

In a spirit of collaboration, I define extraordinary sex therapy here through the lens of each contributor to this issue, as if together they comprise an intelligent and sophisticated kind of convenience sample, n = 12. Think of these practitioners as being asked to describe the proverbial elephant of sex therapy, each from a unique point of view. Their descriptions ring with singular authenticity, depending on their culture, their training, and the particular clients and issues they address. They offer clinical examples and techniques so that readers can incorporate elements of each approach into their own practices. Their collective offerings reveal some cardinal principles of extraordinary sex therapy, all predicated on the understanding that many crucial facts about sexual experience are, in fact, "irrational."

Complex thinking sparks erotic creativity

The issue of sexual complexity is addressed by Alireza Tabatabaie, whose "sexotic therapy" expresses the paradoxical nature of both sexual experience and sex therapy as grounded in his native Iranian culture, and exemplified in Persian erotic poetry. For him, extraordinary sex therapy involves a conceptual framework that acknowledges and celebrates the erotic, and helps couples travel the often surprising distances between intimacy and passion.

Inclusive language expands sexual diversity

Michael Berry and Meg Barker focus on language as a transmitter of sexual information; a vehicle through which to expand norms in a practice of sex therapy where limited language often reflects social limitations and prejudices about sexual diversity. For them, extraordinary sex therapy is based in queer-friendly consciousness and syntax that is plural enough to welcome all genders, orientations, and varieties of relationship, no matter how creative.

New information awakens sexual awareness and desire

Three innovative models address low sexual desire in women. All interweave elements of complexity, collaboration, and nuanced language.

In "Working with Archetypes and an Inner Cast of Characters," Chelsea Wakefield offers a Jungian perspective to unlocking treatment impasses for women and their partners. For her, extraordinary sex therapy means searching for Aphrodite—helping women identify eros-inhibiting patterns of energy and discover their own erotic identities through exploring and playfully engaging the creative realm of the sexual psyche.

Keesha Ewers contributes perspectives of integrative medicine and brain research to post-traumatic dimensions of low sexual desire through her HURT model: Healing UnResolved Trauma. For her, extraordinary sex therapy includes biological, emotional, and relational methods to help women recognize the automatic negative thinking that distracts from pleasurable erotic cues so that they can activate new neuronal paths for pleasure and power.

Lindsay Jernigan's model of Compassionate Authenticity is based on eclectic approaches to moving beyond cultural messages that women ought to sacrifice themselves in the name of caretaking others. In her model, extraordinary sex therapy involves three critical treatment goals for women: 1) Building curiosity about their own sensuality; 2) Differentiating from their sexual partner/s; and 3) Redefining the scope of sexual and emotional caretaking.

Curiosity promotes sexual healing

What is "sex addiction?" Is it an excuse for impoverished impulse control? A symptom of ADHD or PTSD? A sign that a couple is in the wrong relationship? Two authors tackle this contentious subject, each acknowledging the potential for extraordinary healing once the focus is turned from ideological argument to close attention to each client's story.

Paula Hall presents her BERSC model for addressing the biological, emotional, relational, social, and cultural roots of sex addiction. For her, extraordinary sex therapy involves providing a here-and-now opportunity for clients to address old attachment wounds—especially effective in group therapy, which allows shared empathy and emotional attunement among group members.

Ruth Cohn de-stigmatizes sex addiction for a couple, helping them reorganize their story of compulsive porn use and blame into a coherent narrative so that rogue fragments no longer wreak havoc on their relationship. For her, extraordinary therapy for sex addiction means careful history-taking to help clients redefine the roots of their problematic behaviors, then applying a non-judgmental lens to what she calls "the geography of desperation."

Intelligent touch wakes up our bodies

Of all the senses, touch is the first to develop; awareness of touch is as essential to life as to sexual development. Linda DeVillers offers rationale and techniques for teaching sensuous touch as part of sex therapy, where it is too often avoided or assigned as sensate focus homework for clients to fumble through on their own. For her, extraordinary sex therapy includes making sure individuals and couples know how to give—and receive—intelligent touch.

Active education creates active change

Patti Britton and Sarah Bright introduce sex coaching as an active form of sex education. The behavioral elements that coaching adds to effective sex therapy may include beyond-the-office activities such as helping a client choose sex toys, or observational bodywork, such as viewing a client's masturbation patterns. Extraordinary sex coaching involves witnessing, educating, and supporting men, women, and trans clients in their quest for self-esteem and pleasure.

Non-ordinary paths open new sexual vistas

In the next two papers, extraordinary sex therapy is described in non-ordinary terms through aspects of shamanic principles and practice that include the use of plant spirit medicines. Each author offers extraordinary applications of what can transpire when clients dare open the doors of perception to explore the depths of old sexual traumas and vastness of new sexual landscapes.

Yalila Espinoza draws from her ongoing research in Peru, in the Shipibo vegetalista tradition. "Spiritual-Erotic Embodiment with Amazonian Plant Teachers" highlights sexual healing through energetic purification: physical, emotional, mental, and spiritual. For her, extraordinary sex therapy involves increased sensory and cognitive awareness; transforming the relationship with self and others, connecting with subtle energies, and with God.

Linda Savage describes the intersection of shamanic practices and sex therapy during a women's weekend intensive in the San Diego hills, which she co-led with a shamanic elder. Here, extraordinary sex therapy involves yoga breathing, movement, guided meditation, ceremony with plant spirits, and holding space for awakening feminine sexual energy.

Extraordinary sex therapy depends on extraordinary clients

The final offering in this issue is Pamela Henderson's "In Praise of Ordinary Sex Therapy." She eloquently points out what is truly extraordinary about sex therapy: our clients. Which brings us back to our primary task: to focus on the clients we serve.

+ + +

What shines through each of these contributions is that whatever else we do as sex therapists, we must first of all do no harm. *Primum non nocere* is the oath of medical ethics, and is the underlying ethic of sex therapy, whether our primary mode is psychology, sociology, or neurobiology, whether we are psychotherapists, teachers, bodyworkers, or coaches; no matter where we look for information and inspiration—in the literature, in the spirit world, in our own experience.

To do no harm requires that we clear ourselves of whatever keeps us mired in our own dramas so that we can focus always and steadily on the well-being of our clients, not on how much we know (or fear we don't know) as therapists. The core of extraordinary sex therapy is relatively ordinary after all, although it is not always simple to practice. It is that we listen to our clients, create safe space, encourage movement—physical, emotional, mental, and spiritual, and trust our clients to do their own work so we are not working harder in their therapy than they are.

The Gifts We Bring to Our Practice of Sex Therapy

Each extraordinary sex therapist is extraordinary in his or her own way (or "their" own way, in the pluralistic parlance of Berry and Barker). To elicit this point in my trainings, I often ask group members to introduce themselves by saying their names plus one word or phrase that describes the special gift they bring to their practice of sex therapy. This exercise creates an informative positive container for the group and also serves to spread clinical expertise beyond the leader, so that from the very beginning of our training we are modeling a collaborative approach. At a recent training, these were the individual gifts that group members brought into the room:

- Compassion
- Clarity

- Enthusiasm
- Presence
- Curiosity
- Openness
- Heart
- Years of experience
- Understanding
- Listening
- Appreciation
- Warmth
- Firm boundaries
- Acceptance
- Complexity
- Trust
- Surprise

Each statement offered by these therapists suggests a view of sex therapy that is larger than the classic focus, that is: diagnosing dysfunction and helping clients achieve intercourse and orgasm. Rather, the qualities these group members introduced as their gifts suggest dimensions that cannot be graphed or quantified.

Notice, too, that all of these qualities may also make for extraordinary sex as well as extraordinary sex therapy. This is not to suggest that extraordinary sex therapy connects clients and sex therapists in some kind of purient way. Rather, it is to say that to promote positive change for our clients involves more than the models and techniques we use; it also involves the energies we embody ourselves, as therapists. Call it mirror neurons, vibrational resonance, or Freudian transference, our presence may actually spark the change our clients seek—as long as we take the ego out of that statement. When we can step beyond goals and outcomes to encourage (and sometimes surprise) our clients to step into their own experiences of acceptance, trust, compassion, and on and on, we are helping them find their own paths to sexual potential that is beyond count and measure, and most certainly beyond our ability to predict, or sometimes even imagine.

All the approaches and models in this issue of *SRT* are steeped in the consciousness that effective therapy is a complex and collaborative venture we undertake with our clients. Further, they all embrace the concept that sex is not separate from the rest of our lives; sex is energy that exists in relationship—to other beings, to ideas, to the culture we inhabit. Whether such consciousness takes the form of reframing dysfunction, pluralizing our therapeutic language, or broadening the landscapes of desire and therapy itself, extraordinary sex therapy has a common element: a high degree of creative flux. Our meeting place is in the client—body, mind, heart, and spirit. At the same time it is also "out beyond," in that poetic field described by Rumi—embedded in the kinds of questions we ask our clients and ourselves, beyond fixed ideas of what is good sex or bad sex or real sex, or even of what constitutes real sex therapy.

Gina Ogden, PhD, LMFT
Cambridge, Massachusetts
December, 2013

References

Bateson, G. (1972). *Steps to an ecology of mind.* San Francisco, Chandler Publishing Co.

Bass, E, & Davis, L. (1988). *The courage to heal: A guide for survivors of child sexual abuse.* New York: Harper & Row.

Britton, P. (2005). *The art of sex coaching.* New York: Norton.

Daniluk, J. (1998). *Women's sexuality across the life span: Challenging myths, creating \ meanings.* New York: The Guilford Press.

Eisler, R. (1995). *Sacred pleasure. Sex, myth, and the politics of the body.* New York: Harper Collins.

Ellison, C. (2000). *Women's sexualities: Generations of women share secrets of self-acceptance.* San Francisco: Jossey Bass.

Fisher, H. (2004). *Why we love: The nature and chemistry of romantic love.* New York: Henry Holt.

Herman, J. (1992). *Trauma and recovery.* New York: Basic Books.

Jung, C.G. (1970). *Civilization in transition.* In *The collected works of Carl G. Jung.* (Vol. 10). N.Y.: Harper Collins.

Jung, P.B. et al., (2001). *Good sex: Feminist perspectives from the world's religions.* Brunswick, N.J.: Rutgers University Press.

Kaschak, E. & Tiefer, L. (Eds.). *A new view of women's sexual problems.* Binghamton, N.Y.: Haworth Press.

Kinsey, A.C., et al. (1948). *Sexual behavior in the human male.* Philadelphia: W. B. Saunders.

Kinsey, A.E., et al. (1953). *Sexual behavior in the human female.* Philadelphia: W. B. Saunders.

Klein, M. (2006). *America's war on sex: The attack on law, lust and liberty.* Westport, Conn.: Praeger.

Kleinplatz, P.J. (2001). A critical evaluation of sex therapy: Room for improvement. In P.J. Kleinplatz (Ed.), *New directions in sex therapy: Innovations and alternatives* (pp. xi-xxx) Philadelphia: Brunner-Routledge.

Kleinplatz, P. & Moser, C. (Eds.). (2006). *Sadomasochism: Powerful pleasures.* New York: Harrington Park Press.

Komisaruk, B., et al. (2006). *The science of orgasm.* Baltimore, Johns Hopkins University Press.

Maltz, W. (1991). *The sexual healing journey: A guide for survivors of sexual abuse.* New York: Harper Collins.

Masters, W. & Johnson, V. (1966). *Human sexual response.* Boston: Little, Brown.

Masters, W. & Johnson, V. (1970). *Human sexual inadequacy.* Boston: Little, Brown.

McCarthy, B. & Metz, M. 2010. *Enduring desire: Your guide to lifelong intimacy.* New York: Routledge.

Morin, J. (1995). *The erotic mind.* London: Headline.

Ogden, G. (2002). *Sexuality and spirituality in women's relationships: Preliminary results of an exploratory survey.* Working Paper 405. Wellesley, Mass.: Wellesley College Centers for Research on Women.

Ogden, G. (2006a). *The heart and soul of sex: Making the ISIS connection.* Boston: Trumpeter.

Ogden, G. (2006b). The spiritual dimensions of sexual health: Broadening clinical perspectives of women's sexual desire. In M. Tepper & A. Owens (Eds.), *Sexual Health.* (Vol. 4. pp. 131–152). Englewood Cliffs, N.J.: Praeger.

Ogden, G. (2007) (3rd Ed.). *Women who love sex: Ordinary women describe their paths to pleasure, intimacy, and ecstasy.* Boston: Trumpeter.

Ogden, G. (2008). *The return of desire: a guide to rediscovering your sexual passion.* Boston: Trumpeter.

Ogden, G. (2009). It's not just a headache dear: Why some women say no to connecting sex and spirit, in A. Mahoney and O. Espin (Eds.), *Sin or salvation: Implications for psychotherapy* (pp. 105–25). New York: Routledge.

Ogden, G. (2012). Keys to the sexual mysteries: An integrative model for exploring clients' stories. In Kleinplatz, Peggy J. (Ed. Rev Ed.), *New directions in sex therapy: Innovations and alternatives.* Philadelphia: Brunner-Routledge. 337–353.

Ogden, G. (2013). *Expanding the practice of sex therapy: An integrative model for exploring desire and intimacy.* New York: Routledge.

Perel, E. (2006). *Mating in captivity.* New York: Harper Collins.

Perls, F. (1969). *Gestalt therapy verbatim.* Lafayette, Calif.: Real People Press.

Savage, L. (1999). *Reclaiming goddess sexuality: The power of the feminine way*. Carlsbad, Calif.: Hay House.
Schnarch, D. (1991). *Constructing the sexual crucible: An integration of sexual and marital therapy*. New York: Norton.
Zilbergeld, B. (1992). *The new male sexuality*. New York: Bantam Books.

Sexotic therapy: embracing the exotic, irrational and paradoxical experience of living and loving

Alireza Tabatabaie

Faculty of Education, University of Cambridge, Cambridge, United Kingdom

This paper seeks to shed light on an extraordinary therapeutic approach that I refer to as "exotic sex therapy" or "sexotic therapy". This approach originated out of my fascination with the irrational aspects of the "living and loving" experience, developed through my understandings of the scientific and non-scientific literature (particularly Persian love poetry) in this regard, and established through my clinical work. Central to sexotic therapy is a conceptual framework that acknowledges and celebrates the erotic life as a complex, ambiguous, exotic and paradoxical journey. It recognises the inherent challenges and paradoxes of maintaining a balanced passionate and intimate long-term relationship and invites embracing obstacles as potentially constructive and excitement enhancing. In this paper, I start with sharing my experiences and understandings of the relevant literature in Part One, proceed with some clinical discussions in Part Two, and finish by illustrating sexotic therapy with a case study in Part Three.

Part One: On the irrational experience of living and loving

Writing for a special issue (quotes are from the call for contributions) that is dedicated to "extraordinary sex therapy", one that cordially invites the contributor to "expand the conversation about sex beyond [the conventional] measurable outcomes" and seeks to embrace "energy, growth and transformation" and "the irrational facts of experience" (are you still with me?) stimulates a different writing style: one that is extraordinary, energetic, exotic and different from the conventional ways of academic writing. Having said this, and also since I am going to talk about "exotic" sex therapy here, please let me keep this exotic/unusual way of writing.

I just need to tell you something about my background because it is essential to understanding my approach. I was raised in Iran – a country with old civilisation and rich culture in which tradition and modernity coexist simultaneously. I was brought up to accept that life is not a straight flat highway from A to B with extra large traffic signs and excellent visibility. My lived experience was simply complicated. I can probably argue that we – Iranians – in general are not strange to and uncomfortable with uncertainties, ambiguities, complexities and paradoxes; these are, in fact, the heart of our culture (Mottahedeh,

2009). As articulated by one of the most influential modern Persian poets – Sohrab Sepehri (2004, p. 46–48, translations and punctuations modified by me):

کار ما نیست شناسایی "راز" گل سرخ،

کار ما شاید این است

که در "افسون" گل سرخ شناور باشیم.

پشت دانایی اردو بزنیم.

...

کار ما شاید این است

که میان گل نیلوفر و قرن

پی آواز حقیقت بدویم.

Our mission is not to fathom the "mystery" of the red Rose.

Our mission is perhaps

To float in the "charm" of the red Rose;

To pitch our tents beyond Wisdom.

...

Our mission is perhaps

To run between the Lotus flower and the Century

After the Echo of Truth.

In this complex way of conceptualising life, many of us learn how to handle various forces that pull and push us from different directions, some of which are often perceived as contradictory. For example, we learn how to simultaneously adhere to collectivism while maintaining an individualistic approach; or to juggle the structured with the unstructured; or to reconcile the old and traditional with the new and modern; or to live a life in which both your mother and your wife love you! In fact, many of us – Iranians – are brought up to automatically deal with, embrace, and enjoy life as something that is in some way inherently paradoxical; particularly when it comes to the experience of living and loving.

When I was a school-boy, we were taught an old Arabic saying which can be translated as: "man is greedy for what is forbidden". I used this insight to make sense of one of the oldest (and probably most confusing) stories of humankind: Adam and Eve, and the forbidden fruit. They were living in a beautiful garden in heaven that met all their needs.

There were tons of trees in this garden and only one that God had forbidden them to eat from. Between all these fruitful trees, they craved the one they could not eat from the most. . .. and there was temptation; . . . and you know what happened next.

While such a phenomenon – craving the forbidden – somehow made sense to me, as a young adolescent in love with Persian literature, I was still uncomfortable with and confused about the dramatic level of masochism that underpinned Persian love poetry. Let me bring an example: A common portrayal of love in Persian literature is a story of a desperate male figure who is masochistically losing or has lost everything in his life being infatuated by a beautiful (not necessarily) young female figure (although it is a "male" figure in Rumi and Shams's case) that seems to be painfully distant and unattainable, sometimes due to heartlessness and ignorance and sometimes the disapproval of others. Strangely, the more the suffering, ignorance, pain, hurt and cruelty, the greater the passion and infatuation! Let me bring just two examples (and they are countless): first from Rumi – one of the greatest thirteenth-century Persian poets of all time whose work is considered to transcend national and ethnic borders. He articulates, rather beautifully, a lover's address to his/her beloved as:

ای بدی که تو کنی در خشم و جنگ
با طربتر از سماع و بانگ چنگ

ای جفای تو ز دولت خوبتر
و انتقام تو ز جان محبوبتر

نار تو اینست نورت چون بود
ماتم این تا خود که سورت چون بود

از حلاوتها که دارد جور تو
وز لطافت کس نیابد غور تو

نالم و ترسم که او باور کند
وز کرم آن جور را کمتر کند

عاشقم بر قهر و بر لطفش بجد
بوالعجب من عاشق این هر دو ضد

The harm you do in anger and in strife
is sweeter than an ecstasy of harp strings.

Your cruelty is better than a victory,
Your scolding's more desired than life itself.

This is your fire – what does your light look like?
This is the funeral – what's your wedding like?

As for the sweetness which violence holds,
and for your subtlety, none plumb your depths.

I weep and then I fear he/she will believe me,
and then from kindness moderate his/her violence.

I love so much his/her violence and his/her grace –
how wonderful, I love these two extremes! (Rumi, 2006, 1575–1580)

The second one is from the great twelfth/thirteenth-century Persian poet Farid al-Din Attar – the theoretician of Sufism whose influence on Persian poetry and culture is immense:

درد عشق تو که جان می‌سوزدم
گر همه زهر است از جان خوشتر است
درد بر من ریز و درمانم مکن
زانکه درد تو ز درمان خوشتر است

Even if your love's pain that burns the soul
is all poison, it is sweeter than life.

Pour out pain for me and don't offer a cure
since your pain is sweeter than any cure. (Attar, 2007, p. 89)

I would always ask myself, "But why? What on earth is wrong with these ancient Persian lovers!? Aren't these people crazy!? Don't they have any dignity!?" and more questions in this regard. An important point in the verse of many great Persian poets (such as Nizami, Attar, Rumi, Saadi and Hafiz) is the weakness of wisdom and rationality in comprehending and explaining the experience of love. Hafiz, for instance, reminds himself (and us) that "Hafiz! With love's pain, be content; and be silent: / Love's mysteries, reveal not before people of reason" (1891, p. 612); or as Saadi advises, "Wisdom outwears souls/seeking rest, thou need to breed love" (Saadi, cited in Zandi and Yazdani, 2011, p. 39). Who I was to argue with these great figures? But it was just irrational and did not make sense at all... Well, it did not take a long time before I became able to comprehend this myself (if you know what I mean). It was as irrational and paradoxical as it appeared to be; it was painful, and it was pleasurable. In my search for truth in the seeming absurdity and "wrestling for sense in spite of nonsense", logical inconsistency gradually grew into emotional consistency and I found beauty, joy and life (Krûminienë, 2004, p. 32).

As time went by and I grew older, I learnt that this "attraction towards the forbidden and challenging" is not just a Persian phenomenon; it is rather universal, has been probably experienced by the majority of human beings throughout history, and is probably not strange to you. It is probably at the heart of old sayings such as "the forbidden fruit tastes the sweetest", or "stolen water is sweet, and bread eaten in secret is pleasant", or "the grass is greener on the other side of the fence". When it comes to romance and love, it also underpins some of the most everlasting wonders of life – why are we attracted towards the wrong person, the problematic, the difficult, the challenging, and the hard-to-reach? Why the greater the pain, the greater the pleasure? And why although longing craves fulfilment, fulfilment dampens longing? And so forth. Think about the story of Layla and Majnun (Nizami, 1997) for example; or Shakespeare's *Romeo and Juliet*; or Margaret Mitchell's *Gone With the Wind*; even Carrie Bradshaw's cravings for Mr. Big in *Sex and the City*; you name the rest. All these great stories have one thing in common: "attraction towards the forbidden and challenging".

Having suffered/enjoyed this myself, I was always keen to know more about this great mystery of "living and loving". A turning point in my understanding was reading Jack Morin's (1996) insightful – *The Erotic Mind* – during my training as a sex and relationship therapist. In the introduction of this book, Morin looks critically at three major psychological schools of thought in relation to eroticism and sexual fulfilment. First, the "pathology-oriented" approach, highly influenced by essentialism and psychoanalysis, which, as argued by Morin, fails to take into consideration the inevitable unpredictability and dynamic changeability of erotic desires. Keen to put labels on people and stigmatise, the pathology-oriented approach attacks, for example, those attracted to the "wrong" people, those who have the "wrong" kinds of orgasms, or those who express "infantile" or "perverse" sexual preferences such as a strong interest in oral or anal stimulation. This perspective proposes such a narrow path for "normal" and "healthy" erotic development that hardly anyone can fully attain it.

Second, the "neat-and-clean" approach which is more recent compared to the "pathology-oriented" framework and was popular during the era of sexual optimism, experimentation and freedom of the 1960s and 1970s. This approach is mainly influenced by behaviourism and humanism. Behaviourism sees human sexuality as governed by predictable rules of learning and argues that uncontrollable and out of place tendencies of sexual desire can be well managed by the step-by-step methods of reward and punishment. Humanism, optimistically emphasising human nature's inherent tendency towards health, growth and self-actualisation, acknowledges sexual variations and embraces individualism. Both approaches have been highly influential in the development and practice of modern sex therapy, pioneered by William Masters and Virginia Johnson. Masters and Johnson, as noted by Morin, considered sex to be a fundamentally simple "natural" function and held the quite exaggerated view that the removal of inhibiting factors and obstacles (e.g. anxiety, guilt, ignorance or unrealistic expectations) is all that is required for a happy/fulfilling sex life. Morin argues that such an unrealistic "neat-and-clean" perspective, quite popular in today's practice of sex therapy, is so preoccupied with unblocking sexual arousal that it fails to take into consideration its creation, intensification and "irrational power". In the end, he proposes a third perspective which is the focus of the book – "the paradoxical approach".

Morin believes that people's most intense and memorable erotic responses are the result of the interaction of two competing forces: first, an attraction that pulls them towards their object of desire and second, one or more obstacles in their way, resistant to their attraction, in the partner or in the situation itself (such as, doubts on the reciprocity of interest and the desired-one's hesitance, the person's unavailability or inappropriateness, the disapproval of outsiders, the risk of being hurt, or any other impediment to easy access). Morin refers to these as potentially arousal enhancing obstacles and observes (1996, p. 56): "we [may] have a far stronger response to our attractions if they are made more difficult, challenging, uncertain or dangerous by having one or more obstacles to overcome". (Let us go back to the greatest and most passionate love stories of all time and think about the role of obstacles in arousing the passion and infatuation in these cases…). Morin translates this complex concept into a simple formula that is easy and fun to work with. He calls it “the Erotic Equation” (p. 43):

$$\text{Attraction} + \text{Obstacles} = \text{Excitement[orArousal]}.$$

In explaining the erotic equation, he shares with us his insight into human sexuality which is not easy to argue with. He notes (p. 44): “we humans want some restrictions to push against. We just don’t want them to be so harsh that they choke off our sexuality entirely”. He argues that many things that inhibit arousal (such as, for example, doubt, unavailability, distance, anxiety, guilt, etc.) may, under different circumstances, amplify it. He invites us to acknowledge the contradictory and dual nature of erotic life and embrace a “paradoxical approach” towards eroticism; one that while recognising the joys of erotic life, does not deny or downplay its risks.

Morin is not alone in believing that obstacles can amplify excitement, and articulating it. For example, Freud (1922/1953) has also observed that passion must be fuelled by uncertainty and frustration. He notes (p. 213): “Some obstacle is necessary to swell the tide of libido to its height; and at all periods of history whenever natural barriers in the way of satisfaction have not sufficed, mankind has erected conventional ones in order to enjoy love”. Stoller (1979, p. 4) also argues that excitement “implies anticipation in which one alternates with extreme rapidity between expectation of danger and just about equal expectation of avoidance of danger, and in some cases, such as in eroticism, of replacing danger with pleasure”. He adds (pp. 6–7) that excitement “is a dialectic, a rapid oscillation between two possibilities (and their affects). One we tell ourselves has a positive, the other a negative outcome: pleasure/pain, relief/trauma, success/failure, danger/safety. Between the two lies risk”.

The paradoxical effect of obstacles in enhancing arousal is also observed by others through, for example “the Romeo and Juliet effect” (Driscoll, Davis, & Lipetz, 1972) or “frustration attraction” (Fisher, 2004). According to Fisher (2004), adversity heightens the passion in love and when normal, well-adjusted lovers encounter barriers to their attractions and romantic feelings, they may love and desire even more intensely. Discussing the biological basis of frustration attraction, Meloy and Fisher (2005) note that when a reward is delayed in coming, neurons of the brain’s reward system sustain their activation which leads to an increase in the activity of central dopamine that is the main neurotransmitter associated with sexual desire and romantic love (Fisher, 2004).

Theoretically speaking, ironic process theory (Wegner, 1994) and reactance theory (Brehm & Brehm, 1981) have also something to offer. In ironic process theory, the paradoxical effect of thought suppression makes us become preoccupied with something we are asked not to think about (“don’t think about a white bear”). So when we are asked not to think about a particular person (romantically or sexually) as he/she is not “the right one” for us, or when the desired one is made somehow unattainable and distant, our cravings are amplified. Reactance theory assumes that when our freedom to act, think or feel is somehow threatened, we get an unpleasant feeling called reactance, which motivates us to try and regain our freedom by performing the forbidden (Brehm & Brehm, 1981). This may explain why in romantic love we desire more those people whom we feel we should not, cannot or are not supposed to have (Brehm, 1992).

Esther Perel has also discussed the same issue from a different angle. She (2007) assumes that in general, we – human beings – share a fundamental need for security, per-manence, reliability, stability and continuity – qualities that for easy reference I group here as “intimacy” – which pushes us toward committed relationships; however, paradoxically, we also have a strong need for adventure, excitement, novelty and change –

qualities I refer to here as "passion", also for easy reference. Putting the institution of marriage into the socio-historical context, Perel notes that reconciling our need for intimacy and passion into one relationship used to be a contradiction in terms:

> Today, we turn to one person to provide what an entire village once did: a sense of grounding, meaning, and continuity. At the same time, we expect our committed relationships to be romantic as well as emotionally and sexually fulfilling. Is it any wonder that so many relationships crumble under the weight of it all? It's hard to generate excitement, anticipation, and lust with the same person you look to for comfort and stability, but it's not impossible. (Perel, 2007, p. viii)

I agree with her. These two – passion and intimacy – do not necessarily coexist comfortably and peacefully, as they are not associated with the same levels and qualities of arousal, are not regulated by the same neurochemical pathways and are also socio-culturally situated (Diamond, 2004; Fisher, 2004). In fact, as Hatfield and Rapson (1987) observe, passion and desire are most intense when relationships are new and somewhat uncertain. Often over time, as security increases in relationships, passion and desire do not increase linearly; "security frequently seems to give way to sexual boredom" (Hatfield and Rapson (1987, p. 273).

In this context, Perel (2003, 2007) notes, the troublesome aspects of power and control dynamics (such as dependency, surrender, jealousy, aggression, even hostility) that can be an obstacle/challenge to intimacy and security in an egalitarian intimate relationship can, when properly eroticised, be transformed into powerful sources of excitement and become highly desirable. Even extramarital affairs, Hatfield and Rapson note (1987), with all the difficulty and anxiety they create, may revitalise a couple's deteriorating excitement. Like Morin, Perel also invites us to acknowledge these paradoxes and think about ways in which we can mix difficulty with ease and introduce risk to safety, mystery to the familiar, and novelty to the enduring.

Let us go back to our ancient Persian lovers; apparently they were not as crazy as I imagined after all. Rather, they were probably very clever; they just perfectly knew how to use obstacles and pain to add fuel to the fire of their passion! No wonder Rumi says: "I will never exchange your sorrow for the two worlds"; or:

من درد تو را زدست آسان ندهم
دل برنکنم زدوست تا جان ندهم

از دوست به یادگار دردی دارم
کآن درد به صد هزار درمان ندهم

I will not lose the pain of your love easily.
I will not forsake my love till I die.

I have my love's pain as souvenir,
And I will never exchange this pain for countless remedies. (Rumi, 2008, p. 530)

Part Two: Sexotic therapy (exotic sex therapy)

In my clinical work as a sex and relationship therapist I often discuss with my clients that maintaining a contemporary Passionate AND Intimate Relationship (PAIR), one that keeps a balance between security/familiarity and excitement/novelty, one that walks carefully between feeling abandoned and overwhelmed by the partner, one that celebrates individuality and togetherness simultaneously, is NOT a given. It is not an already done-and-dusted framed painting with lifetime guaranty that one finds effortlessly and conveniently hanged on the perfect position of the wall of his/her room. Living a PAIR is creating that framed painting from scratch: obtaining the right painting tools, brushes and colours and preparing properly the blank canvas; then painting a desired picture together with your partner, skilfully; then choosing the right material to make the right frame that is the right size and can hold the painting properly; then choosing the right place on the right wall to hang it on; and then maintaining it constantly with care. I always suggest that you may need to reconsider the painting, change the colours or shapes, erase some parts or add extra bits, depending on your situation; be prepared and open to it. You may need to change the frame as it might break over time... All these stages require continuous education and practice. In my opinion, we do not "get" married; we "do" marriage, everyday. It is a full-time job.

I agree with Morin and others (including Persian lovers) in acknowledging the paradoxical and irrational nature of the erotic life and embracing it. A sexually fulfilling encounter is not necessarily intimate and close (e.g. one-night stand or casual sex); couples whose sex lives are steamy and satisfying might have serious problems when it comes to intimacy and security. On the other hand, a close and intimate relationship does not necessarily mean that the couple have no problem in their sexual functioning. In fact, as discussed above, sometimes the increase in intimacy, closeness and security give way to sexual boredom and desire/arousal difficulties. In my clinical work when relevant and appropriate, I discuss these paradoxes and contradictions with my clients comprehensively. As noted by the twentieth-century philosopher, essayist and poet – George Santayana – "contradiction means only variety, and variety means spontaneity, wealth of resource, and a nearer approach to total adequacy" (cited in Krûminienë, 2004, p. 32). Clients often find this quite useful, comforting and reassuring. They start to make sense of many of their challenges and contradictions. So the first step in my approach is to normalise contradictions and paradoxes (do you remember the first few paragraphs where I discussed my background?), reassure clients and invite them to open a space in their day-to-day life dedicated to reconstructing/maintaining their PAIR.

Central to my approach is constructing balance: a balance between the two forces that while seemingly contradictory are also complementary. If a relationship is problematic on the passion (desire/arousal) side, it may also adversely affect the intimacy side and vice versa. Each PAIR requires good enough amounts of both, agreed and accepted by both parties depending on their situation, to function properly. Such balance is not static; rather, it is a dynamic, fluid, contextualised and person/couple-centred construct. Such endeavour is not easy and requires openness and flexibility. It also requires education. When we plan and implement sex education programmes for young people, we often forget that relationship education is a crucial component of it; what a huge mistake!

In maintaining such a balance between intimacy/security and passion/desire, I often employ an approach that I have recently called "exotic sex therapy" or "sexotic therapy". I was a trainee when I decided to incorporate the conceptual frameworks discussed in Part One and some of the "irrational facts of [the living and loving] experience" (Carl Jung, cited in Ogden, 2012, p. 337) in my clinical work. Resistant to my approach was the mainstream conservative culture of sex therapy that was mainly based on the Western/modern ways of interpreting normality and health; a certain "rational" perspective that is so uncomfortable with ambiguity and paradox and, as noted by Perel

(2003), so preoccupied with solving the conflict by prescribing "mature" and "adult" sexual agendas, that it fails to take into consideration the beauties of human beings' everlasting pleasurable fascination with the unknown and hidden, the mysterious, and the paradoxical.

The term "exotic" is defined by Merriam Webster Dictionary as "strikingly, excitingly, or mysteriously different or unusual". I have called this approach exotic sex therapy for three reasons. First, I personally like the term exotic and have found my clients to get excited and optimistic about an approach that is called exotic! Second, it is an approach that is exotically different from the conventional ways of sex therapy (e.g. sees inhibitions and obstacles as potentially excitement-enhancing, embraces paradoxes, etc.) and employs various exciting, mysterious, unusual, paradoxical and extraordinary (i.e. exotic) perspectives and interventions. Finally, in developing this approach, added to the conceptual frameworks discussed above, I was influenced by Daryl Bem's exotic becomes erotic theory (EBE). In his article – "Exotic Becomes Erotic: A Developmental Theory of Sexual Orientation" – Bem (1996) suggests how biological variables might interact with experiential and socio-cultural factors to influence the formation of opposite-sex and same-sex desire in both men and women. Embedded within his theory and the part that is relevant to my approach is an argument that generalised physiological arousal, produced as a result of perceiving another person or the context as dissimilar, unfamiliar, and exotic can subsequently be experienced as erotic desire (Bem, 2000). I use this theory to suggest that an exotic factor in the other person, in the interpersonal encounter or the environment, can (further) stimulate sexual excitement. Many of us use this concept in our day-to-day clinical practice when, for example, suggesting our clients to "spice thing up" by using erotica or acting out sexual fantasies, or when encouraging them to exercise playfulness and naughtiness (Morin, 1995). Sometimes "bad" is "good" in sex.

In sexotic therapy, the focus is on helping a client/couple whose relationship has been unbalanced (particularly those shifted towards the intimacy, security and familiarity side) to get back on track through exotic interventions that acknowledge and celebrate the erotic life as an exotic, complex, ambiguous, sometimes irrational, and paradoxical journey. Sexotic therapy recognises the inherent challenges and paradoxes of maintaining a balanced PAIR in long-term and invites embracing obstacles as potentially constructive and excitement-enhancing.

Comfort can lead to boredom, so can discomfort lead to excitement and arousal. I often invite couples to explore their sexual life (of course responsibly, consensually and according to their core values) beyond their comfort zone – place-wise or time-wise. For example, I sometimes suggest to couples to take sex out of their bedrooms (of course taking into consideration privacy issue) and using other unfamiliar spaces in the house (e.g., kitchen, living room) that they may find exotic (Well, bedrooms are places that people mostly sleep, how come we expect their sex organs not to?). Changing the time of having sex is also an intervention that can bring novelty and exoticness, and therefore enhance excitement and arousal.

I am particularly interested in using obstacles and challenges and trying to interpret and use them as exotic arousal-enhancing factors acting in favour of my clients instead of against them. Anything that causes a problem can also be a potential remedy. Interpreting problems differently and exotically, they are potentially capable of providing clients with the joy and excitement of "problem solving"; like when we were kids and enjoyed solving a problem and overcoming an obstacle. This is the essence of playing: you face an obstacle, you overcome it, and then there is a reward and you go to the next level; the harder the challenge, the greater the excitement. For example, have you had the experience of prescribing sensate focus exercises for a sexually hypoactive couple or in the case of erectile difficulties, putting a ban on intercourse and they come back having had sex a few times in the past week? Some might refer to this as a paradoxical intervention (LoPiccolo, 1992), but most therapists do prohibit intercourse with a genuine intention of, for example, removing the pressure or relieving performance anxiety; what do the couple do? They see that ban as an obstacle to overcome exotically which enhances their arousal.

I sometimes suggest distance and unavailability. Think about a passionate reunion after a period of time (typical train station scene). There is an old Persian proverb that says: "keep a distance, keep a friend". In our romanticised endeavours in finding the true love and our idealised urges to merge, we may forget that keeping a distance is as important as (and as essential to) seeking closeness. Although some of us probably prefer to believe that a true love is when our lovers cannot possibly live a moment without us, sometimes this "a moment without us" is all they need to truly love us. The challenge here, as Morin (1995, p. 63) notes, is "to find [and keep] an *optimal distance* – one that is neither too close nor too far".

Playing "hard to reach" games which are at the heart of seduction might also be useful: "I know you like me, but you need to fight for me". Silence, although not much celebrated in conventional sex therapy, can also be a change and exotic factor in long-term relationships; it can work as an obstacle in couples' communications whilst having sex and create fun, thrill and arousal. Add having sex in complete darkness to this; the result is sometimes phenomenal.

Having sex semi-naked instead of fully-naked can also be a way of creating distance and unavailability and an effective intervention. Many people find 'partially/almost naked' to be more arousing and sexier than 'fully naked'. In sexualised societies where sex is almost everywhere, sometime not being sexy might be exotically the sexiest way. Sometimes our overwhelmed-with-nudity brains want some obstacles to easy access, so we can live our fascinating potential of imagination and enjoy the thrill of mystery, anticipation and discovery. In this context, modesty can also be sometimes an exotic excitement-enhancing factor.

Here is an interesting one and one of my favourite therapeutic interventions: encouraging a couple to have sex immediately after a heated argument. This is a crystal example of an intervention based on the principles of sexotic therapy on many levels. Why? . . . I leave it to you to answer.

I think I have said enough. I should probably finish soon and let your creativity and imagination flow and fly. Just let me discuss the case of Julia and Richard to put what I discussed above into practice.

Part Three: The case of Julia and Richard

Julia and Richard had been married for 12 years when they attended my clinic for their dissatisfaction with their sex life. A brief assessment revealed that Richard had developed erectile problems (attaining and maintaining). Understandably, this had also affected his sexual desire as well as, not surprisingly, Julia's. His erectile problem had been developed over the past 2 years and he had no difficulty in the first 10 years of their marriage. At the time of the clinical visit, he had problems more than 75% of the time and had already used oral medications without any positive impact. Following a thorough assessment, biomedical issues were ruled out. Relationship-wise, both emphasised that they had a loving and intimate relationship, although this problem had caused some minor relational

Figure 1. Julia and Richard's relationship map.

difficulties. I found their intimacy genuine. Richards's erectile problems had led him to develop fear of failure and performance anxiety.

After an assessment that took two sessions, I discussed with them that a possible explanation to their situation might be that in their gradual transition from the "passionate" couple to the "intimate" couple, they had gone too far towards intimacy, security and familiarity. I comprehensively discussed the paradoxical approach and drew the simple diagram in (Figure 1).

They both identified their relationship with this diagram and seemed to have found it reassuring and comforting. Julia was comforted because she had started to feel unloved and distant. Richard was also comforted because he was seeing their relationship in a different way; "we are too intimate and loving and that's why our sex life is problematic". Too much love and intimacy is often good news for couples and gives them confidence. They were both pleased with the discussion and left the third session. Two weeks later in their fourth session, they discussed the positive effect of the previous session on Richard's confidence and performance. But it was still far from good-enough. I suggested the next time they were having sex, they would not fully undress and would keep their bedroom curtains and window open just a few inches. They were surprised by this and asked for explanation. I just very briefly said: "to put some home-made obstacles in the way of your sex and to add the thrill of potentially being seen while having sex"... they came back the next session, happy and surprised. Richard had been able to properly attain and maintain satisfactory erections on three occasions out of five attempts. What had happened? First, I had perhaps comforted and reassured the couple by providing an explanation about their problem which had a focus on their strengths (intimacy and security) rather than shortcomings; second, I had possibly helped Richard to move towards restoring his confidence; and finally I had probably helped them to use the obstacles (anxiety and fear) that up until that moment had worked against them, for them as arousal enhancing. Anxiety and fear were translated into thrill. They indicated that they had also experienced semi-nakedness as something exotic; a barrier that its novelty had added to Richard's excitement and therefore helped his arousal (erection). In the next few sessions, I helped them to find various exotic ways to develop and expand their erotic experience and find a balance between passion and intimacy.

To summarise, exotic sex therapy or sexotic therapy is an approach that takes into consideration and embraces the irrational, paradoxical and complex nature of the erotic life. It is rooted in an understanding that a sexually fulfilling encounter is not necessarily intimate and close, and a close and intimate relationship does not necessarily mean that the couple have no problem in their sexual functioning. It emphasises the complexities and dual nature of maintaining a contemporary balanced PAIR or marriage. Central to this approach is a balance between the two forces that while seemingly contradictory are also complementary. It invites couples to revisit their relationship and reconstruct their balance, which is fluid and dynamic in nature, with openness and flexibility. A comprehensive discussion of these paradoxes with clients is the first step and can be followed by various exciting, mysterious, unusual, paradoxical, and extraordinary techniques and interventions to help a client/couple whose relationship has been unbalanced, particularly shifted towards the intimacy side, to get back on track.

References

Attar, F. (2007). *Fifty poems of `Attar*. [K. Avery & A. Alizadeh, Eds. & Trans.]. Melbourne: re. press.

Bem, D.J. (1996). Exotic becomes erotic: A developmental theory of sexual orientation. *Psychological Review, 103*(2), 320–335.

Bem, D.J. (2000). Exotic becomes erotic: Interpreting the biological correlates of sexual orientation. *Archives of Sexual Behavior, 29*(6), 531–548.

Brehm, S.S. (1992). *Intimate Relationships*. New York: McGraw-Hill.

Brehm, S.S., & Brehm, J.W. (1981). *Psychological reactance: A theory of freedom and control*. New York: Academic Press.

Diamond, L.M. (2004). Emerging perspectives on distinctions between romantic love and sexual desire. *Current Directions in Psychological Science, 13*(3), 116–119. doi:10.1111/j.0963-7214.2004.00287.x

Driscoll, R., Davis, K.E., & Lipetz, M.E. (1972). Parental interference and romantic love: The Romeo and Juliet effect. *Journal of Personality and Social Psychology, 24*(1), 1–10.

Fisher, H. (2004). *Why we love: The nature and chemistry of romantic love*. New York: Henry Holt.

Freud, S. (1922/1953). A special type of choice of object made by men (contributions to the psychology of love I). In E. Jones (Ed.), *Collected papers* (Vol. 4). London: Hogarth Press.

Hafiz. (1891). *The Divan-i-Hafiz*. [H. W. Clarke, Ed. & Trans.] (Vol. II). Calcutta: Government of India central printing office. Retrieved from http://archive.org/details/thedivan01hafiuoft

Hatfield, E., & Rapson, R.L. (1987). Passionate love/sexual desire: Can the same paradigm explain both? *Archives of Sexual Behavior, 16*(3), 259–278.

Krûminienë, J. (2004). John Donne's Homilies: Paradox as an Instrument of theopoetic evocation. *Literatūra, 46*(4), 29–37. Retrieved from http://www.doaj.org/doaj?func=fulltext&aId=1235210

LoPiccolo, J. (1992). Postmodem sex therapy for erectile failure. In R.C. Rosen & S.R. Leiblum (Eds.), *Erectile disorders: Assessment and treatment* (pp. 171–197). New York: Guilford Press.

Meloy, J.R., & Fisher, H. (2005). Some thoughts on the neurobiology of stalking. *Journal of Forensic Sciences, 50*(6), 1472–1480.

Morin, J. (1995). *The erotic mind: Unlocking the inner sources of passion and fulfilment*. New York: HarperCollins.

Mottahedeh, R.P. (2009). *The mantle of the prophet: Religion and politics in Iran*. Oxford: Oneworld Publications.

Nizami Ganjavi. (1997). *Layla and Majnun*. [C. Turner, Trans.]. London: John Blake Publishing Ltd.

Ogden, G. (2012). Keys to the sexual mysteries: An integrative model for exploring clients' stories. In P.J. Kleinplatz (Ed. Rev Ed.), *New directions in sex therapy: Innovations and alternatives* (pp. 337–353). Philadelphia: Brunner-Routledge.

Perel, E. (2003). Erotic Intelligence. *Psychotherapy Networker, 27*, 24–31.

Perel, E. (2007). *Mating in captivity*. New York: HarperCollins.

Rumi, J. (2006). *Spiritual verses*. [A. Williams, Ed. & Trans.]. London: Penguin Books Limited.

Rumi, J. (2008). *The Quatrains of Rumi: Ruba 'iyat-e Jalaluddin Muhammad Balkhi-Rumi*. [A.G.R. Farhadi & I.W. Gamard, Trans.]. San Rafael, CA: Sufi Dari Books.

Sepehri, S. (2004). *The water's footfall.* [I. Salami & A. Zahedi, Trans.]. Tehran: Zabankadeh.
Stoller, R.J. (1979). *Sexual excitement.* New York: Pantheon.
Wegner, D. (1994). Ironic processes of mental control. *Psychological Review, 101*, 34–52.
Zandi, H., & Yazdani, S. (2011). A Study of Paradox in the Works of Saadi, the Persian poet, and John Donne, the English Metaphysical Poet. Presented at the International Conference on Languages, Literature and Linguistics, Singapore. Retrieved from http://www.ipedr.com/vol26/8-ICLLL%202011-L00016.pdf

Extraordinary interventions for extraordinary clients: existential sex therapy and open non-monogamy

Michael D. Berry[a] and Meg Barker[b]

[a]*Department of Psychology, University College London, London, United Kingdom;* [b]*Faculty of Social Sciences, Open University, Milton Keynes, United Kingdom*

Open non-monogamy is an important and sensitive area for psychotherapists and counselors, as it can challenge the practitioner's personal values, and professional assumptions about dyadic sexual relationships. Additionally, the increased attention to non-monogamy in popular culture, and the sometimes-ambiguous distinction between "monogamy" and "non-monogamy" make understanding the potentials and challenges of non-monogamy a priority for sex therapy specialists. We recommend existential sex therapy as a useful, non-pathologizing model for addressing the needs of openly non-monogamous clients. Both therapists with limited experience working with non-monogamous clients, and those seeking new theoretical frameworks, may benefit from the use of existential sex therapy. We identify core existential therapy principles, including bracketing (i.e. reflectively identifying, and endeavoring to separate out one's own prejudgments and values) and horizontalizing (i.e. working to situate the client's sexual identity within the wider context/horizon of their life experience), as methods for affirming the importance of freedom and belonging in light of the client's subjective, lived experience.

Aside from being heteronormative, love stories are historically dyadic: boy meets girl, they fall in love, and triumph or tragedy ensues as they live happily ever after, or not. The contemporary proliferation of lesbian, gay, bi, trans, and queer (LGBTQ)-oriented art and activism has helped to challenge the heteronormative framework of love narratives. Also, within the discipline of psychotherapy, growing attention to LGBTQ issues has helped show that people rarely, if ever, fit precisely into sexual binaries, and "straight or gay" is an untenably reductive way to view sexual identity. Despite the progress made in issues of sexual diversity overall, and LGBTQ issues specifically, the one-to-one assumption of sexual partnership seems to still be commonplace in the sex therapy field, necessitating the question: how can we effectively and appropriately work with openly non-monogamous and polyamorous clients?

It is important to acknowledge that clinicians have varying degrees of experience, and varying levels of comfort, working with non-monogamous clients. This article is intended primarily for clinicians with a lower level of experience in this area, and clinicians looking for new strategies and approaches in dealing with non-monogamous clients. We recommend existential therapy as a framework well-equipped to deal with both the common elements of human experience – the day-to-day challenges in one's professional or personal life associated with leading a less socially conventional life – and the unique challenges of open non-monogamies – associated with the need to define and establish a framework of personal meaning in relationships that may fall outside many people's (and many psychotherapists') conceptual frameworks. Below, we outline the core principles of existential sex therapy, including the focus on the multiple meanings the client may have surrounding sex, emphasis on the client's unique lived experience, and the importance of considering the client's sexual identity, behaviors and choices within the context of wider, unique lived experience.

Existential sex therapy is grounded in a non-pathologizing model of sexuality, which views human sexual behaviors as existing within a broad and diverse spectrum. This non-pathologizing approach rejects a binary view of "healthy" and "pathological," or "normal" and "abnormal." Instead, the existential sex therapist sees sexuality and sexual behavior as subjectively situated within the context, or horizon, of one's individual life. An underlying core objective of the existential approach is to confront and problematize the non-reflexive assumptions that may be reflected in socially conventional scripts of sexual health and normality. In this regard, our model of existential sex therapy is influenced by the work of contemporary researchers who seek to challenge traditional and non-reflexive notions of sexual health and pathology (e.g. Kleinplatz, 2012; Tiefer, 1995). This non-pathologizing psychotherapeutic model, we contend, provides an extraordinary means for addressing the extraordinary[1] experiences openly non-monogamous clients may bring into the consulting room.

Sex and subjectivity: the heuristic value of labels

Most sexual and relationship therapists are likely to encounter non-mainstream sexualities in their clinical practice. The capacity to deal with evolving normative frameworks, and widely variant client identities, is an essential skill for psychotherapists. Especially when working with diverse clients, even something so familiar as the language that we use has powerful implications. For instance, while terms like "straight" and "gay," or "monogamous" and "non-monogamous" or even "her" and "him" have a heuristic value, they inevitably restrict the ways in which we communicate about – and the ways we conceive of – ourselves and our clients. We might say that such terms are both enabling and constraining, as they enable us to communicate, but they never fully capture the client's subjective experience and identity. This linguistic issue is a clear illustration of the challenges we face when working from an existential framework: our concepts, and the labels we apply, are often inadequate in describing the complex world of sexuality. The very language we use in this paper provides a clear example. Throughout this paper we use the pronoun "they" in favor of the gender dichotomous singular pronouns "she" and "he," in discussing individuals, and in referencing individual clients (in effect, we use "they" as both a singular and plural term). Our hope is that this inclusive language may create a space for clients, and our readership, to self-identify according to their terms of preference, and in accordance with their subjective, lived identities.

Clients may define their identities and sexual practices in reference to particular categories; lesbian, gay, bisexual, queer and trans being common terminology. The burgeoning popular interest in open non-monogamies (Barker & Langdridge, 2010), the increasingly hazy distinctions between monogamy and non-monogamy (Barker, 2011), the problematizing of traditional language and conceptualizations of sexuality, and the increasingly salient presence of such non-heteronormative sexualities in western society make clinical competence in these areas an important priority. As many clinicians attest:

a language for discussing the client's sexuality, shared between client and therapist, is essential. Below, we provide a brief overview of the non-monogamous relationship patterns therapists may encounter amongst their clients, before illustrating the relevant key principles of existential psychotherapy, and showing how they may be of particular use in working with non-monogamous clients.

Non-monogamies

Recent research indicates that non-monogamy is a heterogeneous category, which includes a number of variant relationship arrangements. These arrangements differ with respect to the following: (1) the kinds of relationships engaged in, (2) the degrees of transparency and disclosure involved, and (3) specific terms of mutually-agreed conduct (behavioral "contracts") or the lack of them. In the academic and research sphere, a number of articles and books have begun to explore the issue of non-monogamy (Adam, 2006; Barker & Langdridge, 2010; Brandon, 2011; De Visser & McDonald, 2007; McLean, 2004; Rubin, 2001; Sheff, 2005). Additionally, there is an expanding range of books and publications for individuals involved in, or considering, non-monogamous relationships (Benson, 2008; Matik, 2002; Ravenscroft, 2004; Taormino, 2008). Taken together, these bodies of work seek to disambiguate the high levels of flexibility and variability seen in openly non-monogamous ways of relating.

The most common forms of open non-monogamy in western culture are swinging and open relationships (both of which involve the possibility of sexual encounters outside a primary relationship), and polyamory (which entails being open to a multiplicity of simultaneous love-relationships) (Barker & Langdridge, 2010). Swinging and open relationships involve a primary and enduring partnership, with acceptance of additional sexual encounters or relationships. In both, the primary couple may engage in encounters together or separately from their partner, although swinging implies a shared experience involving both members of the couple, while open relationships do not necessarily connote a shared experience, and may imply more separate/individual extra-relationship activities (Easton & Hardy, 2009; Barker & Langdridge, 2010). It must be noted, however, that the way couples conceive their sexual relationships, and negotiate conduct agreements, can vary widely between couples, and within a single couple, over time (McLean, 2004). Equally, polyamorous relationship arrangements, which can involve multiple concurrent sexual and love relationships, vary significantly. As such, the existential psychotherapist must be prepared to deal with non-monogamous clients phenomenologically, on a case-by-case basis, taking into account the individuality and subjectivity of particular clients.

Within the sphere of open non-monogamies, specialized terms help provide a conceptual framework for understanding the nature of sexual and romantic relationships. Newer terms – such as "metamour" (the partner of one's partner), "monogamish" (a relationship defined by some degree of openness to sexual/emotional relationship outside the couple), and "frubbly" (the sense of pleasure one derives from knowledge of a partner's satisfaction and pleasure with other partners) – have been added to more familiar terms such as "polyamory," "swinging," "dogging," etc. (Richards & Barker, 2013; Ritchie & Barker, 2006).

These types of sexual labels have the potential to be both enabling and constraining; while they offer a conceptual and heuristic value, they are hardly tidy categories. Though such terms enable us to discuss clients' unique, subjectively experienced sexual identities (and therefore it behooves the therapist to inform themselves about open non-monogamies and the common terminology involved prior to working with such clients (Richards

& Barker, 2013), clients are unlikely to fit exactly within a categorical prototype. Just as no client is "just gay," or "just straight," no client is "just polyamorous." As experienced clinicians often observe, clients may self-identify (comfortably or uncomfortably) in relation to particular sexual categories, but what these terms mean, and how they relate to the client's subjective experience of personal identity, will vary – often significantly – from one individual to the next, and within a given individual over time. Thus, clinicians require a psychotherapeutic framework that enables an effective, meaningful understanding of the client's sexuality, as the client lives and experiences it, *phenomenologically* and *subjectively*. Like the subjectivist interpretation of the client's lived experience, a phenomenological understanding of the client's experiences, which we discuss at greater length below, allows the therapist to understand the client's experience in itself, as it is lived by the client (Spinelli, 1989). Existential sex therapy, which draws on the philosophical work of thinkers such as Simone de Beauvoir and Jean-Paul Sartre, and on the psychotherapeutic work of Yalom (1989), Van Deurzen (1997), and others, is a highly useful method for approaching non-monogamous clients (Barker, 2013b).

Existential sex therapy and non-monogamies: an extraordinary framework for an extraordinary client group

Existentialism is grounded in the principle that "existence precedes essence" (Sartre, 1945/2002, p. 20). Philosophically, this means that the individual is thrust into existence, and must develop a personal identity (i.e. essence) by making real, individual choices. The implication, Sartre states, is that, "subjectivity must be our point of departure" (1945, p. 20). Consequently, choice and meaning-making are central to the philosophical views developed by Sartre (1943/2005), and his intellectual companion and lover, de Beauvoir (1953/1997), and to the existential psychotherapy model. "Because human beings have no predetermined essence" Van Deurzen & Kenward (2005) emphasize, "we need to constantly choose our lives, and it is our choices that define us, and our choices that constitute our ever-changing identity" (p. 35). In effect, the therapist must recognize that the client is not reducible to some essential, or fundamental nature, but must be understood in light of these subjective choices, and the meanings of the client's lived experience. To create this existential framework in a sexual therapy session, the therapist might foster a joint exploration of the client's sexual choices in relation to existential themes, in particular meaning-making, and the client's subjective experiences of interconnectedness.

In this regard, bracketing and horizontalization are particularly valuable tools, of especial relevance with openly non-monogamous clients. Bracketing is a therapeutic technique with roots in the phenomenological tradition in philosophy and psychology. Phenomenology, an important foundation of existential psychotherapy, involves understanding experience in and of itself (on its own terms), without deferring to external theoretical frameworks (Aanstoos, 2012). Grounded in this approach, bracketing consists in the suspension, or setting aside, of preconceived notions, prior beliefs, and personal values, and allows the therapist to engage the client openly, a capacity that is particularly important in working with openly non-monogamous clients (Spinelli, 1989). We horizontalize, as Van Deurzen and Adams (2011) write, "when we endeavor to place what is becoming known against a horizon, to contextualize the client's worldview" (p. 50). In addressing the sexual dimension of non-monogamous clients' lives, the therapist will work to situate the client's sexual identity and behaviors within the wider horizon of the client's life. It must be emphasized that within the existential therapy model, even therapists familiar with non-monogamy – and even those who have lived experience in non-monogamous relationships – need to bracket their own beliefs from those of the client. In particular, the many different relational arrangements and subjective experiences within the wider frame of open non-monogamy make bracketing and horizontalizing invaluable to the therapist.

Bracketing and horizontalizing are illustrated in the following example: when working with a couple, one of whom was monogamous and one of whom was non-monogamous, in relation to bracketing, the second author (Meg) needed to reflexively consider both clients' preferred ways of doing relationships in relation to their own, and the potential implications of this for (perceived) alignment. Meg found journal-writing about different understandings of relationships to be a useful practice here. It was helpful for recognizing that Meg was more philosophically aligned with the non-monogamous partner regarding the capacity to love more than one person at once, but also more aligned with the monogamous partner regarding the responsibilities entailed by having "a relationship" with somebody. In relation to horizontalizing, the clients themselves were rather fixated on the monogamy/non-monogamy tension as the issue for therapy. Responding to this apparent fixation, Meg explicitly explained to the clients that (as with any fixation on a sex or relationship problem), it is important for the therapist to get a sense of the whole of the clients' lives and their wider worldviews, in order to understand how this aspect fits within them. This involved encouraging them to create a diagram of all of the important people in their lives (not just romantic partners), asking them to describe a day in their life in detail, and exploring what they valued most in life (both in terms of relationships with others, and in terms of what they wish to achieve, how they would like to look back on their life, and so on). From such explorations it was possible to explore the arenas of life in which each client valued independence over sharing/belonging, and vice versa. Some useful analogies were drawn between the value that the non-monogamous client placed on freedom to pursue their additional relationships and the value that the monogamous one placed on freedom to pursue their sporting activities. It was also discovered that they both valued their shared working lives, and their grounding themselves in this aspect of their lives was a helpful anchor from which to explore their tensions and conflicts.

The client's personhood is inherently self-determined, and the client must be considered in light of their subjectivity. In large measure our aim is to reveal the meanings our clients associate with sexuality and relationships in general, and with the particular sexual and relational choices they might make. In effect, the client may not be reduced to some essential, or fundamental nature, but must be understood in light of the choices and subjective meanings of their lived experience. With non-monogamous clients, we would be apt to inquire about the nature of the client's agreements with their partners. Non-monogamous clients vary with respect to the level of transparency of their sexual partnerships, ranging from a "don't ask, don't tell" agreement to complete transparency (Barker, 2013b). We might inquire how the client envisions their sexual contacts on a continuum of emotional intimacy (Barker, 2011). Some clients might experience a higher level of emotional intimacy with one partner, and other relationships as less intimate. Other clients may experience a high level of emotional intimacy with a variety of partners. From an existential vantage point, it is often of particular value to link the client's sexual choices to the meanings they associate with sexuality and sexual intimacy.

Like all human relationships, open non-monogamy is a dynamic landscape. We might encounter, for example, a client who begins in a "don't ask, don't tell" relationship and shifts towards a higher level of relational transparency, or vice versa. The client's experiences of emotional and physical intimacy are equally dynamic. Considering the client's personal and relational evolution, an existential sex therapist may use meaning as a consistent clinical theme, regularly questioning the meanings (both known and unknown) that the client may associate with sexual choices and behaviors, in order to foster an understanding of how the client's experience of sex and intimacy might vary between partnerships, and within partnerships across time.

In this process of questioning and open exploration, the therapist works to set aside presumptions and to accompany the client in an exploration of their world, maintaining a kind of informed naivety. In dealing with openly non-monogamous clients, the therapist's informed naivety is foundational to a set of therapeutic techniques – bracketing, horizontalizing and verification – which allow the therapist and client to address the client's subjective, lived experience.

This position of informed naivety necessitates that the therapist identify, and bracket off, assumptions and presuppositions about sexual behavior in general, and non-monogamy in particular, to the greatest degree possible. This, as many therapists are apt to note, can be easier said than done. By taking a stance of informed naivety, and using the existential techniques of bracketing and horizontalizing, the therapist endeavors to understand the client on their own terms, and works consciously to avoid imposing presuppositions about "normal" sexual behavior on the client.

Guidelines for intervention

There is no proprietary "existentialist" method for maintaining a stance of informed naivety, or implementing the techniques of bracketing and horizontalizing. Critical self-awareness and reflexivity are fundamental to this process. In our own experience, the use of common professional tools, such as journaling, clinical supervision and dialogue with peers, and inner work practice (such as mindfulness, or one's own psychotherapy) can be invaluable in cultivating informed naivety. By helping therapists maintain a critical orientation towards their clinical practice, such tools can facilitate the reflective practice essential for bracketing and horizontalizing. As with the client, the therapist's professional experience is subjectively based, and inevitably the tools that work best will be highly specific to the individual therapist. The core existentialist themes, including an exploration of meaning as the therapist experiences it, can be highly useful, and are applicable across modalities. Our own reflective and meditative practice, for instance, is methodologically eclectic, but consistently informed and shaped by an exploration of existential themes. For example, both authors of this paper draw on mindful meditation practices (Barker, 2013c) prior to meeting each client in order to be present to them as they are and to resist fixing them according to prior experiences or assumptions (I-thou rather than I-it relating, Buber, 1937/2004). This practice aids bracketing as it is possible to check in about the ways our own assumptions and experiences about relationships may be coloring our expectations of the client. Clients might also be encouraged to briefly return to their breathing (mindfulness) during sessions in order to be better able to empathize with the partner/s positions on issues of tension.

Maintaining a stance of informed naivety is both particularly important and particularly difficult by virtue of the mononormative biases of our culture (Ritchie & Barker, 2006). For instance, a therapist might struggle with biases or prejudices about the "right" kind of sexual relationships. Sexuality can be a difficult topic for clinicians to broach at the best of times. Introducing non-monogamy can be additionally challenging. Some therapists may be inclined to view non-monogamy itself, or particular forms of non-monogamy – such as the "don't ask, don't tell" arrangement – as inherently problematic.

Here, the subjective framework of existentialism can be usefully applied: non-monogamy might not work for the therapist, but it does not have to. It has to be healthy in the context of the client's subjective experience. The experience of non-monogamy, likely, will not have the same meaning for the client as it might for the therapist.

Like the therapist, the client is encouraged to assume an open, self-questioning approach, which evaluates the subjective meaning of their sexual choices, and intimate relationships. As with the therapist's reflective practice, the client's process of evaluative and critical questioning need not follow an exact formula, but may be grounded in exploration of existential themes. Existential principles are conducive to integration, and therapists may benefit from introducing existential questioning alongside an array of counseling interventions. In our own practices, we have found deconstruction of social constructs and conventions to be particularly useful for many openly non-monogamous clients. This social constructionist approach can be particularly helpful vis-à-vis cultural mononormativity, as well as the forms of polynormativity (more rigid ways of doing open non-monogamy), which inevitably spring up when a community is positioned outside of the mainstream (Barker, 2013a). For example, many clients who have come across books and websites on open non-monogamy will get the sense that there is one "right" way of doing this, and it will be important to introduce, and hold onto, the multiplicity of non-monogamies and the sense that one is being chosen at the expense of other possibilities, and that all ways of relating will inevitably have both potentials and challenges attached to them.

The existential approach focuses on the client's lived experience, devoting particular attention to the varied meanings the client may hold regarding sexual relationships and sexual behavior. In light of the powerful stigmas surrounding non-monogamies, it may at times be necessary for the existential therapist to actively affirm the client's open non-monogamy, or other non-normative aspects of sexuality. This type of affirmative stance may have two aspects – deconstruction of certain social constructs, and validation of subjective sexual choices. In the first instance, it may be necessary for the therapist to refute or deconstruct common cultural stereotypes, and problematize the stigmas that surround sexuality. In our experience, this may involve critiquing some of the more prevalent biases clients may encounter, from common mononormative and heteronormative biases to anti-sexual biases in certain aspects of our culture. This may be done, for example, by citing statistics on the commonality of such relationships (e.g. half of gay men have openly non-monogamous relationships), or problematizing the idea that most people are monogamous (e.g. mentioning that half to two-thirds of people who are monogamous have affairs) (Blumstein & Schwartz, 1983; Vangelisti & Gerstenberger, 2004). You might discuss examples of celebrities of fictional characters who are not monogamous or otherwise non-normative sexually, and generally express familiarity with different modes of non-monogamy from your reading in this area.

Our approach to existential therapy holds that a critical understanding of the external sources of mononormativity can help the client attain a higher level of subjective control of meaning-making in their life. The second aspect is one of more direct affirmation – the therapist may legitimate non-monogamies, stating directly that alternative sexualities are, fundamentally, equally legitimate to more socially normative sexual arrangements. Here, the therapist may offer an authoritative-but-balanced view, pointing out that both monogamous and non-monogamous people may have healthy *or* unhealthy relationships, and that this is a function of their specific relationship experience, rather than the number of people involved.

It is important that the therapist address the sexual element of the client's life in a balanced way, by horizontalizing and treating sexuality as an important – but not totalizing or all-encompassing aspect – of the client's life. Thus, with respect to horizontalizing, the therapist must not fixate on the client's non-monogamy, or assume that the non-monogamous relationship arrangement is the central concern in the individual or relational sex therapy (Barker, 2013b). To focus overly on this dimension of the client's sexuality puts us at risk of overemphasizing a single facet of the client's life and obscuring other important issues. Further, overemphasizing the client's non-monogamy puts the therapist at risk of fixating on non-monogamy as the "problem," and may distract the therapist from attending to the complexity of sexual and relationship choices and behaviors. It cannot be overstressed that our model of existential sex therapy is a non-pathologizing approach.

Existential sex therapy's non-pathologizing conceptualization of sexual relationships and behavior benefits from an emphasis on the themes of freedom and belonging – which the (existential) psychotherapist may wish to explore, and return to, with clients as they progress through therapy. For instance, the therapist may wish to invite an exploration of how the client experiences freedom, and a sense of belonging *within* the context of their intimate relationships and *outside* of their intimate relationships, in the other facets of their life. According to Yalom, exploration of freedom and belonging, as a core existential psychotherapy practice, may help to foster an understanding of the client's subjective, lived experience, for both the client and the therapist (Yalom, 1980). In the sex therapy field, we hold, this exploration can help shed light on the unique subjective meanings of sexuality in the client's life specifically, and the way that sex is situated in a wider context of human experience and relationships. In effect, these conceptualizations are grounded in a broader understanding of human experience, which envisions the individual's experience of self as inherently linked to their experience of the other. The implication of this intersubjective experience is that we live in a social world where meaning already exists, and the experience of defining ourselves and our sexual identities is dialectical, in that it occurs in the interactions between ourselves and others. Our quest for belonging, and our freedom to define ourselves and our sexualities is intrinsic to our relationships with others.

Freedom and belonging, within the existential framework, are simultaneously invaluable and challenging. Yalom emphasizes that freedom is no easy thing, writing, "in its existential sense 'freedom' refers to the absence of external structure," with the implication that "the individual is entirely responsible for – that is, is the author of – his or her own world, life design, choices, and actions" (1980, p. 8–9). The consequence is that we therapists as well as clients must determine our own identities, a potentially liberating but also potentially frightening experience. This is particularly true for clients endeavoring to forge or determine extraordinary identities, and so particularly relevant in terms of open non-monogamy. Our clients seek a sense of meaning and belonging in a world that offers social meanings, as determined by others, but no absolute answers. Clients may choose to derive their sense of meaning, and a vital experience of belonging, from embracing openly monogamous lifestyles and identities. They are free to do so, even though the social world may offer meanings that challenge this process. It is important to bear in mind, however, that clients may choose open non-monogamy for different reasons altogether. While it may be invaluable to explore the themes of freedom and belonging with the client, it is the prerogative of the existential sex and relationship therapist to explore what non-monogamy means to the client, and to avoid imposing assumptions about the client's motivation on the therapy process.

Conclusion

Within existential sex therapy the therapist focuses on the client's subjective, lived experience, taking into account all aspects of the client's life, including those which are not immediately sexual. The therapist endeavors to bracket off biases and presumptions, and to control any temptation to overemphasize single aspects, a technique of particular importance when dealing with openly non-monogamous clients. The client's subjective process of meaning-making is a vital topic of consideration in the therapy. The client is seen as an individual who happens to be in a non-monogamous relationship – what this means to them simply cannot be known a priori.

Note

1. The experiences may well not, of course, feel extraordinary to clients, but rather they are extraordinary in the mononormative context of wider culture, which many therapists will occupy. Generally, openly non-monogamous arrangements will feel rather mundane and everyday to the client, unless she/he/they are new to them (Richards & Barker, 2013).

References

Aanstoos, C. (2012). A phenomenology of sexual experiencing. In P. Kleinplatz (Ed.), *New directions in sex therapy* (2nd ed., pp. 51–68). New York, NY: Taylor & Francis Group.

Adam, B.D. (2006). Relationship innovation in male couples. *Sexualities, 9*(1), 5–26.

Barker, M. (2011). Monogamies and non-monogamies – a response to: 'The challenge of monogamy: Bringing it out of the closet and into the treatment room' by Marianne Brandon. *Sexual and Relationship Therapy, 26*(3), 281–287.

Barker, M. (2013a). *Rewriting the rules: An integrative guide to love, sex and relationships.* London: Routledge.

Barker, M. (2013b). Open non-monogamies. In M. Milton (Ed.), *On sexuality: Existential perspectives on psychotherapy, sexuality and related experiences.* London: PCCS Books.

Barker, M. (2013c). *Mindful counselling & psychotherapy: Practising mindfully across approaches and issues.* London: Sage.

Barker, M., & Langdridge, D. (2010). Whatever happened to non-monogamies? Critical reflections on recent research and theory. *Sexualities, 13*(6), 748–772.

Benson, P.J. (2008). *The polyamory handbook.* Bloomington, IN: AuthorHouse.

Blumstein, P., & Schwartz P. (1983). *American couples: Money, work, sex.* New York, NY: William Morrow.

Brandon, M. (2011). The challenge of monogamy: Bringing it out of the closet and into the treatment room. *Sexual and Relationship Therapy, 26*(3), 271–277.

Buber, M. (1937/2004). *I and thou.* (R. Gregor-Smith, Trans.). London: Routledge.

de Beauvoir, S. (1953/1997). *The second sex.* London: Vintage.

De Visser, R., & McDonald, D. (2007). Swings and roundabouts: Management of jealousy in heterosexual 'swinging' couples. *British Journal of Social Psychology, 46*(2), 459–476.

Easton, D., & Hardy, C.A. (2009). *The ethical slut: A practical guide to polyamory, open relationships and other adventures.* Berkeley, CA: Celestial Arts.

Kleinplatz, P. (2012). Is that all there is? A new critique of the goals of sex therapy. In P. Kleinplatz (Ed.), *New directions in sex therapy* (2nd ed., pp. 101–118). New York, NY: Taylor & Francis Group.

Matik, W.O. (2002). *Redefining our relationships: Guidelines for responsible open relationships.* Oakland, CA: Defiant Times Press.

McLean, K. (2004). Negotiating (non)monogamy. *Journal of Bisexuality, 4*(1–2), 83–97.
Ravenscroft, T. (2004). *Polyamory: Roadmaps for the clueless and hopeful.* Santa Fe, NM: Crossquarter Publishing Group.
Richards, C., & Barker, M. (2013). *Sexuality and gender for counsellors, psychologists and health professionals: A practical guide.* London: Sage.
Ritchie, A., & Barker, M. (2006). 'There aren't words for what we do or how we feel so we have to make them up': Constructing polyamorous languages in a culture of compulsory monogamy. *Sexualities, 9*(5), 584–601.
Rubin, R. (2001). Alternative family lifestyles revisited, or whatever happened to swingers, group marriages and communes? *Journal of Family Issues, 7*(6), 711.
Sartre, J.-P. (1943/2005). *Being and nothingness.* (H.E. Barnes, Trans.). London: Verso.
Sartre, J.-P. (1945/2002). *Existentialism and human emotions.* (B. Frechtman, Trans.). New York, NY: Citadel Press.
Sheff, E. (2005). Polyamorous women, sexual subjectivity and power. *Journal of Contemporary Ethnography, 3*(34), 251–283.
Spinelli, E. (1989). *The interpreted world: An introduction to phenomenological psychology.* London: Sage.
Taormino, T. (2008). *Opening up: A guide to creating and sustaining open relationships.* San Francisco, CA: Cleis Press.
Tiefer, L. (1995). *Sex is not a natural act and other essays.* Boulder, CO: Westview Press.
Van Deurzen, E. (1997). *Everyday mysteries: Existential dimensions of psychotherapy.* London: Routledge.
Van Deurzen, E., & Adams, M. (2011). *Skills in existential counselling and psychotherapy.* London: Sage.
Van Deurzen, E., & Kenward, R. (2005). *Dictionary of existential psychotherapy and counselling.* London: Sage.
Vangelisti, A.L., & Gerstenberger, M. (2004). Communication and marital infidelity. In J. Duncombe, K. Harrison, G. Allan, & D. Marsden (Eds.), *The state of affairs: Explorations in infidelity and commitment* (pp. 59–78). Mahwah, NJ: Lawrence Erlbaum.
Yalom, I. (1980). *Existential psychotherapy.* New York, NY: Basic Books.
Yalom, I. (1989). *Love's executioner and other tales of psychotherapy.* New York, NY: Basic Books.

In search of Aphrodite: working with archetypes and an inner cast of characters in women with low sexual desire

Chelsea Wakefield

While much research has been done on sex roles and scripts, an analysis of how archetypes influence sexuality has yet to be articulated. Archetypes are inherent patterns of energy found in the seedbed of the psyche. They have a "felt sense" in the body and move through the psyche shaping perception and motivating behavior. They lie dormant until developmental milestones or life experiences awaken them. This article will describe an archetypal and "inner cast of characters" approach to treating the problem of low sexual desire in women. This method is experiential and acknowledges the range and multidimensionality of human sexual experience. It opens a dimension that can help unlock treatment impasses as the practitioner respectfully engages Sexual Gatekeepers. Identifying the impact of "eros-inhibiting" archetypes and negotiating space for a Sexual Self are part of the work. An archetypal perspective empowers women to define their own erotic identities as they explore the creative realm of the sexual psyche.

Introduction

If I were a visitor from outer space, reading the sexology literature and trying to understand sex on earth, I might conclude that earthlings considered "good sex" to consist of functioning body parts that can achieve penetrative intercourse leading to the production of an orgasm. While the recent Diagnostic and Statistical Manual of Mental Disorders (American Psychiatric Association, 2013) shows some improvement in the awareness that trauma, medical, cultural, situational, and relational factors can interfere with a woman's sexual interest, there is still a strong inference that "normal and healthy" women *should* desire sexual activity on a fairly regular basis (although the exact interval is not specified). If a woman loses interest in sex for over six months, she is considered to be suffering from female sexual interest/arousal disorder. The severity of the diagnosis is framed in terms of the woman's level of distress over this lack of interest: mild, moderate, or severe.

Since the time of Masters and Johnson (1966), sex therapy has retained a strong behavioral component. Sex therapists educate people about sexual physiology, assign sensate focus exercises, micro-track sexual encounters to discern where things are going "off the rails," offering suggestions to resolve specific difficulties, coaching people to become more skilled and sensitive lovers. We encourage partners to talk to each other about their needs, desires, sensations, and responses, and give them permission to explore their sexuality. We also employ cognitive interventions, such as myth-busting, and rework negative sexual messages and inhibiting scripts, in the hopes that clients will begin to experience pleasure and enjoy each other (Annon, 1975; Goodwach, 2005a, 2005b). All of this is good sex therapy.

While sexual health is important, the increasing medicalization of the field reinforces the perspective that sex is something we *do* and that the physical and behavioral aspects of sex therapy are the primary focus of intervention. The sharp focus on heterosexual intercourse also marginalizes other forms of erotic engagement (Kleinplatz, 2001, 2012; Tiefer, 2012). Despite physical health, adequate sexual skills, *and* good relationships, sexual desire disorders or disparities are the most common reason that clients come for sex therapy today. There are numerous theories regarding both cause and cure (Leiblum, 2010).

Something is "off"

In my own practice, confused couples arrive, knowing how to "produce orgasms," even becoming "erotic virtuosos," and yet sex has become lackluster. They often describe a sense of erotic disconnection in which something is "off" or "missing." An increasing number of men are saying that they no longer want to engage with a partner who provides "service sex," but lacks the fire of desire. Women convey that their partner may be "trying," but somehow he or she is "not there" in a way that fulfills their erotic longing. They feel unmet, unmoved, untouched on some level, and ultimately unsatisfied. These mystifying mismatches can lead to withdrawal and sexual despair. It is clear that functioning body parts do not necessarily lead to fulfillment. In a world where information about "how to do" sex is everywhere, clients are bewildered and come to sex therapy hoping for answers.

The need for multidimensional treatment models

There is a conversation among a growing number of sex therapists about the need to develop treatment models that address the multiple dimensions of sexual experience beyond the physical (Basson et al., 2003; Kleinplatz, 2001, 2012; Ogden, 2013; Snell, 2011; Snell, Fischer, & Walters, 1993; Tiefer, 2012). It is important to consider that most of the time sex occurs within close relationships (DeLamater & Shibley Hyde, 2004). Sex is more than a mere progression of actions or behaviors. Sex is a series of *symbolic* interactions, imbued with subjective meaning, which greatly determines whether sex is satisfying or not (Kimmel, 2007; Ogden, 2006, 2008, 2013). When we reduce sexuality to overt behaviors we overlook the wellspring of eroticism and the symbolic richness that sexuality can hold (Bader, 2002; Kleinplatz, 2001, 2012; Morin, 1995).

A Jungian perspective in treatment

It is in the realm of subjective meaning and symbolic richness that I have found my Jungian training to be profoundly helpful, because Jungians are deeply interested in these realms as well as the archetypal energies that underlie and motivate all of life. When looking at sexuality from this perspective, we become aware of the invisible shape/counter-shape dance going on between partners. Sex is not just something that bodies engage in; it is the interplay of projections and longings. It is the underlying dance of the psyches and the energy of the interchange that determines whether sex is imbued with the spark of eros or disengaged and devitalized. The same sexual behaviors can be generated from a range of internal orientations that influence a person's erotic identity as well as the quality of the interchange between partners. In the Jungian world, these internal energies and orientations are referred to as archetypes.

Archetypes and the sexual psyche

People often think of archetypes as categories or roles, but archetypes are more than this. Archetypes are innate organizing forms for the expression of patterns that are enduring in human nature. They are instinctual and outside of cognition. Archetypes are felt in the body and move through the psyche, shaping perceptions and agendas, motivating choices and behaviors. Certain archetypes lie dormant in the seedbed of the psyche, until activated by developmental passages or by the requirements of an environment. The sexual aspects of the psyche are fertile ground for growth and creativity (Qualls-Corbett, 1988; Young-Eisendrath, 1984).

When clients come to me having lost their passion, this unexplored playground of the psyche is where I turn. When it is clear that a woman has never experienced the flame of desire, this is where I turn. I invite individuals and couples into an exploration of the sexual psyche and into the journey of Sexual Individuation.

Individuation is the Jungian term for self-actualization. It involves claiming one's true Self fully, shadow and light, and growing into the true shape of one's "soul print" (Wakefield, 2012). This process cannot be accomplished if the Sexual Self is left out. Sexuality is not just an aspect of individuation; it can be a *means* of self-discovery and individuation. When two people are both on this journey, diving into the depths of the psyche and bringing back pearls of discovery to each other, the relationship is continually fed from a deep, creative source. With each person growing and changing, boredom becomes impossible because they are never engaging the same person twice.

One of my great joys as a sex therapist is in helping women to define their unique eroticism in an archetypal framework, particularly in cases of low sexual desire. We begin by exploring the *archetypal identities* from which the woman is currently sourcing her life. Are they "eros-enhancing" or "eros-inhibiting?" Is her archetypal sexual identity sourced from her core Self, or is it the product of cultural overlays and other people's scripts? From the moment a client enters my office, I am listening with "archetypal ears." Beyond her story and script, I want to know "who" is playing the parts. Who is in her "inner cast of characters" (Wakefield, 2012)? We begin to look behind the curtain into areas of her psyche that are unexplored and undeveloped.

According to Meston and Buss (2009), women have sex for pleasure, but most often they have sex as a means of nurturing, feeling connected to a partner, and deepening the bond of a relationship. Women also use sex to "mate-guard" (protect their territory) and compete, believing that if a partner is satisfied at home, they will not seek satisfaction elsewhere. Sex is also sought to validate a woman's attractiveness, boost her sense of power, satisfy curiosity, and barter for favors and resources. Although pleasing and nurturing a partner is important for most women, it is not enough to sustain long-term sexual motivation, especially in the face of other competing demands on her time and energy.

Everyone's sexuality is unique. When we look below the surface of cultural and partner-pleasing scripts, we begin to discover a client's love maps (Money, 1993), arousal templates (Bader, 2002), and core erotic themes (Morin, 1995). Hendrick, Hendrick, and Dicke (1998) describe six different love styles, and McCarthy and McCarthy (2009) describe four sexual relating styles in couples. Mosher (1980) has outlined three preferred styles of sexual engagement: *sexual trance*, the focus on interior experience and sensations; *partner engagement*, with a preference for lots of eye contact, feedback, and words of endearment; and *role enactment*, where partners enjoy drama, the use of settings, props, ambiance, costumes, erotic talk, and playing with power. In this researcher's way of thinking, each of these styles and erotic dimensions is populated by differing archetypes, each carrying a different sexual energy, each evoking a potentially different response from a partner.

Every archetypal orientation has a "felt sense," an instinctual resonance in the body which shapes behavior, response, script, and interpretation of experience. Most of this material is outside of conscious awareness. Archetypal mismatches create a sense of erotic disconnection that is bewildering to people. Partners may try to communicate that something is "off," but they struggle, because the issue is about energy rather than behaviors, technique, lingerie, or talk. It is difficult to put language to a problem that is about *being* rather than *doing*.

Over the years I have developed a typology of sexual archetypes that conveys the spectrum of possible sexual energies that a woman can carry. When I open this world up to women, they become intrigued. The idea that they have a unique sexual essence and that sex is a realm of creativity sourced from within causes them to feel affirmed, curious, and empowered.

Marie

To illustrate the application of this approach, let us take a 45-year-old woman, whom we shall call Marie. As I describe her case, I will place names of possible archetypes in parentheses. A sex therapist working from this perspective is listening with "archetypal ears" from the onset of treatment, making mental notes of the client's "inner cast of characters" and the parts they play in her sexual story. This awareness of the inner cast and the archetypal energies they carry is held by the sex therapist for later exploration.

Marie sat in my treatment room wringing her hands and looking anxious and sad (Vulnerable Child). Her husband Jack had recently announced that he was bored with their marriage and fed up with her "just lying there" during sex. He disclosed that there was a young woman at the office who had been flirting with him and had told him she thought he was sexy (this female archetype has been called by many names: Sweet Young Thing, Adoring Girl, Desire-Awakening Maiden, Flirt, Brazen Hussy, Seductress, etc.). Jack had always been a loyal, honest, stable guy (Boy Scout). Now he said he wanted some spark in his life. He wanted someone to want him (Jack had entered into the archetypal mid-life re-evaluation that we have come to call the "mid-life crisis"). Marie was shocked, alarmed, and a little bit angry at this disclosure. She was constantly on the run with the children (Devoted Mother) and keeping up with the house (Domestic Executive). She was often exhausted, but had never denied Jack sex when he really wanted it. Jack said this was the problem; she never really wanted sex. (Marie has been "servicing" her partner, as a Dutiful Wife, a particularly "eros-inhibiting" archetype).

I asked Marie how long she had been "providing sex" for Jack and she stated, "Pretty much always." She cared for Jack and she did enjoy the little bit of closeness that sex brought. "He's not exactly Romeo," she sighed (Shakespeare understood archetypes). She stated, "Jack is an accountant," as if this explained everything. "He's a Good Father and Provider" (two of the major "eros-inhibiting" archetypes to be found in men).

When asked if she was orgasmic, Marie sheepishly admitted that she often hurried sex along by faking orgasms. She looked at me knowingly and said, "You know how sensitive men are about these things." (Marie is in the archetype of Reassuring Mother to Jack's

Insecure-Needy Boy. The intent is nurturing, but also condescending, as Marie does not believe that Jack's "fragile ego" could handle the truth).

As we talked about her sexual history, Marie revealed that she once had a boyfriend in college who really "lit her fire." Her mother had not approved of him. "He was a musician, not really marriage and family material." I was encouraged to hear that Marie had once sipped the nectar of Aphrodite. "My mother approved of Jack. She said he was a solid guy with prospects." When I asked Marie if she and Jack had ever shared an erotic experience together she laughed, "I think Jack would find that word inappropriate (he's a Good Boy). As for me, I'm old, tired, and sleep in flannel pajamas (Frump)."

From Marie's report, it sounded like the Good Girl and Good Boy had married. They existed on parallel tracks, shouldering their roles as Provider, Responsible Father, Dutiful Wife, and Devoted Mother (all "eros-inhibiting" archetypes). There was little emotional connection, and neither had ever explored their sexual psyches. I also noted that there was no sense of play in their relationship, an important foundation for becoming Play Mates. Marie and Jack were in mid-life, a time when aspects of self that are yet undeveloped begin pressing for emergence.

Aphrodite and the sexual woman

In the Greek pantheon of Goddesses, Aphrodite is the Goddess of love, beauty, sensuality, erotic attraction, sexuality, creativity, and new life. Aphrodite creatively engaged her chosen lovers and knew exactly who she was and what pleased her (Shinoda Bolen, 1984). Aphrodite energy is the antithesis of the archetypes of Dutiful Wife, Devoted or Selfless Mother, Frump, Victim, or Shrinking Violet.

When a woman comes to me with no sexual interest or desire, I know we are in search of Aphrodite (Stone & Stone, 2000). Before a woman can experience desire, she must experience herself as a Sexual Woman. She has to house an Aphrodite Self as one of her inner characters in order to value her sexuality enough to create protected time and space in which to unfurl her erotic energies and bask in the glories of being embodied.

I like to describe Aphrodite energy as a frequency that clients can tune into, like a station on the radio dial. When a woman is in the frequency of Aphrodite, it is evident to everyone in the room. In my Luminous Woman® weekends, women explore the unique ways in which each carries Aphrodite energy. When a woman steps into this energy, regardless of her age, weight, or other defining features, she begins to take on the sparkle and glow of an irresistible charisma.

Over the past few years, I have been researching the archetypal scope of the Sexual Woman. Her potential resides in the seedbed of *every* woman's psyche, waiting to be cultivated and developed. The bloom of this flower will be unique to the woman. It is helpful for women to know that in ancient times women's sexuality was revered instead of feared (Eisler, 1996).

Here is a list of words that women have used to describe a Sexual Woman who carries Aphrodite energy. She is authentic, imaginative, self-aware, able to negotiate, responsive, sensuous, soulful, rapturous, open, present, joyfully embodied, compassionate, magnetic, intuitive, creative, radiant, luminous, erotic, spontaneous, curious, adventurous, courageous, edgy, humorous, confident, passionate, warm, inviting, intimate, playful, flirtatious, companionable, bold, dramatic, evocative, nurturing, sweet, generous, quiet, mysterious, ethereal, and comfortable in her body.

Another way to think of a woman's sexual energy is in elemental terms. She might be fluid, fiery, earthy, or breezy. If a woman were to describe herself in animal terms, would she be a lost Puppy Dog or a Hungry Tigress, a Shy Doe or Playful Monkey? What is her sexual story and what are the archetypal energies she carries? Fairy tales are embedded in women's psyches. What characters does she identify with? Is she playing the part of Sleeping Beauty, waiting to be sexually awakened, or Cinderella, disappointed and sexually withdrawn because her Prince Charming turned out to be a mere human being. What is her relationship to power? Does she want to seduce or be seduced, initiate or be initiated? In the spectrum of archetypal energies, is she an Earth Mother who loves to nurture, a Playful Kitten who loves to tease and flirt, a Saucy Wench who wants to tussle before she is tamed, or a Soulful Sexual Priestess who invites her partner into transcendent aspects of the sexual mysteries. On the vulnerable side, have her wounds and fears defined her as a Poor Little Match Girl, who does not believe that her flame is enough to light anyone's fire, or a Shrinking Violet (Ogden, 1990), terrified of engaging instinctual energies?

Women can learn about the range of sexual energies they might carry by exploring archetypes in films. Who are the actresses they admire and the parts they play? Lauren Bacall is a smooth, mysterious, smoldering Seductress. Marilyn Monroe carries Sweet Tease, Flirt, and Sex Kitten. Angelina Jolie carries Amazon and Femme Fatale. Meg Ryan is a Pixie or Girl Next Door. Queen Latifa is an earthy, fiery Red Hot Mama; Mae West a Saucy Vamp. Meryl Streep is a Sensuous Goddess who has played a wide range of archetypes (with academy awards to match) embodying boldness, emergence, mystery, warmth, hunger, radiance, vulnerability, longing, and playfulness. In noticing how other women carry sexual energy, clients can begin to understand that each represents a flavor of Aphrodite.

Sexual energies can be cultivated in a woman by studying them and "trying them on." Experiential methods such as Active Imagination (Johnson, 1986) or Voice Dialogue (Dyak, 1999; Stone & Stone, 1989; Wakefield, 2012) are effective ways to do this. In conducting these experiential sessions, the sex therapist can invite a woman to imagine how she might feel if she "housed" this energy. What is the "frequency" of it? How would she carry herself, talk, dress, or act differently? How would she be different with a partner (Wakefield, 2012)? "Trying on" an archetype and exploring it expands a woman's sense of sexual identity and opens her to new possibilities.

Making space for Aphrodite

Before a woman can begin to identify with Aphrodite energy, she must make space in her "inner cast of characters." Certain archetypes can engulf a woman, crowding out her Aphrodite self. Hite (1994), Heyn (1997), and Stone (1997) all discuss how the archetype of the Wife and Mother, severely inhibit a woman's sense of sexual empowerment. In *Marriage Shock: The Transformation of Women Into Wives,* Heyn outlines the gradual erosion of a woman's erotic edge as she becomes a virtuous, self-sacrificing, "proper wife." The Good and Proper Wife is faithful, devoted, accommodating, patient, kind, sexually available to meet a man's needs, but never sexually demanding. We may think the women's movement freed us from this archetype, but "she" still lives in the back recesses of many women's psyches. Her voice is reinforced by another introject that Stone (1997) refers to as the Inner Patriarch. "He" monitors and comments on a woman's behavior to insure that she is conforming to the proper standards of her culture and upbringing.

Another archetype that all but extinguishes Aphrodite energy is the Devoted, Self-Sacrificing Mother. The institution of motherhood is held as almost sacred in this and other cultures. When the Self-Sacrificing, Responsible Mother reigns supreme in a woman's psyche, this energy is deadly to a woman's Sexual Self, her Aphrodite energy. The Responsible Mother puts her children's needs before everything else. To attend to personal needs or pleasure would be "selfish." A woman dominated by this archetype often begins to feel dowdy, less desirable, frisky, or playful. Sex becomes another task on her endless caregiving list.

The couple system itself can become de-eroticized as parental archetypes dominate. The Responsible Provider, Devoted Mother, Administrator, Chauffeur, Disciplinarian, and Soccer Parent begin to displace the Youthful Lovers who once lingered in bed on Saturday mornings, reveling in sensuous delights. Too busy, tired, and preoccupied with task lists, the couple no longer nurtures their erotic connection. They may mourn this loss, but many people believe it to be an inevitable part of becoming Responsible Adults.

Treatment impasses and Sexual Gatekeepers

All sex therapists encounter frustrating treatment impasses. Clients do not always complete homework or implement suggestions. A helpful approach to this is to go in search of inner characters that I call Sexual Gatekeepers. Internal Voices of Warning can escalate at the mere idea of becoming a more openly sexual being. The sex therapist can trace back to a point where treatment seemed to stall out, and ask the client to look inside to see if they can locate a sensation of anxiety, or hear a Voice of Warning, Shame, or Judgment in the background. Gatekeepers try to protect a woman from what they perceive as dangerous to her safety or acceptability. Gatekeepers need to be surfaced and actively engaged, or they will undermine treatment progress.

Women today navigate a bewildering maze of double binds about sexuality. While the media openly promotes sex, exploring new dimensions of sexuality or outright pleasure seeking is still considered questionable for a woman concerned with her reputation. The erotic possibilities that a woman entertains in her private world may never be expressed openly, even in an intimate relationship (Wentland, Herold, Desmarais, & Milhausen, 2009). Many women house an inner character that I call the Reputation Guardian. This Gatekeeper oversees how a woman expresses her sexuality and reminds her of the dangers of becoming "too sexual." The split categories of Madonna and Whore still resonate in the psyches of both women and men. This dichotomy of contrasting archetypes creates anxiety in women as they begin to try on new sexual energies. The Devoted Mother can act as a powerful Gatekeeper, who fears that a woman will abandon her responsibilities to others if she focuses on personal pleasure. Sexual trauma can create Gatekeepers that warn a woman that she is inviting violation if she were to become more sexual.

When a sex therapist encounters a Gatekeeper, respectfully engage them in an experiential dialogue to explore their history, agenda, perspective, and concerns. Recommended experiential methods for doing this include Voice Dialogue (Dyak, 1999; Stone & Stone, 1989; Wakefield, 2012), Ogden's (2013) ISIS Wheel, Gestalt two-chair technique (Resnick, 2012), Hypnotherapy (Phillips & Frederick, 1995), or Internal Family Systems (Schwartz, 1995).

In dialoguing with a Gatekeeper, speak directly with this aspect of the woman's psyche and have the client physically shift to a different position, to emphasize a distinction of this "inner character" from her larger identity. Open with the prompt, "Tell me about yourself," and let the Gatekeeper talk for a while. Follow up with more questions to learn about this inner character's history, how she/he came into being, and what was going on at the time. Ask about teachers and role models to get a sense of "who" you may be talking to. Is this a specific introject from the client's past? If so, you might give the

Gatekeeper this name. Ask questions about how the Gatekeeper is trying to help or protect the client. For example, "What are your concerns for (client's name) as she explores her sexuality?" The goal is to discover what assurances the Gatekeeper needs in order to allow the client to move forward.

Dialoguing directly with inner characters, naming them, and getting to know them surfaces a tremendous amount of material that can then be worked through, to resolve treatment impasses (Wakefield, 2012). Over the years I have dialogued with a wide array of Gatekeepers: Amish Grandmothers, Possessive Fathers, Fire and Brimstone Preachers, Voices of God, Amazon Protectors, Mother Superiors, Militant Feminists, and Disembodied Saints. I have uncovered Proper Behavior Police trying to control a Wild Woman in hiding, fearful that these energies might take over and ruin a woman's life or besmirch the Snow White reputation she has presented to her children.

Marie's Lioness

As a Jungian-oriented sex therapist, I often draw upon powerful dream images to bring new energies into the client's life. Women who are exploring the uncharted territory of their instinctual, embodied energies sometimes bring in dreams of big cats: leopards, panthers, cougars, and lionesses (Stone, 1997). Marie brought in such a dream. She dreamed of a beautiful, sensual, sleek Lioness on the African tundra. This amazing Lioness became the touchstone of her emergent sexuality. We conducted several Active Imagination/ Voice Dialogue sessions where Marie imagined herself becoming the Lioness, experiencing what it was like to be in that energy. During these experiential sessions, Marie's flat, tired eyes took on a warm sparkle, and she became sultry and engaging. The Lioness desired lingering mornings in bed with no kids around. She longed to have her body stroked with firm hands. She wanted to roll around playfully in bed without regard to who was up or down or whether anyone was about to fall off. At the end of these Lioness sessions, Marie was amazed to discover that this potential lived within her, an aspect of her being that felt sensual and timeless. We reflected on how different the Lioness felt from the Dutiful Wife and the Devoted Mother.

We then conducted Voice Dialogue sessions with her Devoted Mother and Dutiful Wife to help Marie separate out from these dominating archetypes and create space for the Lioness in her life. As Marie became more aware of her "inner cast of characters," she decided to become their director instead of being at their mercy. As she integrated the Lioness energy, she found that she began to make time for relaxing baths and basking in the sun. She began to set some boundaries on the archetype of the Devoted Mother as she and her husband spent some relaxing, play-filled weekends away from the children. It occurred to her that by creating a ballet carpool for her daughter, she could recapture a couple of hours for herself, something that never occurred to her when she was being perpetually devoted. Marie used this time to take an exercise dance class and began to experience herself as less of a Frump while enjoying the energies she got going as she moved to Middle Eastern and Latin music.

As Marie became more playfully sensuous, Jack became interested in the "inner cast of characters" model and began to name his own inner cast. Marie and Jack came in for a few couples sessions and began to explore "who" was relating to "whom" in their relationship (Stone, 2000; Young-Eisendrath, 1984, 1993). They learned to shift states into more "eros-enhancing" archetypes. Jack recognized that he too had been trapped in Provider and Parental archetypes. He realized that he had never thought of himself as a sexual being and had not attended to his own need for rest and play. As they began to explore deeper levels of their psyches, they began to break out of the stale bonding patterns and to kindle a sexual flame for the first time in their lives. The temptation of the Sweet Young Thing at the office faded away.

Intimacy in the journey of Sexual Individuation

When a woman begins to understand her sexual essence, her core erotic themes and preferred methods of engagement, she can communicate these to a partner. This is *real* sexual intimacy, as the sharing of this material indicates a willingness to be deeply seen and known. Revealing this depth of the Sexual Self requires a significant degree of individuation work on a woman's part. It also requires patience and compassion for partners, as they learn to dance with emergent energies. Sexual needs and desires may surface that require sensitive negotiations or adjustments in relationship agreements. This is another area that a sex therapist knowledgeable in contemporary relationship work can help clients navigate.

Conclusion

Working with sexual archetypes moves sex therapy beyond a definition of "good sex" based on performance. Incorporating an archetypal perspective in treatment does not supplant current "best practices" of sex therapy, but offers a depth perspective that can enhance other approaches. It moves sex therapy into a multidimensional and integrative view of sexuality that allows for the subjective meaning of fulfillment to be defined by the client. It involves *being* more than *doing* and imbues sexuality and sex therapy with a new creativity. It empowers clients to venture into the sexual psyche to explore and define who they are as sexual beings, to work through intra-psychic conflicts, and to view their sexuality as an unfolding journey that lasts a lifetime, the journey of Sexual Individuation.

The experience of corresponding love maps is one of the most exhilarating experiences on earth and leads to the deepest levels of sexual fulfillment. Corresponding archetypes can transport people into the transpersonal realm. Individuating women want to be seen, known, met, and loved in their full personhood.

Many problems in life can be reduced to a failure of imagination. We get stuck in scripts and stories that are too small for the vastness of our souls. We live in boxes and constructs that limit our creative capacity and potential for fulfillment. The sexual psyche and the range of sexual archetypes available to women are a realm of great potential, largely unexplored. By introducing this perspective, sex therapists can open doorways into this realm, providing helpful maps and reference points for a woman to explore. We can support her, holding space and witnessing her unfolding discoveries as she develops her erotic potential and expands her sexual identity along the path of Sexual Individuation.

Acknowledgements

The author would like to gratefully acknowledge Hal and Sidra Stone, PhDs, and Gina Ogden, PhD, for their ongoing support in the development of a Jungian and archetypal approach to sex therapy.

References

American Psychiatric Association. (2013). *Diagnostic and statistical manual of mental disorders* (5th ed.). Washington, DC: Author.

Annon, J. (1975). *The behavioral treatment of sexual problems*. Honolulu, HI: Enabling Systems.

Bader, M. (2002). *Arousal: The secret logic of sexual fantasies*. New York, NY: Thomas Dunne Books.

Basson, R., Leiblum, S., Brotto, L., Derogatis, L., Fourcroy, J., Fugl-Meyer, K., . . .Weijmar Schultz, W. (2003). Definitions of women's sexual dysfunction reconsidered: Advocating expansion and revision. *Journal of Psychosomatic Obstetrics and Gynecology, 24*, 221–229.

DeLamater, J., & Shibley Hyde, J. (2004). Conceptual and theoretical issues in studying sexuality in close relationships. In J. Harvey, A. Wenzel, & S. Sprecher (Eds.), *The handbook of sexuality in close relationships* (pp. 7–30). Mahwah, NJ: Lawrence Erlbaum.

Dyak, M. (1999). *The voice dialogue facilitator's handbook, Part 1*. Seattle, WA: L.I.F.E. Energy Press.

Eisler, R. (1996). *Sacred pleasure: Sex, myth, and the politics of the body-new paths to power and love*. San Francisco, CA: Harper.

Goodwach, R. (2005a). Sex therapy: Historical evolution, current practice, Part 1. *Australian and New Zealand Journal of Family Therapy, 26*(3), 155–164.

Goodwach, R. (2005b). Sex therapy: Historical evolution, current practice, Part 2. *Australian and New Zealand Journal of Family Therapy, 26*(4), 178–183.

Hendrick, C., Hendrick, S., & Dicke, A. (1998). The love attitudes scale: Short form. *Journal of Personality and Social Psychology, 15*(2), 147–159.

Heyn, D. (1997). *Marriage shock: The transformation of women into wives*. New York, NY: Villard.

Hite, S. (1994). *The Hite report on the family: Growing up under patriarchy*. New York, NY: Grove Press.

Johnson, R. (1986). *Inner work: Using dreams and active imagination for personal growth*. San Francisco, CA: Harper.

Kimmel, M. (Ed.). (2007). *The sexual self: The construction of sexual scripts*. Nashville, TN: Vanderbilt University Press.

Kleinplatz, P. (2001). A critique of the goals of sex therapy, or the hazards of safer sex. In P. Kleinplatz (Ed.), *New directions in sex therapy: Innovations and alternatives* (pp. xi–xxxiii). Philadelphia, PA: Brunner-Routledge.

Kleinplatz, P. (2012). Is that all there is? A new critique of the goals of sex therapy. In P. Kleinplatz (Ed.), *New directions in sex therapy: Innovations and alternatives* (2nd ed.) (pp. 101–118). New York, NY: Routledge.

Leiblum, S. (Ed.). (2010). *Treating sexual desire disorders: A clinical casebook*. New York, NY: Guilford Press.

Masters, W., & Johnson, V. (1966). *Human sexual response*. New York, NY: Bantam Books.

McCarthy, B., & McCarthy, E. (2009). *Discovering your couple sexual style*. New York, NY: Routledge.

Meston, C., & Buss, D. (2009). *Why women have sex: Understanding sexual motivations – from adventure to revenge (and everything in between)*. New York, NY: Times Books.

Money, J. (1993). *Love maps: Clinical concepts of sexual/erotic health and pathology, paraphilia, and gender transposition in childhood, adolescence, and maturity*. Buffalo, NY: Prometheus Books.

Morin, J. (1995). *The erotic mind: Unlocking the inner sources of sexual passion and fulfillment*. New York, NY: Harper Perennial.

Mosher, D.L. (1980). Three dimensions of depth of involvement in human sexual response. *The Journal of Sex Research, 16*(1), 1–42.

Ogden, G. (1990). *Everywoman's guide to understanding sexual style and creating intimacy*. Deerfield, FL: Health Communications.

Ogden, G. (2006). *The heart and soul of sex: Making the ISIS connection*. Boston, MA: Trumpeter.

Ogden, G. (2008). *Return of desire: A guide to rediscovering your sexual passion*. Boston, MA: Trumpeter.

Ogden, G. (2013). *Expanding the practice of sex therapy: An integrative model for exploring desire and intimacy*. New York, NY: Routledge.
Phillips, M., & Frederick, D. (1995). *Healing the divided self: Clinical and Ericksonian hypnotherapy for post-traumatic and dissociative conditions*. New York, NY: Norton.
Qualls-Corbett, N. (1988). *The sacred prostitute: Eternal aspect of the feminine*. Toronto: Inner City Books.
Resnick, S. (2012). *The heart of desire: Keys to the pleasures of love*. Hoboken, NJ: Wiley.
Schwartz, R. (1995). *Internal family systems therapy*. New York, NY: Guilford.
Shinoda Bolen, J. (1984). *Goddesses in everywoman: A new psychology of women*. New York, NY: Harper Perennial.
Snell, W. (2011). Multidimensional sexual self-concept questionnaire. In T. Fisher, C. Davis, W. Yarber, & S. Davis (Eds.), *Handbook of sexuality-related measures* (3rd ed.) (pp. 537–540). New York, NY: Routledge.
Snell, W., Fischer, T., & Walters, A. (1993). The multidimensional sexuality questionnaire: An objective self-report measure of psychological tendencies associated with human sexuality. *Annals of Sex Research, 6*, 27–55.
Stone, H., & Stone, S. (1989). *Embracing our selves: The voice dialogue manual*. Novato, CA: Nataraj.
Stone, H., & Stone, S. (2000). *Partnering: A new kind of relationship: How to love each other without losing yourselves*. Novato, CA: Nataraj.
Stone, S. (1997). *The shadow king: The invisible force that holds women back*. Novato, CA: New World Library.
Stone, S. (2000). *The shadow king: The invisible force that holds women back*. Novato, CA: New World Library.
Tiefer, L. (2012). The "new view" campaign: A feminist critique of sex therapy and an alternative vision. In P. Kleinplatz (Ed.), *New directions in sex therapy: Innovations and alternatives* (2nd ed.) (pp. 21–35). New York, NY: Routledge.
Wakefield, C. (2012). *Negotiating the inner peace treaty: Becoming the person you were born to be*. Bloomington, IN: Balboa Press.
Wentland, J., Herold, E., Desmarais, S., & Milhausen, R. (2009). Differentiating highly sexual women from less sexual women. *The Canadian Journal of Human Sexuality*. Retrieved from http://www.thefreelibrary.com/Differentiating+highly+sexual+women+from+less+sexual+women.-a0217847386
Young-Eisendrath, P. (1984). *Hags and heroes: A feminist approach to Jungian psychotherapy with couples*. Toronto: Inner City Books.
Young-Eisendrath, P. (1993). *You're not what I expected: Learning to love the opposite sex*. New York, NY: Morrow.

An integrative medicine approach to the treatment of HSDD: introducing the HURT Model™

Keesha Ewers

The Institute for the Advanced Study of Human Sexuality, San Francisco, CA, USA

Female sexual interest and arousal disorder (FSIAD), formally known as hypoactive sexual desire disorder (HSDD), is the most common complaint reported by women experiencing sexual dysfunction. In spite of this, FSIAD/HSDD is still considered treatment refractory and sexual health is only addressed by 35% of medical providers in about 75% of the time.

Intrusive automatic negative thoughts (ANTs) are the number one barrier to healthy female sexual desire (FSD), and relationship satisfaction is the number one barrier to decreased FSD. Women with persistent ANTs struggle to forgive, lack emotional intimacy in romantic relationships, and report relationship dissatisfaction, depression, and anxiety. ANTs can hijack adaptive information processing through rumination on past hurts, which can result in FSIAD/HSDD. Given the complexity of FSD, an individualized, integrative, interpersonal neurobiological model is called for in the treatment of FSIAD/HSDD.

Dyadic cohesion is an important predictor of FSD. The HURT (Healing Un-Resolved Trauma) study investigates the importance of emotional intimacy in partnered sex and how emotional hurt contributes to ANTs and FSAID/HSDD. Further, the HURT study investigates the role that releasing hurt, confronting the self (MIRROR exercise), and subsequent forgiveness may play in reversing FSIAD/HSDD and offers an accessible integrative treatment model for patients, medical providers, and therapists. The HURT model bridges the gap between medicine and psychotherapy, providing treatment for women who are suffering with decreased FSD and FSIAD/HSDD.

Introduction

Hypoactive sexual desire disorder (HSDD) is the most common reported form of female sexual dysfunction. *The Diagnostic and Statistical Manual of Mental Disorders* (*DSM–5*; American Psychiatric Association, 2013) recently redefined HSDD and renamed it female sexual interest and arousal disorder (FSIAD). I agree with the change, but given that the data referred to in this article is based on a study conducted under the *DSM–4* ((1994) definition, and for purposes of continuity, I will use the old nomenclature.

Though estimates of the prevalence of HSDD vary widely, it may affect as many as 55% of women worldwide (Richters, Grulich, de Visser, Smith, & Rissel, 2003). A number of factors may contribute to HSDD, but among the several potential barriers to female sexual desire (FSD), one stands out far above the rest: rumination on intrusive automatic negative thoughts (ANTs) during sex (Carvalho & Nobre, 2010). “I'm not satisfying my partner.” “I'm not getting turned on, when will this be over?” “I have so much stress at work and now you want me to do what?” Such ANTs, which are significantly more common in women with HSDD, distract a woman from erotic cues, which is at the crux of HSDD.

What causes ANTs? Their source typically lies in past emotionally hurtful experiences that are stored maladaptively in the brain, with resulting negative self-attributions (Shapiro, 2001). Though these past hurtful experiences may include traumas associated with post-traumatic stress disorder (PTSD), more often they are simply distressing life events. In fact, distressing life events can generate as many PTSD symptoms as traumatic events do (Mol et al., 2005). This suggests that past emotional hurts (including those within a dyadic relationship) have a significant impact on female neurobiology, relationship health, and level of sexual desire. Thus, evaluating past and current emotional pain, subsequent ANTs and negative attributions of self and sexual partner and level of relationship satisfaction are a key in the search for a real solution to HSDD in women.

Decreased FSD and HSDD in medicine today

Sexual problems are associated with relationship problems, interfere with overall health, and are a marker for other undiagnosed comorbid medical conditions. It is therefore an important priority for healthcare professionals to manage the sexual health concerns of their patients. Yet sex is addressed in medical visits by only 35% of primary care providers about 75% of the time (Nazareth, Boynton, & King, 2003). Time constraints, the belief that sexual history is not relevant to the chief complaint, and embarrassment of the clinician and/or client are all reasons cited for this oversight (Kingsberg & Knudson, 2011).

Another problem is the lack of training the mainstream medical providers receive regarding sexual issues. What little sex education medical providers and therapists receive is typically rooted in the linear Masters and Johnson sexual arousal model, in spite of the current research on FSD, which shows that many women follow a more circular sexual arousal/desire cycle, that women's sexual desire is more likely to be triggered than spontaneous, and that women exhibit a variety of motives for sexual engagement (Basson, 2008; Ogden, 2006). Often, even if women do not feel desire, they have been shown to have a *willingness* to engage in sexual activity with the belief they will become aroused and sense desire "soon" (Ganz & Greendale, 2007). The Masters and Johnson sexual arousal model is largely inadequate, when it comes to realistically addressing issues of FSD.

Sex therapy and medicine are also chiefly practiced within a framework of deficiency or dysfunction rather than a framework that facilitates personal growth in an individual, which can then allow for greater intimacy in partnerships. Given the complex nature of FSD, it is no surprise that the attempts made to cram a simple treatment plan into a 10–15 minute medical appointment, or even hour-long therapy appointments, have failed in a health care system that is pharmaceutically and procedurally driven. In my practice of integrative medicine, I find that women are frustrated about having been prescribed antidepressants (whose number one side effect is low libido), hormones (with controversial outcomes), and lubricants (that do not work).

Medical science and behavioral science have yet to find clear common ground both clinically and in the research literature – and this is not serving women with decreased sexual desire or FSIAD/HSDD. The integrative treatment model proposed in this article is based on research from the HURT study that is in press at this time. What follows is a brief overview of the study, the model that emerged from the study, and a case study for medical providers and therapists that could provide the common ground needed to really help women with decreased sexual desire.

New HSDD study: the HURT Model™

This is a pilot study that examines the impact of held-onto emotional hurt on FSD with the intent to help therapists and medical providers promote better health, increased self-awareness, personal growth, and enhanced intimacy for the women who suffer as a result of past and current emotional hurts and unsatisfactory sex lives. This study was inspired by hundreds of frustrated women who were not experiencing successful outcomes, in spite of trying many of the available treatments for HSDD and "doctor shopping" over a course of years. The lack of efficacious treatment options currently available for women with decreased sexual desire sent me to the literature for answers. Four main questions came out of a thorough review of literature on FSD:

(1) What role does emotional intimacy with an intimate partner in a committed relationship play in FSD?
(2) Does emotional hurt affect FSD?
(3) Does forgiving improve FSD?
(4) What can be done to improve treatment outcomes for women with HSDD?

A small, correlational, pilot study ($n = 89$) was designed and conducted using three validated survey tools: the Decreased Sexual Desire Screener), the Emotional Intimacy Scale, and the Transgression-Related Interpersonal Motivation Scale-18 Item form. In addition, a series of qualitative inquiries that encompassed the domains of the preceding four research questions (HSDD, emotional intimacy, emotional hurt/trauma, and forgiveness) were asked.

The hypotheses of the study were the following:

(1) Since emotional intimacy is a primary motive for women in committed relationships to engage with their partners sexually, and many women measure their relationship satisfaction level (another primary predictor for FSD) in terms of how much emotional intimacy they have within the relationship, emotional intimacy will be correlated with HSDD.
(2) It is established that neuroticism and ANTs are the most prevalent barriers to HSDD. It is predicted that held-onto hurt could be a factor in rumination and subsequent ANTs that are seen in women with HSDD.
(3) Forgiveness will be positively correlated with a reduction in decreased FSD.

The reasons given for HSDD by the women of this study could be grouped into four categories in order of the most common to the least common: (1) ANTs, (2) emotional barriers, (3) relationship dissatisfaction and stress, and (4) physical causes.

This study affirmatively answered the research questions and validated the hypotheses. In addition, this study revealed that in this sample of women:

(1) The women unwilling to let go of hurt(s) were less likely to engage in sexual activity with a partner after an interpersonal transgression (decreased FSD).
(2) The greater the perception of magnitude of hurt, the greater the decrease in FSD.

(3) The women who reported greater HSDD secondary to past hurts also reported greater effects of perceived magnitude of current emotional hurt affecting sexual desire.
(4) The women with decreased FSD secondary to past transgressions were more likely to be affected by hurt, and less likely to let go of hurt in the present than the women who had been able to continue with a satisfying sexual relationship after forgiving their partners of the past.
(5) A willingness to forgive significantly predicted whether a satisfying sexual relationship could be continued.
(6) The women who felt more emotionally intimate with their significant other were more likely to be benevolent (i.e., more likely to forgive) toward their transgressor.
(7) The women with HSDD were more likely to be vengeful or avoidant than benevolent with transgressors who were significant others.

The question we could then ask is why do some women hold onto hurt, with resulting inhibition in sexual desire, while others release hurt and have healthy sex lives.

HSDD, held onto hurt, and the neuroendocrine system

Women with HSDD focus more on overthinking their responses, which interferes with normal sexual response (Arnow et al., 2009). The more ANTs they have, the lower their subjective arousal will be, and the higher their levels of stress. A woman will focus on dealing with her stressful thoughts rather than on erotic feelings, thus continuing the HSDD cycle. Additionally, women with HSDD have trouble decoding physiological information and deciding whether it relates to sexual desire. A study by Laan demonstrated this through findings that showed women lubricated vaginally while watching pornography, while their brains failed to register arousal (Laan, Everaerd, van der Velde, & Greer, 1995). This discrepancy could be explained by the impact stress has on the prefrontal cortex (PFC).

The PFC translates stressful experience into adaptive behavior, a dynamic that women with HSDD struggle with. This is due to ANTs, difficulty decoding physiological information, and trouble staying focused on the erotic situation at hand. The brain structures that process stress, like the PFC and amygdala, affect the neurotransmitters that impact sexual desire (dopamine, norepinephrine, and serotonin) and the hormones that regulate the sexual response system (cortisol, estrogen, and testosterone). Body–brain integration plays a major role in the adaptation to stress, both past and present (Mora, Segovia, Del Arco, de Blas, & Garrido, 2011). Women do not need to experience distressing events in real time for the elicitation of stress-related cortisol release and activating autobiographical memories of past threats is sufficient. Mental rehearsal of stressful memories elicits cardiovascular reactivity (McNally et al., 2004) and women who ruminate about traumatic life events, including interpersonal transactions that are painful but not traumatic (McCullough, Bono, & Root, 2007), experience elevated levels of cortisol. Rumination and stress-related cortisol secretion lead to the activation of the autonomic nervous system, particularly the sympathetic nervous system (fight, flight, or freeze). A vigilant, self-protective stance toward future threat that uses rumination as the cognitive mechanism for reactivating the prior memory in order to prevent future hurt (McCullough et al., 2007) is an example of a maladaptive memory loop (MAML) that keeps the first trauma in real time in the brain and the autonomic nervous system on alert for ready re-activation.

The autonomic nervous system on constant alert can have an adverse effect not only on FSD, but on female reproductive hormone levels as well.

The acronym for maladaptive memory loop (MAML) sounds like *mammal* when sounded out. Remember that mammalian survival is dependent on the quality of our social bonds (Panskepp, 1998). It is even argued that the neuroarchitecture for the experience of broken social bonds or rejection (social/emotional hurt) overlaps with the same brain function experienced with physical hurt (Eisenberger & Leiberman, 2004). The difference is that emotional and socially painful events are heightened with rumination or repetitive memory triggering, the memories becoming intrusive or ANTs. We are hardwired to remember hurts so we do not repeat them. Rumination, or repeatedly reflecting on emotional hurts, changes fear and anger into ANTs, resulting in the delayed emotion of unforgiveness (Worthington, 2003), and according to the literature, a reduction in sexual desire for women. Thus, MAMLs in women are synonymous with negative emotions with resulting negative attributions, rumination and ANTs, autonomic nervous system activation, unforgiveness, and therefore, potentially with HSDD/FSIAD (see Figure 1).

Forgiveness as a treatment for HSDD

When even mental rehearsal of a negative memory can elicit a stress response, how much more likely to elicit such a response is an actual marital conflict? There is near universal agreement among clinicians that marital conflict is a major cause of HSDD (McCullough et al., 1998) and can predict the end of a relationship (Gottman & Levenson, 2002).

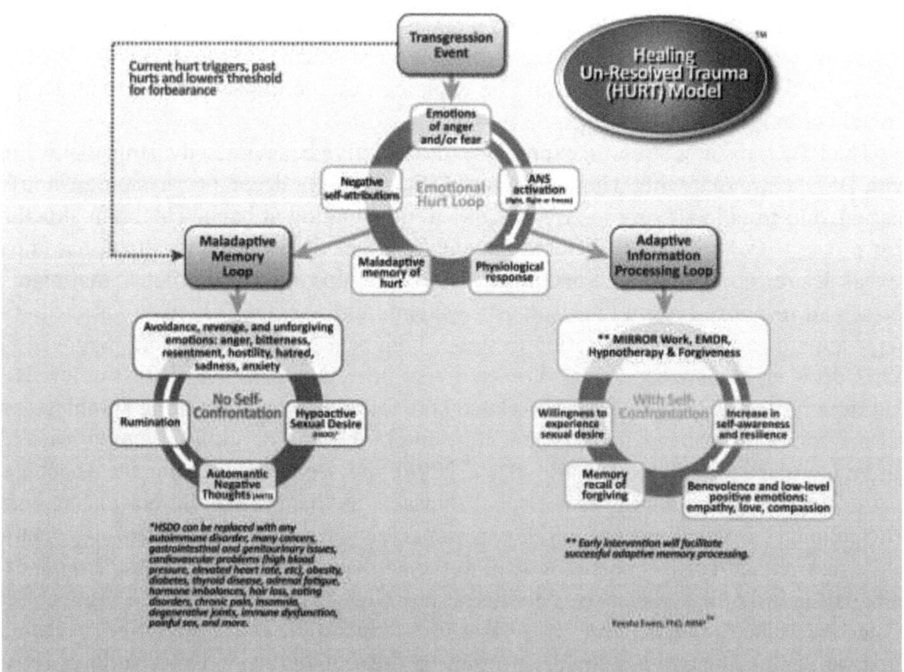

Figure 1. The HURT model.

Yet marital conflict is also an unavoidable by-product of interpersonal relationships (Fincham, 2000) and an opportunity for self-differentiation and growth within the relationship (Schnarch, 2009). The process of self-differentiation requires an ability to self-confront if significant others are not to be held responsible for a lifetime of transgressions resulting in emotional pain. Self-confrontation is a technique for behavior modification that depends on a person's recognition of and dissatisfaction with inconsistencies in his or her own values, beliefs, and behaviors, or between his or her own personal system and that of a significant other (Mosby Medical Dictionary, 2009). From the process of self-confrontation can emerge the emotional space for forgiveness and subsequent release of held onto hurt.

Forgiveness can be defined as:

> A willingness to release the hurt, resentment, negative judgment, and/or indifferent behavior we have toward someone who has injured us, while simultaneously confronting the self and taking responsibility for our own growth. Forgiveness means developing empathy, compassion, generosity, and even love; understanding that fear and love cannot co-exist in the same thought or breath. Forgiveness is not about forgetting or condoning transgressions that have caused pain or ignoring hurt. It is NOT reconciliation, which is not possible unless the transgressor has authentically apologized, taken responsibility for wrong-doing, and established trustworthiness and physical, emotional, and spiritual safety. (Ewers, in press)

Forgiving involves engaging in the cognitive, emotional, and/or behavioral work necessary to reframe a transgression so that neurobiological and endocrine responses are no longer negative. The goal of forgiveness is to grow and learn from hurtful events and release any stored negativity from the body and mind that can cause the victim further pain in the future; this will require a certain degree of self-differentiation and the ability to self-confront. According to Bowen, a person with a well-differentiated *self* recognizes her realistic dependence on others, but can stay calm in the face of conflict, criticism, and rejection. People with a poorly differentiated *self* depend heavily on the acceptance and approval of others (Bowen, 1978).

Given the overlaps noted in the literature on the neurobiological changes in response to trauma, distressing life events, relationship distress, and decrease in emotional intimacy between partners, HSDD, personality traits, and forgiveness, it is not surprising that a willingness to let go of hurt could positively affect levels of FSD. Research suggests that if rumination lessens over time, women will become more forgiving and can let go of their hurt (McCullough et al., 1998, McCullough, Root, Tabak, & Witvliet, 2009).

The HURT model

The HURT model is one way of conceptualizing an integrative approach to the treatment of decreased FSD. It is based on the principles of Interpersonal Neurobiology, a way of integrating interdisciplinary sciences to find common ground in understanding human experience (Siegel, 2010). This reflects the vision of integrative medicine, which takes into account all aspects of a person's life and seeks the root cause of illness rather than just symptom management. If HSDD is conceptualized as a sexual issue that is the result of the inability of the neuroendocrine circuitries to integrate with the complex nature of sexual response encompassing physiological, psychological, emotional, spiritual, and relationship components (Meston & Frohlich, 2000), then an individualized integrative (spiritual and intimacy-based) model for the treatment of low sexual desire must be adopted in order to provide an efficacious solution to HSDD.

The theoretical framework that results from integrating the current scientific understanding of FSD, emotional intimacy, the impact of distressing life experiences and/or trauma has on the brain and body, and the role of forgiveness and trauma release methods is as follows:

> Female sexual desire emerges from an integrated interpersonal neurobiological mind, brain, body connection, as well as from a strong individualized spiritual connection with healthy interpersonal and self-confrontational communication tools in place. This integration helps the individual adaptively process the inevitable emotional hurts that will occur in interpersonal relationships and establish and maintain emotional intimacy, positive attributions for self and other, self-differentiation, and safety for both partners. (Ewers, in press)

Implementing the HURT model in clinical practice

One of the easiest ways to organize information, whether it's during a 15-minute medical appointment or a 60–90 minute therapy session, is to use the adapted functional medicine matrix (Figure 2). This matrix comes from the Institute for Functional Medicine and has been adapted to include sexual health, partner intimacy, and attributions for self and other.

This matrix illustrates the complexity of any imbalance, whether HSDD or a medical diagnosis, such as hypertension. Hypertension is not *caused* by a shortage of an antihypertensive drug in the body, any more than erectile dysfunction for men is caused by a shortage of one of the popular pharmaceuticals prescribed in medicine today. HSDD is also

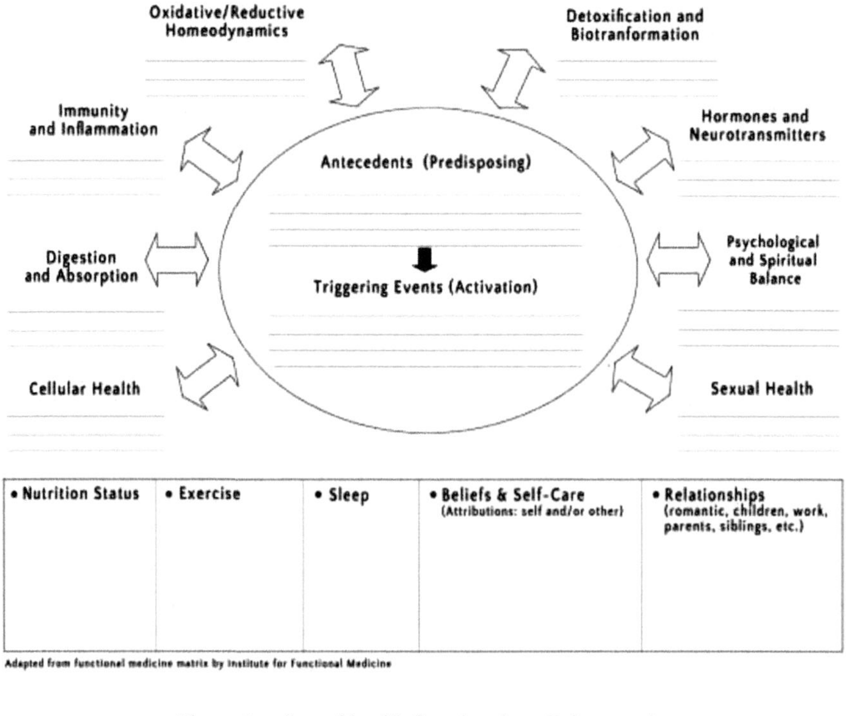

Figure 2. Sexual health functional medicine matrix.

not a shortage of a drug in a woman's body; it is a complex issue that will have a root cause. Having a road map to use is useful when diagnosing and treating imbalances. The functional medicine matrix is just such a tool. Asking your client open-ended questions that incorporate each of the eight categories of the matrix will ensure that a holistic history and assessment have been performed.

Here is an example of how to assess and triage FSD using an integrative medicine approach.

Triaging decreased female sexual desire

(1) What are the chief complaints in the client's words? List in order of distress for the client. A thorough history will allow the use of the adapted functional medicine matrix pictured in Figure 2.
(2) Populate the matrix by filling in:
    i. The eight categories.
    ii. The antecedents.
    iii. The triggers.
    iv. The contributing lifestyle factors.
(3) When working with FSD, pay particular attention and ask about:
    i. ANTs.
    ii. Negative attributions for self and other.
(4) If negative attributions are present for self or other:
    i. Use the HURT model and select the adaptive information processing (AIP) strategies appropriate for your client (as shown in Figure 1).
        a. The MIRROR exercise (ME) for self-confrontation and release (described below).
        b. Eye movement desensitization reprocessing (EMDR) (Shapiro, 2001)s or hypnotherapy if appropriate for trauma release.
        c. Forgiveness.
    ii. Clear negative attributions for self and other as they arise in treatment.
(5) Use the ME (self-confrontation), trauma release techniques, and forgiveness as the conversation uncovers where the client is in her self-responsibility and self-differentiation process, as well as with her spirituality and personality needs.
(6) If you are not trained in trauma release or functional medicine testing, refer to providers trained in the skills needed to help your client heal fully from the inside out.
(7) Websites for training and/or referral:
    i. ME skills training and the HURT model training: www.fernlifecenter.com
    ii. EMDR training or to find a professional: http://www.emdr.com/
    iii. Functional medicine training or to find a functional medicine provider: http://www.functionalmedicine.org/

When a woman comes into my integrative medical clinic, she has already been asked a series of questions via her intake paper work. Her reasons for coming in are listed in order of importance (chief complaints), and she has rated on a scale of 1–10 (with 10 the best and 1 the worst) her satisfaction with her personal growth, her family and friends, her finances, her romantic/significant other, her sex life, her job, her health, her stress coping ability, and her mood. She has filled out a food diary for me, given me an addiction and eating disorder history, her ways of coping with stress, a medication and supplement list (past and present), and she has filled out open-ended questions that include questions about spirituality. Because I am interested in the answers to these and other questions, before I ever meet her, her paper work gives me a good idea about her level of self-differentiation, her willingness to self-confront, personality traits, and any medical/surgical or comorbid conditions that might be contributing to decreased FSD.

I then populate the adapted functional medicine matrix for assessment and diagnosis and as a way to organize an individualized treatment plan based on the context in which decreased FSD is occurring for each individual woman. I re-tell her story from the matrix back to her to verify I have it right and for additional information she might want to add. I then order several diagnostic tests, as needed, in order to get a comprehensive picture of the woman sitting before me so we can get to the bottom of her issues as quickly as possible. These may include, but are not limited to the following:

- Nutrigenomics (genetic testing).
- Food sensitivities (food = mood).
- Adrenal stress index with expanded hormone panels (both salivary and plasma).
- Comprehensive thyroid and iodine level testing (including free T3 and T4, TSH, TPO, and RT3).
- Urinary neurotransmitters (depending on self-reported mood stability).
- Inflammatory markers (hsCRP, SED rate, homocysteine).
- Detoxification pathway indicators (liver and renal function, colon transit testing).
- Autoimmune markers: I find women with HSDD seem to be more reactive on many levels and have a higher than average incidence of autoimmunity.
- Comprehensive stool analysis as needed.
- Methylation testing: DNA methylation is one of the methods used to regulate the expression of genes and since HSDD and depression are linked, this can be important as the heritability of depression for women is 40% (Davidson, 2013).
- Standard blood work (Hgb A1c, Chem panel, CBC, Vit D, Vit B-12 and folate, lipids, GGT, and an iron panel).

The next step is to use the HURT model and ME to transform MAMLs into AIP networks. The AIP model was developed for therapists to address the overall clinical picture. This includes the past experiences that contribute to a client's current difficulties, the present events that trigger MAMLs, as well as to develop more adaptive neural networks of memory in order to enhance positive responses for the future (Shapiro & Laliotis, 2011). A primary difference between AIP and MAMLs is the ability to **self-confront**. Self-confrontation is the willingness to see one's own role in MAMLs, and the desire to take responsibility for the suffering that occurs from the re-triggering of old hurts. Relearning in an AIP way leads to stronger neural networks and freedom from held-onto hurt. This can be achieved using the ME in either medical office visits or therapy sessions.

Using the MIRROR exercise for self-confrontation

Case study. Megan was a 37-year-old woman who came into my office with fatigue and low libido. After doing the initial interview, filling in the adapted functional medicine matrix for sexual health, and ordering a battery of lab work that matched her history and physical, I saw her for her second visit. Her lab work had revealed a previously undiagnosed autoimmune disorder and a genetic marker that required a specific diet. During the course of the conversation with Megan, I gently told her that one of the reasons I see autoimmunity in women and the number of food sensitivities she had (intestinal permeability syndrome) was because of rigid patterns of thinking that contain intrusive negative thoughts and negative attributions for self and other.

She began to cry and acknowledged this was true for her. She told me her story of sexual abuse by her brother and the neglect she felt from her mother. I asked what she believed about herself when she thought of each of these people, and she responded that she "wasn't important" and "didn't feel safe a lot." I asked if she felt this way with her husband, and she was able to identify examples readily, registering surprise that she had never made the connections on her own. I scheduled her for EMDR, installed a calm, safe place for her in that session, and taught her containment (i.e., to place any overwhelming memories into a "container" that would be processed in her next therapy session). She was able to repeat back to me how these events in her past, how her current triggers with her spouse, and how her physical issues were all related to the MAMLs she had created. She was excited to learn to move to the AIP loop using the HURT model.

After one session of EMDR, we moved to the ME so she could see how it worked. The essence of the ME can be found in the letters of MIRROR: Mental Image Revealing Rumination (of) Object (to) Release. MIRRORing allows the client to move from judgment to self-awareness and responsibility taking. This is not a linear process and will happen in a spiral fashion as the client moves toward spontaneous self-confrontation and becomes more and more self-differentiated.

When I teach a client to MIRROR, I start with a distressing life event that is more annoying than traumatic to get her used to the process; for example, the experience of someone cutting you off on the freeway. I ask the client to tell me what negative attributions she would apply to this person. Examples I hear are, "rude," "impatient," and "self-centered." I then ask the client to find these same attributions in herself. As humans we all have the same personality traits, we just manifest them differently and at varying levels of intensity. An easy way to get a client to be able to MIRROR is to model the exercise yourself by sharing ways you have been rude, impatient, or self-centered in the last week or so. This requires a healthy level of differentiation and willingness to self-confront and self-reveal as a medical provider or therapist.

After practicing with low-level events, we moved to Megan's childhood sexual abuse. Looking in the mirror at her transgressor meant that Megan looked for the negative attribution she had applied to him and continued to ruminate about. Here is how I approached Megan with MIRRORing this event:

Doctor: Megan, what would drive your brother to abuse you?

Megan: He was evil.

Doctor: Ok, but what would be a personality trait that would drive him to behave in an evil way?

Megan: I have no idea.

Doctor: (using the technique of self-disclosure to help guide the client) Alright, well when I did this work around my own childhood sex abuse, I decided it must be about the misuse of power.

Megan: Oh, yes, I guess that's true. He was trying to get power because he had been abused too.

Doctor: Good. Now, if you were to look in the MIRROR and take from this some learning for yourself about your own personality traits and thoughts, how do you misuse power? Remember that Hitler also misused power. I likely misused power before breakfast today, but haven't bought tanks and taken over Poland or killed anyone. You will do it differently than your abuser, but you will find how you, too, misuse power if you look hard enough, since all humans have similar personality traits that we manifest in different ways.

Megan: Well, okay, I see what you are driving at. I guilt trip my daughter when she doesn't do what I want her to do; I know it's wrong, but I seem to do it as a habit.

Doctor: Good. Are there any other personality traits in your brother that could contribute to his behavior?

Megan: Yes, he was angry and mean.

Doctor: Are you ever angry or mean? Remember that you will be angry and mean differently than your brother was.

Doctor: Yes, I am that way with my husband a lot.

Doctor: Great job, Megan. So now you have just joined the human race and are not placing yourself above your transgressor by sitting in judgment. We often use that as our only source of power if we have been victimized, and it's not a healthy strategy. I will help you with boundary setting and other strategies for getting what you want later. So now, can you forgive yourself for guilting your daughter?

Megan: Yes, it's hard though. It makes me sick to think it's an abuse of power to do that, but I see that it is now. It also makes me see other places I do this with my husband. I use sex to get what I want too.

Doctor: Good. It will be necessary for you to forgive yourself and your transgressor in order to move those ANTs out of your mind, which will free you from triggering every day to life events around you, which sets your sympathetic nervous system off, which activates your hormone axis in a depleting way. Remember, though, forgiving your transgressor does NOT mean you are forgiving his actions, nor does it mean you need to reconcile. Reconciliation only happens if your transgressor is trustworthy and care-worthy. Forgiveness can happen without any contact with your transgressor. It is simply letting go of negative attributions toward him and toward yourself.

This is a snippet of a typical session using the MIRROR exercise. There will be more time spent in discussion of insights or roadblocks as they arise. Megan was motivated to look in the MIRROR because she was physically sick, her relationship was failing, and she was discovering that her lack of boundaries and codependency were affecting many areas of her life. Her willingness to move into an AIP model from her MAML pattern through self-confrontation allowed her work to progress. Every victory she made empowered her to look in the MIRROR and self-confront more readily.

Eventually, I saw Megan with her husband in couples counseling, and we were able to address their relationship issues. Megan and her husband began to see conflict as an opportunity to look in the MIRROR and to grow as individuals, and as a couple, as self-differentiation grew through the process of self-confrontation.

Today, Megan is free from autoimmunity, is healing her leaky gut, eats according to her APOe genetic type, feels energetic most of the time, and gets excited to look in the MIRROR when she is triggered so she can begin to transform whatever shadow trait she is projecting onto another. Most relevant to this article, she reports both a willingness to experience sexual desire and a satisfaction with her sex life. She has learned to reframe the people who hurt her as her teachers, and distressing events as opportunities for enhancing her self-awareness, rewiring her brain, and creating AIP networks. Self-confrontation and subsequent forgiveness allows her to free herself from ANTs, bitterness, and resentment, and to set healthy boundaries resulting in a supportive and nurturing community in which she finds herself hurt less and less. She has learned how to be powerful without being a victim.

Conclusion

The results of the HURT study along with my clinical and medical experience and examination of the literature reinforce for me that neither psychotherapy nor medical intervention alone is sufficient for the lasting resolution of sexual problems (McCabe et al., 2010). Recently, psychologists have reached a consensus that research has seriously neglected the strengths of human behavior (McCullough et al., 2007). It is argued that many psychological modalities have focused mainly on reducing aggression, psychopathies, and vices instead of emphasizing positive experiences that improve quality of life. The process of MIRRORing (self-confrontation) aids in self-differentiation, and forgiveness creates a practical and positive psychological response to interpersonal hurt. Combined, these result in a positive impact on physical, emotional, and mental states that contribute to health and sexual functioning.

The HURT model (Figure 1) illustrates the rewiring of the brain through AIP networks that replace MAMLs from past distressing life events (which can be triggered by a current emotional hurtful event). The difference between adaptive and maladaptive responses is the process of self-confrontation. When working with a client, if her HSDD is sourced in an MAML, and is being triggered by persistent emotionally hurtful experiences with a current sexual partner, she can be taught to self-confront in order to reach forgiveness for past transgression(s). This process disengages her nervous system and physiological responses from the past trauma and replaces her rumination on hurt and negative self-attribution(s) with positive self-attributions. Replacing negative feedback loops with positive ones increases her emotional resilience and self-differentiation, which can lead to a willingness to experience sexual desire. Tools for trauma release and healing negative self-attributions can include the ME, EMDR, clinical hypnotherapy, and the Integrating Sexuality and Spirituality Wheel (Ogden, 2013).

The more that self-confrontation and subsequent forgiveness is used with trauma release for rewiring the brain, the more likely women will be to willingly experience sexual desire. As research consistently shows, for most women, sexual desire is not always spontaneous, but a response to her cultural cues, level of relationship satisfaction, perceived level of emotional connection to her partner, degree of self-differentiation, feelings of safety and security, her physical, emotional, mental and spiritual health, and above all, her thoughts and beliefs (automatic thoughts and attributions) about herself and her partner and her willingness to self-confront, let go of rumination, and forgive when she has been hurt.

Acknowledgements

I would like to thank the researchers who have gone before me and Dr Gina Ogden for her unflagging support of this study and her expansion of sex therapy; her visionary path of combining spirituality and sexuality is what inspired me to start along this path of research. I would also like to convey my special thanks to Alexander Kohorst, the statistician who willingly re-ran my data and found the missing links, and my editor, who is also my life partner and biggest fan, Ajayan Borys.

References

American Psychiatric Association. (1994). *Diagnostic and statistical manual of mental disorders* (4th ed.). Washington, DC: Author.

American Psychiatric Association. (2013). *Diagnostic and statistical manual of mental disorders* (5th ed.). Arlington, VA: American Psychiatric Publishing.

Arnow, B.A., Millheiser, L., Garrett, A., Lake Polan, M., Glover, G.H., Hill, K.R., … Desmond, J.E. (2009). Women with hypoactive sexual desire disorder compared to normal females: A functional magnetic imaging study. *Neuroscience, 158*(2), 484–502.

Basson, R. (2008). Women's sexual function and dysfunction: Current uncertainties, future directions. *International Journal of Impotence Research, 20*, 466–478.

Bowen, M. (1978). *Family therapy in clinical practice*. New York, NY: Jason Aronson.

Carvalho, J., & Nobre, P. (2010). Gender issues and sexual desire: The role of emotional and relationship variables. *Journal of Sex Medicine, 7*(7), 2469–2478.

Davidson, R. (2013). *The emotional life of your brain: How its unique patterns affect the way you think, feel, and live-and how you can change them*. New York, NY: Plume.

Eisenberger, N., & Leiberman, M. (2004). Why rejection hurts: The neurocognitive overlap between physical and social pain. *Trends in Cognitive Sciences, 8*, 294–300.

Ewers, K. (in press). The impact of held-onto hurt on female sexual desire.

Fincham, F. (2000). The kiss of the porcupines: From attributing responsibility to forgiving. *Personal Relationships, 7*, 1–23.

Ganz, P., & Greendale, G. (2007). Female sexual desire-beyond testosterone. *Journal of the National Cancer Institute, 99*, 659–661.

Gottman, J., & Levenson, R.W. (2002). A two-factor model for predicting when a couple will divorce: Exploratory analyses using 14-year longitudinal data. *Family Process, 41*(1), 83–96.

Kingsberg, S.A., & Knudson, G. (2011). Female sexual disorders: Assessment, diagnosis, and treatment. *CNS Spectrums, 16*(2), 49–62.

Laan, E., Everaerd, W., van der Velde, J., & Greer, J. (1995). Determinants of subjective experience of sexual arousal in women: Feedback from genital arousal and erotic stimulus content. *Psychophysiology, 32*(5), 444–451.

McCabe, M., Althof, S.E., Assalian, P., Chevret-Measson, M., Leiblum, S.R., Simonelli, C., & Wylie, K. (2010). Psychological and interpersonal dimensions of sexual function and dysfunction. *Journal of Sex Medicine, 7*(1 Pt 2), 327–336.

McCullough, M.E., Bono, G., & Root, L.M. (2007). Rumination, emotion, and forgiveness: Three longitudinal studies. *Journal of Personality and Social Psychology, 92*, 490–505.

McCullough, M.E., Rachal, K.C., Sandage, S.J., Worthington, E.L. Jr, Brown, S.W., & Hight, T.L. (1998). Interpersonal forgiving in close relationships: II. Theoretical elaboration and measurement. *Journal of Personality and Social Psychology, 75*, 1586–1603.

McCullough, M.E., Root, L.M., Tabak, B., & Witvliet, C.V.O. (2009). Forgiveness. In S.J. Lopez (Ed.), *Handbook of positive psychology* (2nd ed.), pp. 427–435. New York, NY: Oxford.

McNally, R.J., Lasko, N.B., Clancy, S.A., Macklin, M.L., Pitman, R.K., & Orr, S.P. (2004). Psychophysiological responding during script-driven imagery in people reporting abduction by space aliens. *Psychological Science, 15*, 493–497.

Meston, C., & Frohlich, R. (2000). The neurobiology of sexual function. *Archives of General Psychiatry, 57*(11), 1012–1030.

Mol, S.S., Arntz, A., Metsemakers, J.F., Dinant, G.J., Vilters-van Montfort, P.A., & Knottnerus, J.A. (2005). Symptoms of post-traumatic stress disorder after non-traumatic events: Evidence from an open population study. *British Journal of Psychiatry, 186*, 494–499.

Mora, F., Segovia, G., Del Arco, A., de Blas, M., & Garrido, P. (2011). Stress, neurotransmitters, corticosterone and body-brain integration. *Brain Research, 1476*, 71–85.

Mosby Medical Dictionary. (2009). Retrieved from http://medical-dictionary.thefreedictionary.com/self-confrontation

Nazareth, I., Boynton, P., & King, M. (2003). Problems with sexual function and people attending London general practitioners: Cross-sectional study. *BMJ, 327*(7412), 423–429.

Ogden, G. (2006). *The heart and soul of sex: Making the ISIS connection*. Boston, MA: Shambhala.

Ogden, G. (2013). *Expanding the practice of sex therapy: An integrative model for exploring desire and intimacy*. New York, NY: Routledge.

Panskepp, J. (1998) *Affective neuroscience: The foundations of human and animal emotions*. New York, NY: Oxford University Press.

Richters, J., Grulich, A., de Visser, R., Smith, A., & Rissel, C. (2003). Sex in Australia: Sexual difficulties in a representative sample of adults. *Australian and New Zealand Journal of Public Health, 27*, 164–170.

Schnarch, D. (2009). Intimacy and desire: Awaken the passion in your relationship. New York, NY: Beaufort Books.

Shapiro, F. (2001). *Eye movement desensitization and reprocessing: Basic principles, protocols and procedures* (2nd ed.). New York, NY: Guilford.

Shapiro, F., & Laliotis, D. (2011). EMDR and the adaptive information processing model: Integrative treatment and case conceptualization. *Journal of Clinical Social Work, 39*, 191–200.

Worthington, E.L. (2003). *Forgiving and reconciling: Bridges to wholeness and hope*. Madison, WI: InterVarsity Press.

Compassionate authenticity: a treatment model for working with women with low libido

Lindsay B. Jernigan

Eastern View Integrative Medicine, South Burlington, VT, USA

Women often report taking care of others at the expense of their own well-being in the name of being compassionate. As a result, they may experience a drop in vital energy, including a drop in sensual energy and libido, and a rise in resentment towards their sexual partners, ultimately leading to a lack of satisfying sexual relationship for both partners. A theoretical framework is proposed based on the author's original idea of compassionate authenticity. According to this theory, the most compassionate act a partner can give is one's own authentic presence in the relationship, as this promotes genuine intimacy and sensual flow. This paper guides the reader in the application of the compassionate authenticity treatment model to work with clients with low libido. The model involves the intentional application of an eclectic approach that addresses three critical treatment goals: (1) building acceptance of and curiosity about one's sensuality; (2) differentiating from one's sexual partner/s; and (3) redefining sexual and emotional caretaking.

Our deepest calling is to grow into our authentic self-hood, whether or not it conforms to some image of who we ought to be. As we do so, we will not only find the joy that every human being seeks – we will also find our path of authentic service in the world.

Parker Palmer

Compassionate authenticity

Compassionate authenticity is a treatment model that I developed to help women with low libido experience desire, arousal, and rewarding sexual relationships. The model involves working, via an eclectic range of treatment modalities, on three interrelated goals: (1) building the client's acceptance of and curiosity about her sensuality; (2) differentiating from her sexual partner/s; and (3) redefining sexual and emotional caretaking to include authenticity rather than self-sacrifice.

The compassionate authenticity model is born from my observation, from my work with hundreds of women and couples over more than 15 years of practice, that my clients experience deeper and more passionate connection, more robust desire, and more active and enjoyable sex lives when they act on their own sensual wishes and in alignment with their own emotions; in other words, when they give themselves permission to bring their authentic selves to the bedroom.

Psychologists have long recognized that *authenticity*, or the alignment of external behaviors with internal experiences, is an important ingredient of optimal health (Rogers, 1961). Also recognized is that *compassion*, the desire to reduce the suffering of others, is a fundamental trait of the female gender role across many cultures (Gilligan, 1993), and can be a relational skill that promotes supportive and loving relationships (Jordan, Kaplan, Miller, Stiver, & Surrey, 1991; Miller & Stiver, 1997). But with alarming consistency, my female clients present in therapy having sacrificed their sexual authenticity to what they believe is compassionate caretaking of their partners' sexual needs. They have internalized the message that they should silence, adjust or give up parts of themselves in order to keep their sexual partners happy and to maintain connection, and that to not do so is "selfish."

I consistently observe, in my clients and in the literature, that clients who have sacrificed their authenticity report feeling out of touch with their own vital energy – with their creativity, with their emotions, with their passions, with their bodies, and with their sensuality (Perel, 2006; Rogers, 1961; Schnarch, 1997; Schwartz, 1995). My female clients, in particular, frequently present in therapy with low libido and high levels of resentment, anxiety, and avoidance in their sex lives. Sex has become something they do for their partners instead of for themselves, and often something they do not want to do at all. Rather than fueling connection as they intended to do, these clients, by withdrawing their own authentic selves from the relational equation, are prohibiting real intimacy and robbing their partners of gratifying connection, as well.

The compassionate authenticity treatment model offers an alternative form of caretaking: one in which authenticity is encouraged not only because it enhances one's own well-being, but also because it is a gift to one's partner, providing the possibility of truly intimate connection. Because multiple theories of psychology and psychotherapy address the importance of authenticity to well-being, there are a slew of clinical approaches to draw on that are appropriately suited to the model; I use the approaches that are most authentically suited to me in my work. The compassionate authenticity model provides a map, and clinicians can use and combine many different treatment techniques to build the road to authentic sexuality.

Through the case example that follows, I will describe how the compassionate authenticity model was born out of my clinical observation, and tell the story of one woman's transformation through the process.

Case example: compassionate authenticity and the treatment of low libido in Anna

Initial presentation and the birth of a treatment model

Anna first came to me as a 24-year-old woman married to her high school sweetheart, Derek. She told me tearfully that her marriage was falling apart because she did not want to have sex. She summed up the conflict poignantly: "He wants it all the time, and I consent even though I don't want to." Anna said Derek approached her in ways that felt intrusive and lacked emotional connection (e.g. grabbing at her body), and that he was typically "pushy." She had developed an anxious response to his sexual approach, and she pathologized herself deeply for her pattern of anxiety and disengagement, insisting sadly, "there is something wrong with me." She primarily wanted to "fix" her "problem" so that she could ease her husband's "frustration." He had recently upped the ante by stating that he might leave the marriage because he felt unwanted, sexually, and wanted a more "passionate" sex life that "makes me feel like a man."

Upon assessment, Anna stated, "I hate sex and I have for a few years." She had begun dating her husband at the age of 17; he was her first boyfriend and first and only sexual partner. Initially, sex was a source of pleasure and connection for both of them. This changed when she became a college student, also working hard to pay her way through school. She was exhausted, depleted, and overly busy. "He saw sex as a way to connect, and I didn't. I felt like it was an obligation." That feeling of obligation stuck with her and became a core foundation of their sexual dynamic. She said, "I have to have sex with him, otherwise he gets anxious, and feels rejected and sad." He would then become angry, criticize her for being "unsexual", blame her for his own unhappiness, and withdraw. For herself, she said sex is "nothing positive. I don't enjoy it. But it makes him happy so I try."

In Anna's initial story, I recognized a cycle of experience that I had heard from many women before. She believed her sexual feelings (in her case a lack of sexual interest and anxious avoidant responses) were inherently bad, and she felt ashamed. She pathologized herself and focused on changing or hiding her feelings, rather than exploring them. Because she felt responsible for the emotional and sexual welfare of her husband, she acted in ways that were incongruent with her internal experience, agreeing to sex she did not want to have in the name of taking care of him and protecting their relationship. As she silenced and judged her authentic experience, she grew distant from herself, and she lost touch with her body, her emotions, and her sensuality.

I realized that this was a common presentation. Despite a wide variety of early sexual experiences, of dynamics in current sexual relationships, and of sexual styles and preferences, many women were presenting with the same pattern: (1) they were ashamed of their sexuality; (2) they felt responsible for their partners' sexual happiness; and (3) they acted inauthentically in the name of taking care of their partners. These common experiences looked to me like spokes on a wheel, each reinforcing the next in a cycle of withdrawal (see Figure 1). As the consistency of this cycle became increasingly clear, so did the compassionate authenticity treatment model. Each stage in the cycle of withdrawal presented itself as a place for clinical intervention; the cycle could be reversed by spinning the wheel in the other direction, drawing clients back into closer and more authentic contact with their sensual selves.

And so the treatment goals that make up the model were born. Reverse the cycle of sexual withdrawal and increase authentic sensual flow by helping the client to (1) build acceptance of and curiosity about her own sensuality; (2) differentiate from her sexual partner; and (3) redefine caretaking to support authenticity as an act of compassion (see Figure 2).

Stage 1 of therapy: addressing each treatment goal

Treatment goal 1: build acceptance of and curiosity about her sensuality

Anna was initially hesitant to allow herself to feel curious about her sexuality because she thought she "should" feel something different from her current state of anxiety and avoidance. She was ashamed, and avoiding feelings such as anger, sadness, and fear – all of which were authentic experiences related to her sexual experiences in her marriage. I shared psychoeducational information about the negative consequences of emotional suppression on mental and relational health, explaining that her pattern of emotional suppression could be contributing to her feelings of anxiety and disconnection from Derek (Gross & Levenson, 1993; Salters-Pedneault, Tull, & Roemer, 2004).

Figure 1. The cycle of sexual withdrawal.

We discussed the potential benefits of increasing her emotional range. I used a metaphor. She wanted to experience more passion, an emotion in the "high end of her range." But she was not allowing herself to express painful emotions in the "lower end of her range." I described her emotional energy as being like a square graphic on a computer screen: she could shrink or grow the whole square by "dragging the corner in or out," decreasing or expanding her emotional range. "But," I continued, "you don't get to just raise up the top; that would distort the square." In the name of rediscovering her passion "at the top of her emotional range," she began to risk expressing feelings in her "lower range" – her feelings of sadness, anger, and fear present in her sexual dynamics with Derek.

I used humanistic therapy, an approach designed to support people's natural drive to develop into their healthiest selves through non-judgmental support (Rogers, 1961). In Anna's case, the goal was to help her connect with her "real self" – her genuine feelings and wishes as she really experienced them – particularly her wish to stop having sex against her own consent. The unconditionally accepting therapeutic environment provided a venue where she could explore this emotional experience without self-reproach.

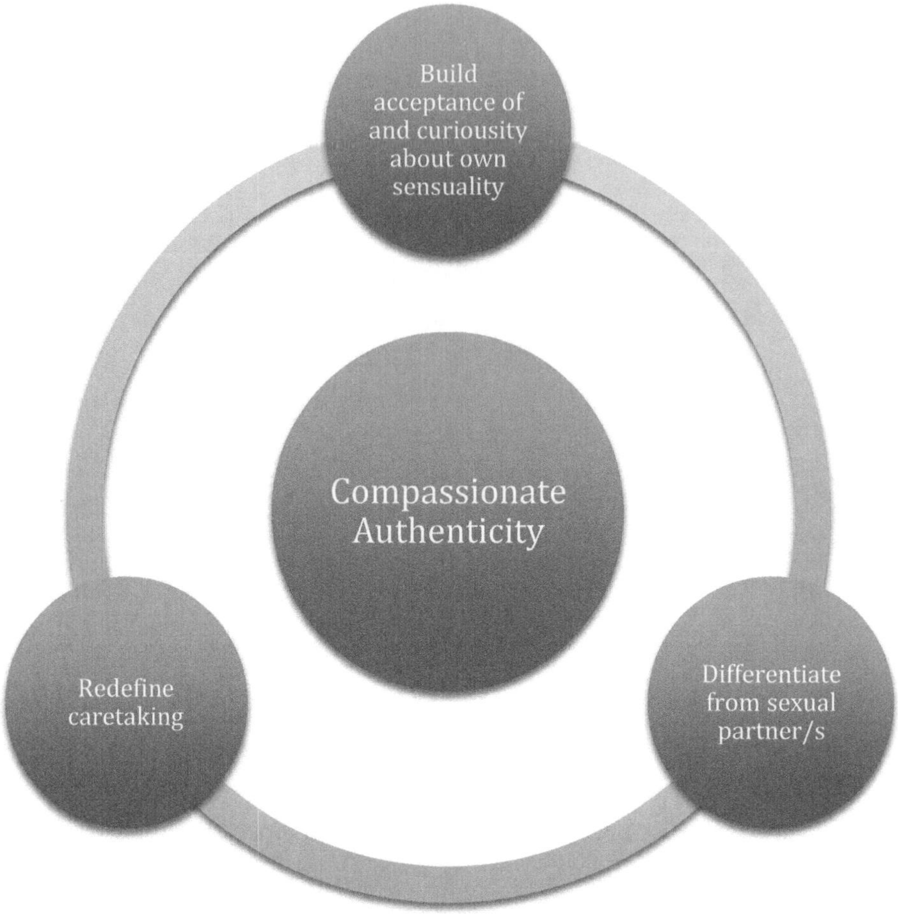

Figure 2. The compassionate authenticity treatment model.

By reflecting back and empathizing with her emotional experiences as she risked expressing them, I guided her to trust her own feelings, even her feelings of sexual withdrawal, as an important source of information and a valuable piece of her emotional and sexual self.

We also used Internal Family Systems (Schwartz, 1995) techniques of listening to "parts" of her that had developed, and of understanding their individual efforts and purposes. We listened to the "part" of her that was overriding her own wish to not have sex and "makes (her) do it" to protect her husband from rejection, and to protect herself from his anger. We listened to the "part" of her that quietly cried inside of her while having sex she did not want to have. And we listened to the "part" of her that got angry on her own behalf and felt resentful and bitter towards her husband. Using these same techniques, we tapped into a core part of her that could feel compassion and concern for all of these parts, and could understand her own complex internal experience. Anna began to feel more love and acceptance for herself and her current sexual experience, and could see her sexual withdrawal as an understandable and adaptive response to unwanted sexual contact.

We built on her new capacity to recognize and tolerate her emotions via mindfulness skills training, the practice of sitting with feelings without judging them or identifying with them (Kabat-Zinn, 1990), and through anxiety management and emotional tolerance skills, such as diaphragmatic breathing, body scans, and grounding in the present through her senses. She used these skills again later in therapy when she was ready to break the conditioned anxious response she felt in response to the thought of sexual contact. We practiced identifying her feelings, and recognizing the bodily sensations that accompany them: "I can tell I'm feeling anxious because my chest is tightening and I feel hot; I am really sad, and I can tell because I have a lump in my chest and I feel like I want to cry; I feel really ashamed. . .I feel sick to my stomach, and my head feels heavy."

Anna engaged in the narrative therapy technique of externalizing the problem to de-identify with her anxious response to sexual approach (White, 2007). She could locate her anxiety as separate from herself; she could explore its shape and size, the speed at which it moved, its weight, and its color. This allowed her to maintain her sense of self as separate from the anxiety, and to learn more about the role the anxiety was playing for her. She saw her anxiety as a steel wall that came down in front of her "all of a sudden" when she felt her partner approach. She could recognize that it was playing a protective role, and that by learning to honor her own truths, specifically, by allowing herself to say no to sex when she wanted to, she could eliminate the need for that protective wall. We spent time carefully "getting to know" her "anxiety" so that she could distinguish a conditioned anxious response (an involuntary tightening in her body that prevented her from feeling pleasure) from a "limit" that was important to honor (the feeling of authentically wanting to stop). One was anxiety that she wanted to manage and overcome using her anxiety management skills; the other was her authentic sexual self. Anna no longer identified these as one in the same.

Treatment goal 2: differentiation

Once Anna was more able to sit with her own uncomfortable experiences, it was time to help her differentiate from her husband: to become more comfortable sitting with *his* uncomfortable experiences. She invited Derek to join her in therapy, and differentiation was the goal of the couples work.

Murray Bowen defined differentiation as the capacity to see one's own emotional and intellectual functioning as separate from that of one's relational partners' (Bowen, 1978). Anna, like many female clients in my practice, found this challenging. She had internalized the message that it was her job, as a compassionate partner, to protect Derek from pain and discomfort; this belief fueled her pre-therapy behavior of having sex she did not want to have so that he could avoid feelings of rejection, fear, abandonment, and anger. Feeling responsible for someone else's emotional experience and acting inauthentically "because he needs me to" is what Bowen called *enmeshment*. For Anna, the result of enmeshment was feelings of resentment and disconnection; she resented that she "had to" have sex against her own will, and she felt lonely and disconnected from her partner. He proliferated this enmeshment by blaming her for their lack of sexual connection rather than looking at his own contributing behaviors, and by holding her responsible for his resulting feelings. In the face of ensuing conflicts they would both withdraw, as if the only way to regain responsibility for themselves was to no longer be in relationship to each other. Bowen called this *estrangement*.

I demonstrated their pattern of enmeshment and estrangement, and the alternative of differentiation, by moving my hands. I held my hands up, palms towards each other. "My left hand is you, Derek, and my right hand is you, Anna," I said. "Anna, when you do something you don't want to do because you think you have to for him, you make *him* responsible for *you*, and you lose part of *yourself* in *him*" – I tipped my hands slightly and interlaced the tips of my fingers. "And Derek, when you tell Anna she has to have sex with you to keep you happy, you make *her* responsible for *you*, and you lose part of *yourself* in *her*." I slid my hands closer together so that the bases of my fingers were interlaced, my hands making an "X." "This is your model of closeness, but look how little contact there actually is. The only point of contact between these two hands is the base of the fingers where they intertwine."

"This is a pretty locked up place to be," I continued, making my hands push and pull against each other to demonstrate that they were stuck. "And when you want to get out of this trapped place, it feels like you have to go like this" – I flung my arms open so that my hands were as far apart as they could get, demonstrating estrangement. "And from way out here, you guys both feel pretty disconnected and lonely. I hear that neither of you really likes either of these options." They agreed.

Now I held my hands up again, palms facing each other. "Differentiation means you are each responsible for your own feelings, and for acting in ways that feel okay to you. Then you can choose to share yourselves with each other fully, when you want to, like *this*." I pressed my hands together, palm to palm. "Pulling out of that enmeshed place can feel scary, because it feels like separation. But you can choose to be separate *and* connected. Look at how much contact there is between these two hands if they come together while they each maintain their own boundaries and edges."

They understood, and we had created a shared image and understanding of the goal of differentiation. This provided leverage, as we continued, to point out moments of enmeshment and estrangement and to practice interacting in differentiated ways – owning, taking responsibility for, and sharing their feelings. Anna and Derek practiced listening to each other without defending themselves, and expressing themselves without attacking each other. And they shared their hopes and dreams for the relationship and their appreciations of each other, allowing them to feel connected in ways that did not violate either person's boundaries.

Family sculpting, a technique of placing themselves and each other in positions to physically demonstrate their dynamics (Satir & Baldwin, 1984), further helped the couple embody the sexual dynamics they were enacting: Derek was encroaching and overpowering Anna in an effort to get her to give him the feelings he wanted, and in response she was shrinking into a ball, getting smaller, and moving farther away. We identified the need for Derek to engage in his own therapeutic process to learn to differentiate – to learn some new ways of pursuing his own masculine and vital self that he craved, other than "getting it from her."

Derek made changes outside of their sexual relationship to create opportunities to feel the masculine energy he had previously sought exclusively from their sex life. He began pursuing hobbies he had put aside and dreams that he had tabled – for example, he began weight lifting, and joined a pick-up ice hockey league. He realized he could generate contact with his masculine energy, and then choose to share it with Anna, rather than making her responsible for this part of him. A few weeks later they repeated the sculpting exercise, and embodied a budding new dynamics: as he began to fill his own space rather than encroaching on hers, she felt more safety to expand back into *her* own space. This was the space she needed to begin to develop authentic connection with herself, and to then be able to step towards him, as he ultimately wished for, but on her own terms.

Treatment goal 3: redefining caretaking

I referred Derek on for individual therapy to continue his work, a recommendation he chose not to pursue, and I resumed working individually with Anna. Although Anna was making progress in her effort to differentiate from Derek, she was easily triggered to feel that it was her job to meet his sexual needs, even when she did not want to. She feared that she was "not a good wife" if she did not make herself sexually available to him on his terms. And as soon as she acted inauthentically in the name of caretaking, her sensual self would shut down – the cycle of withdrawal would begin, again.

To intervene in this cycle, we worked on redefining caretaking. Using feminist therapy, the practice of exploring how gendered expectations, roles, and cultural politics affect one's personal development and relational life (Brown, 2009), we articulated the messages that shaped Anna's beliefs about her role as a woman and a wife. For example, like so many of my female clients, she had learned that caretaking means taking care of others *instead* of taking care of herself, and she had learned that it was her job to sacrifice her authentic self in the name of connection. She reflected on the disempowering personal impact of this cultural and political message. She observed that when she silenced herself to take care of Derek she felt increased resentment and anxiety. She further observed that when she acted inauthentically – in ways that were not true to her internal experience, she felt lonely and disconnected; she created the very disconnection she feared.

In contrast, she recalled that when she had practiced differentiated communication in the couples work, she had felt more love, patience, and curiosity towards Derek. Using cognitive-behavioral therapy, an approach that alters maladaptive and distorted thoughts (Beck, 2011), we used her positive experience with differentiation as evidence to disprove the idea that self-sacrifice is compassionate. We replaced that distortion with the articulation of her new experience: when she brought her authentic self to the relationship with Derek, she felt closer to him.

The next step was to test out the veracity of her new thought, that authenticity is an act of compassion because it breeds intimacy. We turned our focus back to her lack of desire. What would happen to her desire if she applied her new thought process? Could she increase her sexual desire by bringing herself more authentically to their sexual relationship?

I used experiential exercises to give Anna the opportunity to practice bringing her authentic sensual self to the relationship. Derek joined us for a session, and he and Anna engaged in a basic tantric touching exercise in which they took turns touching each other's forearms in varying ways, giving and receiving feedback about their experience of the touch. This exercise helped Anna make space for her authentic sensual self rather than only being in service to her partner – to notice what she liked and did not like, and to practice giving voice to her preferences.

I sent them home with an assignment intended to expand on their experience with the tantric exercise, and to give Anna more space to explore her sensual power. With his consent, Anna tied her husband's hands together and covered his eyes with a blindfold so that she felt sure he could not encroach on her space or pace their sexual contact in a way that felt intrusive. As per the assignment, she then did "whatever she wanted," listening only to her own sensual impulses. She was instructed that she could touch him or not, be close or be far away, kiss him or not, etc. She was further instructed that she could stop the exercise at anytime, and in fact, should stop the exercise when she wanted to, because the key to the exercise was acting on her own wishes. We reviewed her anxiety management skills from earlier in the treatment so that she could manage and proceed past automatic anxious responses when she chose to do so.

Anna reported about her experience the next week. "It was like a switch got flipped; I started out a bit tentative, and then at some point something changed and I was *really* into it. And Derek was pretty psyched, too!" This was a foundational moment in which Anna experienced for herself that bringing her authentic sexual self to the bedroom was indeed a gift for both herself and her partner.

Stage 2 of therapy: gaining momentum

Anna's sensual reawakening was, at times, a painful process. Rather than being a purely joyful reunion with her sensual self, she initially discovered additional layers of sexual shame that she had been avoiding. Early exposure to pornography, a family legacy of sexual abuse, and her mother's fear of sexually transmitted diseases and unplanned pregnancy left Anna with the feeling that sex, pleasure, and her body were "dirty" and "unsafe." We returned to the first treatment goal: building acceptance of and curiosity about her sensuality. Just as we had worked on reducing shame about her sexual withdrawal at the beginning of therapy, we now worked on reducing shame about her sensual vitality.

I introduced Anna to the ISIS Wheel of Sexual Experience, an experiential treatment tool that allows clients to explore their sexual responses along four integrated dimensions of self: body, mind, heart, and spirit (Ogden, 2006, 2008, 2013). To create an ISIS Wheel we laid down four long ribbons like spokes on a wheel, forming four equal segments, which we labeled Body, Mind, Heart, and Spirit. Anna brought in two objects to use in the Wheel – one that represented the feelings of shame and "dirtiness" she wanted to release, and the other representing the feeling of sensual freedom that she wanted. Anna's first object was a "dry, old, yucky, and crumbling" leaf. Her second object was a silver, shiny tube of mascara, which she described as "bold, sexy, and confident."

I asked her to hold the leaf and walk around the wheel, paying attention to her experience in her body, mind, heart, and spirit as she circled. When asked where the leaf "belonged," she said she noticed that the "dirty leaf is a trick of the mind." She stood in the Mind quadrant with the leaf and spoke from the part of her that had learned to fear sex. She was able to honor that her mind had worked hard to protect her from destructive forces like sexual abuse, disease, and unwanted pregnancy. We renamed those experiences she wanted to avoid "gloob," and distinguished "gloob" from the empowering, pleasurable experience of consensual sex. This gave her a way to thank her protective parts while not allowing them to inhibit her desired sensual flow: she could protect herself from "gloob," and still enjoy sex. She was accepting her protective parts without judgment, while also making space for her sensuality to be experienced as something inherently good rather than dangerous.

As she had done with the leaf, she held her mascara tube that represented "bold, sexy, and confident" sensuality, and circled the wheel, noticing how she felt in body, mind, heart, and spirit. In the Body quadrant she physically enacted "bold, sexy, and confident." She stood tall, rolled back her shoulders, and noticed what it felt like to feel beautiful. In the Mind quadrant, she noticed a new sense of "quiet" – as her bold, sexy, and confident self, her mind was free of fearful chatter. And she described feeling "joy and lightness" in her heart and spirit. She was particularly surprised by this piece of her experience, because it was such a stark contrast to the feelings of dirtiness and shame that she previously associated with her sensuality. She was now experiencing her sensuality as a positive and enriching part of her integrated self.

The ISIS Wheel also provided an unexpected differentiation experience. Although Anna worked the Wheel individually, she chose to invite her partner to be a silent observer of this session. This created a rare opportunity for her to focus on her own experiences while being witnessed by her partner, without doing any work to manage *his* experience. And it provided him an opportunity to learn about deeper layers of his wife's feelings. Anna and Derek were simultaneously more separate than their historical dynamics allowed them to be, while also generating an experience of sharing and knowing each other on unusually deep and intimate levels.

At the end of her journey in the ISIS Wheel, Anna considered what she wanted to do with her old, brown, dead leaf. With a smile and some surprise she said brightly, "I want to throw it away!" In a spontaneous act of differentiated caretaking, Derek silently handed her the trash bin.

Stage 3 of therapy: establishing new patterns

Anna is now in the process of establishing new patterns reflective of her therapeutic growth. Having made space for herself to reacquaint with her sensuality, she is taking risks to learn more about her body and her pleasure. She soaks up psychosexual education about erogenous zones and gives herself increasing amounts of permission to experiment with, to engage in, to initiate, and to say "no" to sex.

Her growth led to new patterns in other areas of her life, as well. Paralleling her increased sensual authenticity, Anna made a big change in her professional life. She had remained for years in a job that exacerbated a chronic pain condition in her hands, out of a sense of obligation and responsibility to her employer. However, as she developed compassionate authenticity, she learned to be her authentic self in the name of connection, pain and all, rather than sacrificing self in the name of caretaking others. Anna made an important decision to leave her job.

A cascade of invigorating and rewarding risk-taking experiences followed, both in and out of the bedroom. She took a new job that had previously intimidated her, and developed a whole new set of skills and a sense of competence and efficacy; she reestablished a relationship with an estranged sister through open and honest communication; she made changes to her physical appearance that made her feel "bold and sexy" like her mascara tube; and she bought a vibrator and invited her husband to help her use it.

Anna's path is certainly not without bumps and challenges. She and her partner continue to struggle with the dynamics between them. She reports that Derek still encroaches on her physical space in ways that feel intrusive, and then she feels blamed for not reacting in a sexually welcoming way. However, her response to this dynamics is very different from it was at the outset of therapy. Instead of silencing herself in the name of connection, she now speaks honestly about her feelings, and about her sexual wishes and boundaries. She believes that it is ultimately a compassionate act to respond authentically, even if it leads to conflict. And she faces those conflicts directly, with curiosity about Derek's feelings, and clarity about and faith in the validity of her own. Her libido is active, she enjoys her sensuality, and when she chooses to, she shares it with her husband, on her own terms.

Conclusion

I use the compassionate authenticity model to treat low libido in women with widely variant stories. For instance, the model helped Karin, who had muted her sexuality because she feared her sexual dominance was inappropriate and would threaten her partnership. It helped Maria, who had closeted herself, shutting down her sexuality altogether because she feared that her love and sexual desire of women was sinful and would shame her Catholic family. It helped Marika, who had judged and punished herself for fantasizing about a man who was not her husband, assuming her thoughts were destructive to her partner. The compassionate authenticity model provided a framework to guide all of these women towards sexual freedom and vibrancy.

I have found that the compassionate authenticity model can be generalized and applied to the treatment of issues beyond sexual functioning, as well. The gendered message that women should sacrifice themselves in the name of caretaking is broad reaching, and my female clients present having sacrificed more than their sexual selves; they report ignoring their physical and emotional needs, their creative callings, and their instincts and intuitions, all in the name of taking care of others. I have used the compassionate authenticity treatment model to help clients improve self-worth, reduce resentment of their parenting duties, deepen intimacy with family and friends, generate creativity, and make difficult life decisions based on their own intuition.

The model of compassionate authenticity can be used by clinicians trained in a variety of therapeutic approaches, and with widely variant techniques. It is a circular model, and the treatment goals can be addressed in any order, and in a non-linear progression. If a client is not progressing, I try a different entry point; all of the treatment goals, when integrated with each other, ultimately lead to the same end point.

I find, as treatment progresses, that the work often becomes less defined by one clinical goal at a time. Breakthroughs and insights relevant to one goal quickly lead into growth in other areas. As clients move closer to their authentic selves, the process builds momentum. It becomes a spiraling progression, with the goals flowing into one coherent thought: "I am good, including my pain, so sharing myself as I really am is an act of kindness." The model reframes what it means to be compassionate, giving women a critical alternative to the perceived options of selflessness and selfishness: authenticity.

Acknowledgements

I would like to thank my colleagues and friends who provided both encouragement and editorial suggestions for this article, including Helen Whybrow, Alice Pollvogt, Sarah Spink, Carmen Walker, Emily Miller, Tasha Lansbury, Sara Mason, and Ciara Byrne. I would also like to acknowledge the mentorship and guidance provided by Gina Ogden, which has helped me raise up my own authentic voice.

References

Beck, J.S. (2011). *Cognitive behavior therapy: Basics and beyond* (2nd ed.). New York, NY: Guilford Press.

Bowen, M. (1978). *Family therapy in clinical practice*. New York, NY: Aronson.

Brown, L.S. (2009). *Feminist therapy*. Washington, DC: American Psychological Association.

Gilligan, C. (1993). *In a different voice: Psychological theory and women's development*. Cambridge, MA: Harvard University Press.
Gross, J.J., & Levenson, R.W. (1993). Emotional suppression: Physiology, self-report, & expressive behavior. *Journal of Personality and Social Psychology, 64*(6), 970–986.
Jordan, J.V., Kaplan, A.G., Miller, J.B., Stiver, I.P., & Surrey, J.L. (1991). *Women's growth in connection: Writings from the stone center*. New York, NY: Guilford Press.
Kabat-Zinn, J. (1990). *Full catastrophe living: Using the wisdom of your body and mind to face stress, pain, and illness*. New York, NY: Delacorte.
Miller, J.B., & Stiver, I.P. (1997). *The healing connection*. Boston, MA: Beacon Press.
Ogden, G. (2006). *The heart and soul of sex: Making the ISIS connection*. Boston, MA: Trumpeter Books.
Ogden, G. (2008). *The return of desire: A guide to rediscovering your sexual passion*. Boston, MA: Trumpeter Books.
Ogden, G. (2013). *Expanding the practice of sex therapy: An integrative model for exploring desire and intimacy*. New York, NY: Routledge.
Perel, E. (2006). *Mating in captivity: Unlocking erotic intelligence*. New York, NY: Harper.
Rogers, C.R. (1961). *On becoming a person: A therapist's view on psychotherapy*. New York, NY: Houghton.
Salters-Pedneault, K., Tull, M.T., & Roemer, L. (2004). The role of avoidance of emotional material in the anxiety disorders. *Applied and Preventive Psychology, 11*(2), 95–114.
Satir, V., & Baldwin, M. (1984). *Satir step by step: A guide to creating change in families*. Palo Alto, CA: Science and Behavior Books.
Schnarch, D. (1997). *Passionate marriage: Keeping love and intimacy alive in committed relationships*. New York, NY: Holt.
Schwartz, R.C. (1995). *Internal family systems therapy*. New York, NY: Guilford Press.
White, M. (2007). *Maps of narrative practice*. New York, NY: Norton.

Sex addiction – an extraordinarily contentious problem

Paula Hall

The Clarendon Centre, Leamington Spa, Warwickshire, United Kingdom

Sex addiction is a phenomenon that has a variety of names and even more meanings depending on who you talk to, and each of these interpretations impacts the clients who seek help. There are many different models of addiction, such as the biological, moral or social models that are often not useful when thinking about sex, but by adopting a comprehensive model for describing addiction, both clients and therapists can be helped to consider the multiple layers of compulsive sexual behaviour. Furthermore, to date there have been no models for assessment and treatment that incorporate attachment, trauma and the social context which can help therapists and clients identify and consider the most appropriate, and most urgent, therapeutic objectives.

Introduction

Sex addiction, sexual compulsivity, hypersexuality, problematic sexual behaviours – or whatever you want to call it – continues to be a highly controversial problem (Ley, 2012; Moser, 2013). So when clients present with difficulties with their sexual behaviour, they come not just with the problem and a range of names for it, but also with a range of diverse opinions. In this paper, I offer two models: one for defining sex addiction and other for assessment and treatment. It is hoped that by looking at sex addiction through a different lens, focus can be turned back to the meaning of the condition to the clients, rather than the nomenclature chosen by the therapist.

Whilst clients may describe their behaviour as feeling out of control, they will be challenged to consider if this is really true. Also, is the term "addiction" just an excuse for their impoverished impulse control or poor morality? Or a mask for a deeper unmet need? Or perhaps it is part of their biological heritage from an alcoholic father? Or a narcissistic or attachment wound from their absent and neglectful mother? A symptom of attention deficit hyperactivity disorder (ADHD)? Or a consequence of post traumatic stress disorder (PTSD)? Or are they just acting like a "typical bloke"? Or a sexually liberated woman? A victim of social stigmatism? Or in the wrong relationship? Or not ready to settle down?

And what about the partners? Unlike most other addictions or compulsive behaviours, sex and porn addiction affects a couple's relationship in the most intimate of ways. Even when no physical infidelity has occurred, many partners report feeling hurt and betrayed, saying that porn has robbed them of their sex life, as their partner's libido and arousal wanes. What meaning do they give to their predicament? Some find the label sex addiction an easier pill to swallow than accepting what they often see as the "darker side" of their partner or worse still, a failing within themselves or their relationship. They too are affected by the controversies that abound in public and professional discourse and whilst some couples share the same frustrations at the lack of consistent information and therapeutic approaches, for others those differences drive them further apart.

The BERSC model

In an effort to provide a more comprehensive and inclusive approach, I have found it useful to use the BERSC model (Figure 1) to explain the complexities of sex and pornography addiction. The BERSC model (Hall, 2013) is an expansion of the biopsychosocial view of sex addiction (Hall, 2011) and explores five significant influences, namely biology, emotion, relationship, society and culture. All sexually compulsive behaviours are complex and whilst the addiction model is increasingly recognised in the United States and focuses on changes in the brain (Kor, Fogel, Reid, & Potenz, 2013), this should not be used to the exclusion of other factors. Addictions are frequently used to regulate emotional states (Adams & Robinson, 2002) and in relationships, compulsive behaviours may be used to create or regulate intimacy. The social context of easy availability and opportunity is perhaps the biggest modem influence, but in addition to that it is important to note the individual cultural influences of clients as they relate to gender, family system, faith, work environment or peers.

Using the BERSC model can also be a useful tool for reducing shame and provide a template around which to consider options and motivation for change. Sex addiction is not only impacted by each of these five factors, but in turn, the behaviours also influence

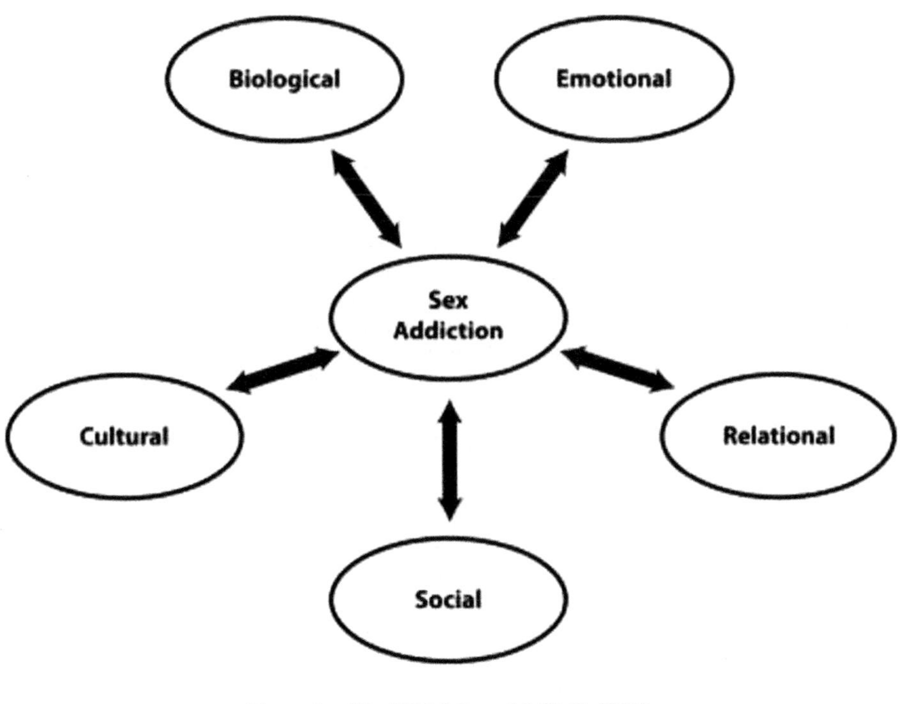

Figure 1. The BERSC model (Hall, 2013).

these factors. For example, compulsive use of pornography or adult hook-up applications may affect a person physically if they are not getting enough sleep or placing them at risk for contracting sexually transmitted infections (STIs). It may affect a person emotionally through increased feelings of anxiety, depression or shame. The behaviours may have negative consequences on primary relationships and on social systems, and it may impact individual cultural systems such as religious values and work ethics. By exploring each of these elements, a client can be helped to consider how big a problem the problem is, and also for whom the problem is a significant issue.

Case example

Jon and Amanda came for couple counselling 8 months after Amanda had discovered that Jon had been visiting prostitutes for 7 years of their 12-year marriage. She had always known that he'd watched pornography when she was away on business and on occasions had "caught" him watching it late at night when he said he was working. It had always frustrated her as she felt he probably used porn more than he said and suspected it contributed to his lack of desire for her. The couple had had numerous arguments about it over the years but she'd concluded it was "what men do" and had resigned to put up with it. But 8 months ago, the day after Jon had stayed up late again to do work, Amanda found he'd left his smart phone at home and she decided to look through the history. Not only did she find pornography in his browser history but also links to sex worker sites and explicit emails.

Jon was mortified when Amanda turned up at work with his phone and confronted him with the content. At first he tried to deny knowledge of its existence but quickly realised this was futile and tearfully confessed all. Amanda kicked Jon out of the house immediately saying she never wanted to see him again and she would do everything in her power to prevent him from seeing their children. Like many men in Jon's situation, he could not offer any explanation for his behaviour. He swore on his children's lives that he loved Amanda and the children and would do anything to get them back. Adding that he hated what he was doing and enjoyed sex with her more than anything else. He said he wanted to stop and had tried to stop on many occasions but always ended up going back again. As far as Amanda was concerned, this was just more lies and deceit and she was not going to be taken for a fool any longer.

That had all been 8 months ago. Since then Jon had been on a recovery course for sex addiction. He had stopped "acting out", both with sex workers and with porn, and he understood why he'd done what he'd done. Furthermore, he was confident that he wouldn't do it again and wanted to work on rebuilding Amanda's trust and their marriage. During the 8 months they'd been apart, Amanda had started coming to terms with what had happened and had done some reading on sex addiction. She explained that she didn't want to throw the good stuff in their marriage away and admitted that apart from Jon's secret other life, their marriage had been good and she wanted to do the best for the children. But like many partners she struggled with the addiction label. "Isn't that just an excuse?", she asked, "a way of not accepting responsibility?. She still had so many unanswered questions: "How could he have kept going back to visiting prostitutes if he didn't enjoy it?", "How did it all start"? "How can he possibly love me and do something that he knew would break my heart?"

Before Amanda could seriously consider getting back together, she wanted to fully understand how they'd got where they were – the BERSC model provided an objective tool, not just for understanding sex addiction, but more importantly for Amanda, for understanding Jon's addiction.

We started by exploring the latest thinking in terms of the neurobiology of addiction, and in particular, the role of dopamine in the reward system part of the brain (Berke & Hyman, 2000; Kuss & Griffiths, 2012). Jon talked about his father's alcoholism and his adult diagnosis of ADHD and I explained that there were indications that both of these may contribute to a biological disposition towards addiction, though more research are still required, especially with sex and pornography addiction. Amanda was also comforted to hear how dopamine is a chemical associated with motivation, drive and wanting, rather than satiation, pleasure and liking. And hence addictions are often characterised by an overwhelming drivenness to do things that don't necessarily provide enjoyment or satiation. And how the reward is in the brain, not in the genitals. As an ex-smoker, this resonated with Amanda as she recalled the times she smoked in spite of chronic bouts of tonsillitis. We also looked at biological principles of escalation and reduced impulse control.

Emotionally, Jon had always struggled with assertiveness and managing anger and he explained to Amanda that he had always used some kind of acting-out behaviour when he felt frustrated or powerless. His father had at times been a violent man and Jon was determined not to follow that path. But regrettably he had not found a healthy way to manage anger and so, ever since adolescence, he'd self-soothed either with alcohol, computer games, exercise or porn. Anger had also been an ongoing issue within their relationship. Amanda had also come from a home with violence and was determined never to be the victim as she'd seen her mum become. She had often accused Jon of being too passive or even a wimp and saw herself as having to be the strong one who took control. She confessed that in arguments she had often pushed Jon to see how far she could go and usually lost respect because he would never fight back – whilst realising that if he did, she might respect him even less. They both recognised that the issues between them had worsened since the children were born and they had increasingly polarised in their views of what appropriate discipline and assertiveness meant.

By now, Amanda understood addiction much more and was beginning to see that Jon had probably had a number of issues for many years that he sought to soothe, but in an unhealthy way. "But why sex?", she asked, "Why choose the thing that would hurt me most? This was where the social and cultural parts of the BERSC model are often the most useful. Because of Jon's family background he knew the risks of alcohol and so had steered clear of this. He had also been a budding footballer in his teens and he remembered the team coach constantly warning him against drugs lest he became a heroin junkie like the coach's brother. Jon had started using paper porn early in adolescence, and by the age of 14 or 15 he remembered he'd developed the habit of going to his room to look at porn whenever the parents argued. He had continued to use porn occasionally and had never considered it a problem until he got a laptop and broadband for a new sales job 10 years ago. The new job involved long periods of time away from home in strange hotels with nothing to do. There were also regular sales meeting and nights out for the sales team where visiting strip clubs was the norm. Jon said his time in the company which spanned a further 5 years was a complete eye opener with colleagues who talked freely about porn and casual sex. At first he had resisted their encouragement to fully "join the team", but regrettably his issues with non-assertiveness did not help, and so he gradually extended his boundaries until he'd completely crossed the line. "I'd opened Pandora's box", Jon said, "and I couldn't get the lid on again".

I continued working with Amanda and Jon over the next few months as they talked through not only the past, but also what they would need for the future. Amanda continued to fluctuate between rage and despair, but the occasions became less often and less severe. And Jon and Amanda began to get back in touch with the good times too. When they left they were still in the process of rebuilding trust with appropriate accountability measures, but both were confident that they were definitely heading in the right direction.

The OAT model

Another model that I find useful for exploring therapeutic objectives and priorities regarding sexual addiction is the OAT model (Figure 2), which classifies the primary drivers of addiction as opportunity induced, attachment induced or trauma induced – or a combination of each. Historically, sex addiction was seen as a disorder of intimacy and attachment

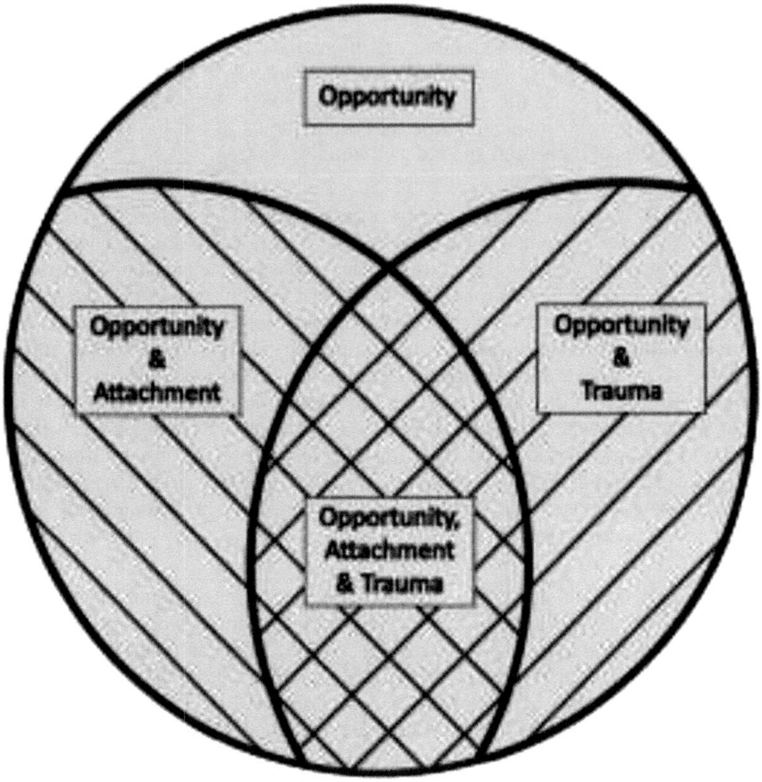

Figure 2. The OAT model (Hall, 2013).

(Flores, 2004; Hudson-Allez, 2009), but the profile of those with addiction is changing. The increased availability of pornography and other sexual stimuli via the internet and smart phone has significantly increased the accessibility and the opportunity to become "hooked". Easy access to high-speed, ever-changing and infinitely novel pornography is often referred to as a supernormal stimuli (Barret, 2010), and there are suggestions that compulsive use of the internet and pornography can actually change the structure of the brain (Doidge, 2007; Kuss & Griffiths, 2012), and in its wake comes an increase in clients with no previous attachment difficulties. There are also a number of clients presenting who have found pornography an effective tool for managing hyper-arousal and hypo-arousal states post trauma (Fisher, 2007), only to find that this self-medication can create additional difficulties.

The OAT model can also be used to help both client and therapist to explore the predisposing, precipitating and maintaining factors of the behaviour and develop a tailored treatment approach. For example, those who present with an attachment-induced addiction may benefit from psychodynamic work on early childhood wounds and may also identify feelings such as loneliness, rejection or lack of autonomy as key triggers for their behaviour. Those with a pure trauma-induced addiction may require body work to relieve physical symptoms as well as lifestyle changes to minimise common triggers such as stress and anxiety. In my experience, a psycho-educational approach to explain the neurobiology of craving and impulse control as well as establishing relapse prevention strategies is also essential for any presentation of compulsive sexual behaviours.

Case example

Tim was a 36-year-old man, married for 6 years with two children aged 1 and 3. He initially presented with erectile dysfunction but detailed assessment revealed that he had no problems with erections to pornography which he was now accessing most evenings for 3 or 4 hours at a time. He was very aware that his pornography use was getting in the way of him having sex with his wife and realised he'd got himself into a Catch 22. Watching increasingly hard-core porn was making him feel numb when having sex with his wife, but because sex with his wife was now so difficult, he was watching even more porn. In fact, the only times he could get an erection with his wife now was if he fantasised about porn which left him feeling guilty and distant from her. The problem had been gradually worsening over the past 3 years until it came to a head a month ago when his wife had begged him to get some help.

Detailed history taking revealed that Tim had enjoyed a relatively stable and happy childhood and adolescence and, on the whole, he was a confident and content man. His marriage was also a happy one and he still felt a strong sexual attraction to his wife. Over the years he had used porn occasionally and had no issues with it. There was a period of time in his early 20s when porn use had become quite an issue for him but he had managed to control it without help and had hoped he could do so again. Using the OAT model and assessment questions tailored to explore attachment and trauma issues revealed that Tim's pornography addiction was trauma and opportunity induced. When he was 25, Tim had been in a serious car accident. He had been the passenger when the car veered off the road into a tree, killing his best friend instantly. He had been trapped in the car for 6 hours before help came and he was cut free. Tim spent a month in hospital with multiple fractures and it was a further 6 months before he was able to walk unaided. It was during this time that his pornography use exploded. "There was nothing else to do", Tim explained, "and it stopped me thinking". Tim shared how terrified he had been whilst trapped in the car. He knew his friend was dead and there was nothing he could do. By the time the emergency services turned up Tim said he had already given up. As he retold the story, he almost physically shrank, cold and motionless, his voice becoming quieter and more monotone. He was dissociating.

Over the coming weeks, we used the OAT model to explore how he had used pornography to manage his hyper-arousal and hypo-arousal states immediately after the trauma; motivational interviewing techniques were useful for getting him in touch with the resilience he'd shown in the early days and the resources he'd used to stop his porn use and get into relationships again. Having initially thought there was no explanation for why he started again, he remembered that it was after the traumatic birth of their first daughter who had gone transverse in labour and was then in an incubator for the first 3 months of her life. He saw how this experience had triggered his old trauma and he began also making connections to everyday triggers of when he feels trapped, helpless or powerless. He also recognised that what in the past he had named as boredom was actually something much greater than that. It was a fearful emptiness and numbness that unconsciously reminded him of those hours in the car. Social changes in accessibility to pornography gave him the explanation he needed for why he had failed to stop alone. Ten years ago, his porn use had been restricted to magazines and videos that he had to leave home to go and buy, but now he had broadband and a smart phone, and infinite, boundless access.

Over the coming weeks of therapy, we used a combination of sensorimotor techniques to work on the trauma and psycho-educational addiction treatment principles to help Tim understand why his pornography use had escalated and impacted his erections. We also explored how he could avoid his triggers and develop alternative strategies for managing the unavoidable ones. Six months after stopping pornography use, Tim's erections were back to normal and he was once again enjoying sex with his wife.

Group work

During the past 10 years that I have specialised in sex addiction, the most "extraordinary" therapeutic approach I have discovered has been group work. Group work has been the backbone of addiction services for many years (Miller, 2005; Nerenberg, 2002), and therefore, felt like an appropriate extension to individual work. And whilst the group will never be an alternative to individual therapy, in my opinion, it serves a number of unique and essential functions. I have found group work for sex addiction to be profoundly powerful as it breaks through shame and isolation in a way that individual therapy cannot replicate. And by providing the opportunity to address old attachment wounds in the here and now, it creates a space for shared empathy and emotional attunement between group members that the boundaries of a professional therapeutic relationship do not allow. Furthermore, group becomes what Yalom described as a microcosm of the real world where members can experience, and be seen to experience, how they operate in the real world. And a place where Yalom's 11 therapeutic factors: instillation of hope; universality; imparting of information; altruism; the corrective recapitulation of the primary family group; development of socialising techniques; imitative behaviour; interpersonal learning; group cohesiveness; catharsis and the existential factors, are interplayed (Yalom, 1985). Witnessing the openness, courage and humility of group members as they share and grow together have undoubtedly been one of the greatest privileges of my career.

Conclusions

It may be many more years before we reach consensus on what to call sex addiction, and we may never find a definition or diagnostic model acceptable for diagnostic and statistical manual (DSM). But does that really matter? Bereavement is not in DSM and neither is relationship breakdown but we still provides help for those who struggle with these issues. Some prefer an existential or systemic approach; others focus on attachment or changing thinking patterns. And some will use outcome measures to assess the efficacy of their therapy. It is my hope that while research continues to establish a more accurate definition of sex addiction and wider understanding, we, in the sex therapy community, will remain open minded and focus our attention on the needs of clients.

References

Adams, K., & Robinson, D.W. (2002). Shame reduction, affect regulation, and sexual boundary development. *Clinical management of sex addiction* (pp. 67–87). New York, NY: Brunner Routledge.

Barret, D. (2010). *Supernormal stimuli, how primal urges overran their evolutionary purpose*. New York, NY: Norton.
Berke, J.D., & Hyman, S.E. (2000). *Addiction, dopamine, and the review molecular mechanisms of memory* (pp. 515–532), vol. 25. Cambridge, MA: Neuron.
Doidge, N. (2007). *The brain that changes itself*. New York, NY: Penguin.
Fisher, J. (2007). *Addictions and trauma recovery*. New York, NY: Basic Books.
Flores, J.P. (2004). *Addiction as an attachment disorder*. New York, NY: Jason Aronson.
Hall, P.A. (2011). A biopsychosocial view of sex addiction. *Sexual and Relationship Therapy, 26*(3), 217–228.
Hall, P.A. (2013). *Understanding and treating sex addiction*. London: Routledge.
Hudson-Allez, G. (2009). *Infant losses; adult searches: A neural and developmental perspective on psychopathology and sexual offending*. London: Karnac Books.
Kor, A., Fogel, Y.A., Reid, R.C., & Potenz, M.N. (2013). Should hypersexuality disorder be classified as an addiction? *Sexual Addiction & Compulsivity, 20*(1–2), 27–47.
Kuss, D.J., & Griffiths, M.D. (2012). Internet and gaming addiction: A systematic literature review of neuroimaging studies. *Brain Science, 2*(3), 347–374.
Ley, D.L. (2012). *The myth of sex addiction*. New York, NY: Roman & Littlefield.
Miller, G. (2005). *Learning the language of addiction counselling*. Hoboken, NJ: John Wiley & Sons.
Moser, C. (2013). Hypersexuality disorder: Searching for clarity. *Sexual Addiction & Compulsivity, 20*(1–2), 48–58.
Nerenberg, A. (2002). The value of group psychotherapy for sexual addicts. In P. J. Carnes & K.M. Adams (Eds.), *Clinical management of sex addiction* (pp. 183–198). New York, NY: Brunner Routledge.
Yalom, I.D. (1985). *The theory and practice of group psychotherapy* (3rd ed.). New York, NY: Basic Books.

Calming the tempest, bridging the gorge: healing in couples ruptured by "sex addiction"

Ruth Cohn

Independent Practice, San Francisco, USA

Frequently couples seek marital therapy for the painful impact of one partner's "sex addiction." Disagreement abounds in both the clinical world and the larger society, about what the designation "sex addiction" actually means. A variety of diagnostic categories are subsumed under it, creating confusion about both its causes and effective treatments. The current paper proposes precise definition and diagnostic language regarding a range of compulsive sexual behaviors. It maps a model for understanding and treating compulsive sexual activity in marital therapy in a stepwise sequence, beginning with careful history taking and diagnostics of both partners, identification of the mutually reinforcing relationship dynamics keeping destructive behaviors in play, processing of underlying psychological and developmental roots of such behaviors, cultivation of empathy and trust, and revitalizing of the couple's sexual relationship. The method is illustrated with a case history.

This journey began some years ago when a man in a distant coastal town called me inquiring about couples' therapy. Initially, I thought he was requesting a referral near his home, but he and his wife proceeded to make the 6-hour round trip to my office weekly for the next year and a half. Since then, I have gotten similar calls – one from a man in a treatment program in the Southwest, another from Europe, a third from two hours away in the South Bay Area, a fourth from the East Coast, and more. Usually, the husband in these heterosexual couples has made the call, and the presenting complaint has gone something like this: "I'm a sex addict. Can you help us?"

The geography of desperation

What prompts people to reach out across the miles and traverse great distances for psychotherapy? Initially, I thought it was shame that inspired people to flee their communities to unearth painful problems of compulsive sexual behavior. However, now that I have done a fair amount of work with this population, I have concluded that desperation is the root cause of their long-distance search. They find themselves casting an ever-wider net as they emerge from unhelpful and even damaging treatment experiences closer to home.

I have several objectives for this article, recognizing that space constraints limit my examination of each. Among my goals are myth-busting about, and destigmatizing, a deeply misunderstood affliction; proposing guidelines for precise diagnosis, offering a new clinical lens through which to view couples' dynamics, and mapping an effective course for treatment.

Does "sex addiction" exist?

Over the last decade or so, "sex addiction" has become a near-colloquial term in both the popular and clinical literature. It has about the same accuracy of meaning as the old term, "nervous breakdown." Presumably, everyone knows what *they* mean by it, but it stands on no nosology, data or uniformly accepted definition. Even the DSM-5 Revision Committee argued vociferously about whether "sex addiction," in fact, exists, and if so, what to call it and how to treat it. Meanwhile, titillating, menacing, and often incriminating popular depictions abound. Of course, there is a category of incontrovertibly dystonic sexual behaviors that engender great shame and remorse, both on the part of the sufferer and others. However, the confusion surrounding these behaviors only compounds the pain.

Insofar as the there is a self-reinforcing dopamine surge that accompanies many sexual behaviors, particularly those involving orgasm, the addiction model can appear to fit. However, that is probably as far as it goes. By definition, addictive disease involves the following.

- *Tolerance*: meaning that over time, more of the substance is required to get the same result.
- *Withdrawal*: meaning that a distressing physiological reaction accompanies discontinuation of use, which makes stopping difficult and painful. Addiction is also
- *Progressive, chronic, and fatal*: the disease gets worse over time and is incurable.

As we will see, most sexually compulsive behavior simply does not fit the criteria for addiction. Wrongly applying the label "addiction" can demoralize, complicate, deter, or derail recovery efforts.

What is in a name? The quest for precise diagnosis

Perhaps the most notable expert on sexual compulsivity is Eli Coleman of the University of Minnesota, who has written extensively and authoritatively on this subject, and has consulted to the DSM revision committee. Says Coleman:

> Disagreement exists as to whether compulsive sexual behavior is an addiction, a psychosexual disorder, an impulse control disorder, a mood disorder, or an obsessive compulsive disorder... I now view the behavior as having a multitude of causes and presentations... (Coleman, 2003, p. 12)

> While I continue to use the term compulsive sexual behavior, I hope it is understood that it is still a set of symptoms waiting for a better term to replace it. (Coleman, 2003, p. 13)

I have adopted Coleman's use and rationale for the term, not knowing of anyone with whom I agree more, and also for want of a more exact term.

In his quest to find suitable language and descriptive criteria, he has been one of the strongest proponents of precise and accurate diagnostics. He bemoans the vast variety of behaviors randomly tossed under the "sex addiction" umbrella, as evidenced in my own practice.

My client, Alex, spent over $50,000 an year on exclusive, high-end escorts; another client, Joseph, harbored a secret life of anonymous sex with men during much of his forty-year married life. My client Oscar, meanwhile, carried on a series of sequential "fatal attraction"-like affairs over his 15-year marriage, while Eric escaped into years of fantasy Internet liaisons. All of these men were tagged with, and dogged by, the "sex addict" label. Each had very different problems. Each had his recovery delayed and his life unnecessarily derailed by misdiagnosis and misdirected treatment. All resolved the behavior and healed their marriages once the underlying problems were identified. That is what they had in common.

Just as a "nervous breakdown" *could* be a psychotic break, a lapse into dysfunctional depression, a series of debilitating panic attacks, a dramatic trauma re-enactment, or a suicidal episode – all calling for vastly different treatment approaches. Therefore, compulsive sexual behaviors can be a manifestation of a wide range of problems. Such behaviors may be an expression of obsessive compulsive disorder (OCD), attention deficit disorder (ADD), social anxiety, post traumatic stress disorder (PTSD) re-enactment, attachment trauma, dissociative behavior, or a host of other named and unnamed diagnoses. By lumping them all together, treatments become generic, cookie-cutter projects that are unlikely to hit the curative mark.

Coleman specifically distinguishes between paraphilic and nonparaphilic compulsive sexual behavior:

> Paraphilic behaviors are unconventional sexual behaviors that are obsessive and compulsive. They interfere with love relationships and intimacy.
>
> Nonparaphilic compulsive sexual behavior involves conventional behaviors which, when taken to an extreme, are recurrent, distressing, and interfere with daily functioning. (Coleman, 2003, pp. 13–14)

What I find most destructive about the addiction model is the notion "once an addict, always an addict," meaning that we cannot cure but at best merely arrest the disease. Although this model may accurately describe alcohol and drug addiction, my experience is that compulsive sexual behavior *can*, in fact, be healed once and for all. In my experience, the doctrine of incurability often serves as permission for the sexually compulsive person to "continue to fail." Likewise, it provides permission to the hurt partner to continue to suspect, condemn, and view the partner who practices compulsive sexual behavior through a pathological or "perpetrator" lens. Each of these forms of permission, based on a false premise, can doom the healing process for the individuals and relationships.

So what *is* compulsive sexual behavior, if not an addiction? I view this behavior through the lens of affect regulation. We will say more about this "new lens" in the next section. For now, it may be useful to consider who it is that determines that there is a "problem."

If one spouse masturbates multiple times per day and the other spouse has a moral or religious anti-masturbation stance, or simply feels left out, that partner may be the one assigning the label of pathology or addiction. What if the masturbation involves explicit sexual visuals? Or what if one partner has a vastly stronger libido than the other? Does that make him or her a "sex addict" or the other a sufferer of "hypo-sexual desire dysfunction?" We need to ask: who is defining the problem?

In our field, diagnostics can be an unscientific and vaguely defined endeavor, possibly affixing stereotypical labels onto clients and/or becoming a mechanical way to view, assess, and treat them. Yet with compulsive sexual behaviors, the lumping of many varieties into one category – addiction – and assigning the treatment approaches applied to substance abuse, often misses the mark widely. These behaviors are extremely diverse, encompassing multiple affairs, viewing pornography, e-mail relationships, utilizing sex workers, masturbation with or without visual stimulation, or frequenting clubs and/or other venues where anonymous or recreational forms of sex are available. It may involve wanting – or not wanting – to stop. Rather than automatically labeling this cornucopia of behaviors "addictive," let us get curious instead.

> (i) ndividuals may have a conflict with their values and those of their partner, family, or culture. Sometimes the problem is a matter of interpersonal or intercultural conflict. (Coleman, 2003, p. 16)

Applying a new clinical lens

When I first see a couple who present with the problem of "sexual addiction," my mind comes alive with questions – none of which I ask immediately. But silently, I'm wondering: How often does the behavior occur? Is it a way to manage stress or relieve tension? Is it a way to stimulate a sluggish brain and enliven a hypo-aroused or "flat" nervous system? Might there be autoimmune, adrenal, or nutritional factors, or a biochemically based dysregulation? Is the behavior a "solution" to a sexual dysfunction or a sexless marriage? Is sex an obsession and a variation of a ritualized OCD activity? Thinking this way begins a process of understanding the client, and begins to point toward appropriate treatment.

From the very first session I attempt to establish myself as a neutral party, stressing that mine is a "no-blame" paradigm with no "problem child." This can be a hard sell. Many treatment approaches view the partner with the compulsive behavior as, in the words of one client, the "bad dog!" And many spouses feel so bitterly and heinously "done to" as to be absolved of any responsibility to help heal the relationship.

A no-blame approach means that although neither partner is responsible for the behavior of the other, each *is* responsible for his or her own reaction to the other's behavior. Dynamics between the partners do reinforce and perpetuate the problematic behaviors of both. I assess what each partner views as the problem, and what each desires as the ultimate outcome, while also attempting to discern what I can about their self-perpetuating cycle of suffering.

Next, I obtain a full history of each partner. Depending on the individuals (and the level of antagonism between them) I might see them together, or separately, for history-taking. My preference is to see the couple together as there may already be a fair amount of secrecy or suspicion between them. In addition, often they learn things about each other that they never knew, which can forge vital curiosity, and possibly even empathy and understanding.

Sometimes, however, there is too much rage or defensiveness to make conjoint history-taking workable.

In the sexually compulsive partner, I usually find a desperate attempt to self-regulate or manage intense affects and body states. Beneath that, however, is nearly always some expression of trauma. It may be attachment trauma owing, for example, to a parent who was physically intrusive and emotionally neglectful, a parent whose rage was overwhelming, or a parent who was seductively over-stimulating or sexually abusive. There are countless variations.

Sometimes in dissociated states, sometimes in fits of rage or desperation, the sexually compulsive person re-enacts trauma stories. Invariably, they are unconscious. Identifying trauma as the root of sexual compulsivity can often shift the lens for both partners. I emphasize to clients that "the nature of trauma is to re-enact the trauma." (van der Kolk,

1980, p. 283.) Often, trauma is logged in memory in a fragmented, incomplete, sensory, emotional, visual, and energetic way, like a broken necklace whose beads roll around chaotically. The task is to restring them into a coherent narrative so that the trauma story can be logged and laid to rest in autobiographical memory, instead of remaining unconscious and perpetually vulnerable to restimulation.

When the behavior is reframed as the desperate urge to give words and meaning to a personal tragedy that has never been consciously recognized, let alone shared with another living soul, it becomes an intimate communication instead of a punishing "acting out." Both partners may be empathically amazed, moved and deeply saddened by the finally known and understood life events.

Of course, sexually compulsive behavior is not always a manifestation of unhealed trauma. In some cases, the behaviors are an expression of OCD, or a reaction to a sluggish ADD brain. Sometimes symptoms requiring specialized treatment interventions, constellate around trauma, such as extremes of dissociation or depression, and we must address that. My experience most often is that a trauma story is being "told," as in the example of Marco and Francine, below.

Marco and Francine: the impact of hidden trauma

History

My couples' treatment approach draws on the work of Harville Hendrix (Hendrix, 1988), which assumes that the dynamics of the couple are shaped by the dynamics of each of their early object relations and childhood experiences. Problems spring from the interplay between the residual emotional vulnerabilities and dysregulation of the two of them. When the past is laid to rest and old fear quieted, they can find calm and restore love and intimacy. I assume that both partners contribute equally to the difficulty, and I routinely say to any designated identified patient, "Don't be greedy, you can only have half."

Marco was a child of massive trauma. His father was a fighter pilot who was gone for months at a time, with Marco aware from a very early age that whenever his father left on a mission, or really any time he left home, he might never return. Recurring nightmares of crashing planes are among his earliest memories. His mother, left alone with five children, was alcoholic and erratic, ultimately abandoning the family and moving with a boyfriend to a distant town. Marco, the youngest, was sent to a boarding school, where he was sexually abused by the teacher who was kindest to him. At various points in his childhood, he felt as if his mother's intent had been to "destroy me and my whole family."

Marco's absent father was larger than life. During the rare times he was around, he was authoritarian and difficult to please. He also drank a lot, which made him unpredictable. Nonetheless, Marco idealized and adored him. When his father abruptly died, not in the ever-dreaded plane crash but of a sudden and aggressive cancer, Marco, then 16, was devastated. First, he'd endured his mother's abandonment, then his abrupt separation from his siblings, and now his worst fear had been realized: his beloved father was gone. It seemed to Marco that all relationships were in one way or another ripped away, that loss was the one constant.

Shortly after his father's death, Marco went out for cross-country and spent many hours of his days in intense training. He didn't know whether he was running from or running to something, just that it brought him some modicum of relief from his chronic internal state of overwhelm.

Later, he found that sex had a similar calming effect on his nervous system, especially when he was free of much consideration of the feelings or idiosyncrasies of a partner. Marco's sexual compulsivity involved numerous, intense sequential affairs. Invariably, the female partner made the seductive approach. In the last and most dramatic of these affairs, Marco's lover made repeated, vicious phone calls to Francine, taunting her about her failure as a wife and sexual partner, and threatening to come to their house and make an explosive scene.

As noted earlier, careful and thorough history-taking is a vital first step in our work. Obviously, it is a powerful vehicle for creating an empathetic connection with any individual who comes into therapy, but in this work it may be even more essential and challenging. Many clients arrive demoralized, shame-ridden, and defensive from humiliating prior-therapy experiences. Perhaps the compulsive partner was viewed as the "problem child" or "bad dog." Perhaps the victimized partner received the message "You're sick for sticking around with this loser." One wife I saw was told by a prior therapist, "Your husband is toxic! What are you going to do?" She was horrified, scared and bitterly embarrassed that she still loved him. What did that mean about her? Often, both partners enter my office expecting to be shamed and punished once again. Marco fully expected condemnation and reproach from me.

Second, compulsive sexual behavior routinely involves lying, a challenge at best if it seeps into psychotherapy. So the opportunity to seed the essential therapeutic alliance in the process of history-taking is especially valuable. My aim is to create a space that is safe enough to make honest disclosure possible.

Third, I am listening for the context, the soil from which the behavior patterns sprang. Whether the behavior is some variation of sexual compulsivity, or whether it is the tolerance for a sexually compulsive partner's betrayals, deceit and absence, there is invariably some foreshadowing or antecedent embedded in the story.

Finally, I am listening for the tenderest vulnerabilities engendered by personal history, which later kindle and inflame the reactivity that will fuel the couple's core destructive dynamic. I will say more about this later. For now, suffice it to say that the task of history-taking requires great thought, care and attention to what may initially seem to be a mass of extraneous details.

To summarize, the initial interview with each partner, always at least 90 minutes, has the multiple objectives of:

- initiating a safe relationship;
- embarking on diagnosis;
- searching for clues about the roots of the behaviors; and
- gathering information that will shed light on the couple's relationship dynamic.

Needless to say, this work requires great care, energy, thought, patience and self-regulation on the parts of all three participants.

Marco's initial call to me had a tone of urgency and fear, a response to Francine's disgusted anger and exasperation. He scheduled his individual appointment for as soon as I could arrange it. The history-taking was somewhat like witnessing the collapse of a house of cards. On the outside, Marco appeared indomitable, with his Ivy League doctorate, remarkable athletic accomplishments and astonishing accumulation of wealth. Underneath his successful, dignified exterior, however, was an abandoned, rejected, lonely little boy, wracked with fear, shame, and loss.

My initial, impressionistic view of Marco was that he had a wildly dysregulated nervous system, and, like many severely traumatized individuals, had spent his life on a mad quest to calm down. He had endured a cascade of erratic and ruptured attachments, with chronic insecurity and fear beginning early in life, and shocking losses of important attachment figures. His relationship template was "No one takes the time to know you" and "Nobody sticks around." To him, it made no sense to put all of one's eggs in a single relationship basket. If called upon to give Marco a diagnostic label, I would have placed him on the spectrum of post-traumatic stress disorder, with the prominent symptoms of hyperarousal, hypervigilance, intrusive memory, and bouts of dissociation.

It took much longer to schedule Francine's session. She viewed couple's therapy as something she had to endure because her husband was sick and irresponsible and needed to change – period. She did not think she needed therapy, and resented how much time and effort was required of her to address *his* problem. Besides, she had spent – in her opinion, wasted – enough time and money on this issue and had no reason to believe this bout of therapy would be any more useful than the others. Angry and deeply skeptical that a therapist recommended by Marco's analyst could be helpful to *her*, she was grudging and cool. But she came.

Francine was strikingly attractive and stylish. I have observed that in all the couples I have seen for this problem (all of whom have been heterosexual), the women have been extraordinarily attractive. No excuse about the partner's physical attributes being a reason for sexual activity outside the marriage, would fly very far in these couples. Francine was petite, exquisitely fit, and dressed with artistic flair. She was also bitter and wary, more interested in talking about Marco's sordid behavior than about her own history.

As is often the case, Francine did not believe she had much of a story of her own. Her childhood, as she described it, was undramatic. "Nothing happened to me." These words are a flag that the client might in fact be a child of neglect, whose traumatic past is about *missing experiences* and holes in the fabric of daily life, rather than traumatic occurrences. Francine was the quintessential child of neglect who slipped under the family radar unnoticed, raising her younger siblings and filling in the gaps in the parenting she herself received.

Francine's parents divorced when she was eight, at which point her father disappeared from her life. "But that happened to many kids," she said, shrugging. She gave no thought to having to cook and keep house as her mother worked 12-hour shifts as an ER nurse, having to sign herself up for school each fall, or never having a parent present at any performance or athletic event. She had given little thought to the fact that she'd temporarily lost her hearing and ability to speak when she was five and it had been a month before anyone had noticed.

Competent, self-reliant, and proud, Francine had no awareness of how enraged she was about her past. She truly did not believe she had been angry "before Marco gave me something to be angry about."

The early loss of her father had prepared Francine for Marco's long and frequent "business trips," which felt familiar and normal to her. She was accustomed to raising children singlehandedly and thanklessly, having her accomplishments and talents go unnoticed and her pain and ailments ignored. She'd felt proud and safe that she didn't need anyone's help. In her mind, Marco continued to increasingly demonstrate that she needed him "like a fish needs a bicycle." She had little awareness that somewhere deep inside, there lived a little girl who longed to be taken care of, cherished, and spoiled.

Crashing planes meets fish without bicycle

Locating the core dynamic

Marco and Francine's core dynamic emerged early on in our work. By "core dynamic" I mean the primary repetitive cycle or pattern of conflict that imbues almost any topic, and results in ever-increasing disconnection and demoralization. It's that same tired fight that couples have over and over again on any and every subject, becoming terribly upset, and gridlocked in the process. A thorough and thoughtful history makes it easy to spot. In the usual chicken-and-egg manner, the self-perpetuating destructive cycle re-enacts the worst of each partner's childhoods (Cohn, 2011, pp. 53–63).

Marco perceived Francine's confident and unmistakable independence to mean that she had no need for him at all. This belief stirred his fears of rejection, abandonment, and loss, which led him to avoid the house as much as he could. Marco's absences increased Francine's imperious and autocratic running of the home, which contributed to more distance and anger and deepened Marco's wish for warm, vulnerable companionship. The distance continued to widen. Confrontations about each other's behavior grew ever louder, sharper, and more contemptuous.

To interrupt the seemingly endless volley of blame and accusation, I asked each partner to describe the depth of feeling that each suffered as a result of the pattern. The feelings invariably hearkened back to childhood experiences and we were able to wend our way back to deeply buried stories, some of which Marco and Francine had never shared with each other. In my experience, it is the childhood stories that elicit tears and empathy, the moments of deep emotion that begin to heal both the injured relationship and the addled brain of compulsivity. It is deep and powerful work, not for the faint of heart. Thoughtful and conscientious self-care and support on the part of the therapist are of the essence.

Marco's most recent affair had a sadistic quality, and Francine was haunted by the violent phone calls of his affair partner. In Francine's recollections of the traumatic calls, she described feeling as if this woman was "trying to destroy me and our family" – interestingly, using the very words that Marco had used to describe his mother.

As the elements of re-enactment and projective identification fell into place, Marco's trauma story came into focus. The experience of the "kindly," exploitative teacher coming on to him in boarding school was repeatedly re-enacted in the opportunistic approaches of powerful, flattering women with their own agendas. With deep pain and shame, he recounted his childhood experiences to Francine in our sessions.

Marco had never before had words for what he felt was his mother's calculated crushing of his soul. He had never actually talked about her biting, confusing, and insulting verbal abuse, her seeming to take pleasure in making him feel worthless, ugly, and incompetent. By inadvertently creating that experience inside of Francine, he felt that someone, at long last, knew and understood his devastation. In deeply emotional sessions, we were able to link the compulsive adult behaviors to the childhood trauma, with Marco re-experiencing powerful affects, visual and sensory memories. Gradually, as Marco recounted his trauma stories in words, he found that he no longer needed the compulsive behaviors. Their function accomplished, the behaviors were finally laid to rest.

To keep things in perspective, I emphasized to the couple many times that this trauma re-enactment and projective identification were not excuses for the pain and betrayal Marco had visited on Francine. They did not "make it OK"; they simply made it intelligible. At the same time, Francine recognized that she had been entrusted with her husband's story in a way no one ever had before. She had been worthy of his deepest trust and able to understand and know him this profoundly, which gave a new and powerful meaning to their terrible and protracted rupture.

By bringing together the present-day stimulus and emotions with the antecedent childhood memory, even asking them to register the body experience, understanding the meaning, and all in the presence of an empathic other – this is how we process trauma. We are integrating fragmented elements, constructing a coherent narrative, and evolving new meaning for both the original experiences and the more recent experience of the couple. As I explained to Marco and Francine, moments of deep empathic feelings are emotional markers or indicators of significance in the brain. This is how we fundamentally change the relationship. With sexually compulsive clients whose compulsivity is rooted in trauma, this process extinguishes the flame that fuels the behaviors.

Francine had been obsessed with details. She wanted to know absolutely every indiscretion that Marco had ever committed. She had read on the Internet that the gold standard for "sex addiction" treatment is when the addict takes a lie detector test. She insisted that if he really loved her, he would do that for her to win back her trust. Marco was appalled at the idea, feeling that he was being treated like a criminal. The most nightmarish of his prior treatment programs had included a lie detector test as part of its protocol, and he viewed the therapist there as a ghoul and a fiend.

As we deepened into Francine's feelings, we learned of the secrets lurking in the shadows in her family that she did not discover until she was 18. At that time, she found out that her father "all along" had another whole family, and that when he left Francine's family it was to be with them. She reacted by becoming fiercely distrustful, adamant about keeping the truth transparent and visible at all times. She was terrified and devastated by the depth of the deception in her marriage. Now, Marco understood better why. He could see that the deceit was even more painful to his wife than the infidelity had been. We began to work on how he could reassure her of his honesty, and how she, in turn, could reassure him of his value and his place in her world.

Learning repair

Processing and integration open a channel for true relationship repair, which for many of our clients is an entirely new experience – one never learned in their families-of-origin. What is required is an authentic understanding of how both partners were hurt. Again, it is often a hard sell convincing "victimized" partners that they, too, played a role in the couple's unhealthy dynamics. Incensed and deeply hurt, they do not want to accept any blame for the heinous behaviors they so despise.

And they are *not* to blame, much as their compulsive partners may have claimed at times. However, they do, in fact, have a role in keeping the core dynamic in play. Repair is about empathic understanding and ownership of one's own part of the devastating history of one's relationship. It is not about who behaved worse and who suffered the most. It is a journey of humility and of learning the elusive art of true apology on both of their parts. It is rarely quick or easy. When undertaken with commitment and perseverance, however, it can be transformative.

Often, couples must build a new sexual relationship from the ground up. Perhaps the sex had never been good between them. In Marco and Francine's case it had been once, but the lovemaking had stopped years ago when the compulsivity came to light. Francine was haunted by the details of Marco's affairs that she had insisted upon knowing. She was also worried about being compared with other women, whom she could only imagine. And it took a while before she could begin to trust that it was really over, and make herself vulnerable to her husband again.

I recommended a tantra workshop in Hawaii, where in a whole new setting with a new set of skills, they could begin to renew their sexual relationship. As calm grew between them, they were ready to deepen their sexual interaction and experience a different and trusting closeness. A new way of starting that focused on connection, presence, and spirituality was appealing to them. During their glorious and successful trip, Marco proposed to Francine again, and they planned a recommitment ceremony to signify the birth of a whole new marriage.

Now, more than a year post-therapy, Marco's compulsive sexual behavior has not returned. He continues to self-regulate with ultra-athleticism: with Francine's support, he is currently training for a 100-mile (in one stint!) foot race. And he is supporting and coaching her as she trains for her first marathon. Marco continues to work hard in therapy. Francine, meanwhile, continues to process her own history of profound neglect, and how it prepared her for Marco's long absences and being left to fend for herself and their children. They celebrated their renewed marriage vows and are actively creating their envisioned new marriage, replete with fun, companionship, satisfying co-parenting and lively, intimate sex. They are happy and hopeful. For me, the measure of a successful outcome is a renewed (or new) and safe closeness, trust, and a measure of joy. Usually that brings with it a rhythm of regular and mutually satisfying sexual and emotional activity.

Mapping a course

Working with couples who struggle with sexual compulsivity is a delicate and difficult challenge. Research states that most unhappy couples have suffered for at least 6 years before seeking therapeutic assistance (Gottman, 2002, p. 35). My own experience is that these couples have struggled a decade or more and have made more than one, often tragic, attempt at treatment. They may be skeptical, resigned, or worse. I warn them that both partners will need to make a big investment of time and energy. Our goals, very briefly, are:

(1) to identify the couple's core dynamic and its expression of each partner's personal history;
(2) to translate the meaning of each partner's problematic behavior: what is the story that each is attempting to tell?
(3) to put language and affect to the trauma stories; building an empathic connection between the partners; linking the unwanted behaviors to the trauma stories;
(4) to integrate trauma memory, behavior, affect, and meaning in shared moments;
(5) to make a shared commitment to eradicating the unwanted behaviors;
(6) to apologize, forgive, and renew trust and commitment;
(7) to create a new sexual relationship between the partners.

I warn couples (and remind myself) that it will not be easy or quick. Certainly, my intention is not to imply that all compulsivity is rooted in trauma, or that all couples can effectively process their histories, change behavior, forgive, and live happily ever after. Admittedly, those who have the resources to travel great distances and engage in long-term therapy are a select subgroup. This is the population I know best. My intention here is to encourage exploration, creativity, hope, and dialog about the nature and healing of these complex and painful life dramas.

References

Cohn, R. (2011). *Coming home to passion: Restoring loving sexuality in couples with histories of childhood trauma and neglect* (pp. 53–63). Santa Barbara: ABC CLIO, LLC.

Coleman, E. (2003). Compulsive sexual behavior: What to call it, how to treat it. *Siecus Report, 31*, 12–18.

Gottman, J. (2002). *The mathematics of marriage*. Cambridge: MIT Press.

Hendrix, H. (1988). *Getting the love you want*. New York: Henry Holt and Co. LLC.

Van der Kolk, B. (1980). *Traumatic stress: The effects of overwhelming experience on mind, body and society* (p. 283). New York: Guilford.

Getting in touch with touch: a use of caressing exercises to enrich sensual connection and evoke ecstatic experience in couples

Linda De Villers[a,b]

[a]*Graduate School of Education and Psychology, Pepperdine University, Los Angeles, CA, USA;* [b]*Department of Psychology, Santa Monica College, Santa Monica, CA, USA*

Of all the senses, touch is the first to develop; it is the most essential to life and a requirement for normal development. Interpersonal touch, including sexual touch, is also the most controversial of the senses, perceived by some as uncomfortable or threatening, and by others as the epitome of sublime pleasure and connection with a partner. An extraordinary and basic way sex therapists can enrich the sexual connection between couples is to introduce caressing exercises that are not goal focused on arousal and orgasm. Caressing exercises assist couples in moving beyond any negative or ambivalent attitudes toward partnered touch, often bringing them to levels of sensual awareness and tactile pleasure that are new and delightful.

The primacy of human touch

Our sense of touch is called the "mother of all senses" (Montagu, 1986). It is the first of the senses to develop in the womb; by the eighth week of gestation it develops in the cheek, with the genitals and palms next in line (Patterson, 2007). With millions of specialized tactile receptors located throughout the body, the skin, through which the touch receptors are activated, is the largest of all the sense organs.

Touch is also the most essential to survival; recognition of its necessity traces back to ancient Greece, in Aristotle's *De Anima* (Harvey, 2003). We can live without vision or hearing. We can also "...thrive on tasteless food and get along without smelling the roses" (Brynie, 2001, p. 20), but without touch, our very survival is at risk; without pain receptors sending messages to the somatosensory cortex of the brain, alerting us of danger, the body cannot protect itself. Those who suffer from congenital analgesia, a rare genetic disorder, cannot feel pain and are prone to severe bodily injury that is frequently life threatening.

Numerous studies have long established that healthy infants are born with a fully developed sense of touch, and that touch is essential to normal physical, cognitive, emotional, and social development (Hertenstein & Weiss, 2011; Montagu, 1986). Failure to be adequately touched in infancy poses serious health risks, including "failure to thrive," which often leads to death (Bowlby, 1969; Spitz, 1946). The classic rhesus macaque ("monkey") studies of Harlow and Harlow (1962) found that infant macaques deprived of "contact comfort" suffered a reduction in levels of essential growth hormone.

The Harlow and Harlow results also established that close bodily contact, "contact comfort," is more important than food in forming an attachment bond. Nurturing human caregiver–infant touch is equally essential in creating a secure attachment that becomes the basis for getting close to others, including the ability to establish an adult intimate relationship. Touching and intimacy go "hand in hand." When early experiences of touch are abundant and loving, we come to associate touch with trust, safety, warmth, closeness, and serenity. Recent research has confirmed that oxytocin is released during interpersonal touch and "…promotes a feeling of calmness, pleasantness, and mild euphoria" (Floyd, 2006, p. 104).

Touch receptors and sensation

Both free nerve endings and specialized touch receptors reside just below the epidermis. They are sensitive to temperature, limb position, pain, vibration (Ruffini corpuscles), indentations of the skin (Merkel's disks), pressure (Pacinian corpuscles), and Meissner's corpuscles. Pacinian and Meissner's corpuscles are especially concentrated on hairless, "glabrous skin" portions of the body, including the lips, face, eyelids, tongue, fingertips, palms of the hands, soles of the feet, nipples, inner labia, clitoris, and penis. They are particularly sensitive to light touch, low-frequency vibration, or brief taps on the skin (Carlson, 2010). The fingertips, clitoris, and penis have the highest concentration of free nerve endings and specialized touch receptors.

Various touch receptors and free nerve endings produce the sensations of pressure, temperature, movement, vibration, itch, and tickling. However, it is only through our perception, or interpretation, of the sensations produced by stimulation of the receptors that we impute meaning. For example, there are no specialized tactile "pleasure" nerve endings per se; instead, we perceive certain kinds of touch as pleasurable, or sadly, do not.

Perception and the multiple interpretations of touch

Cultures vary in the extent to which they avoid or embrace touch and experience it with positive affect. Four factors account for most of the cultural variations: latitude, collectivism, gender, and religion (Hertenstein & Weiss, 2011). Degree of proximity to the equator, as expressed by latitude, is the most significant factor. Cultures closer to the equator are generally "high-touch" cultures, while those that are distant engage in far less interpersonal touching. Various hypotheses have been put forth to account for this geographic distinction, from greater exposure of skin to the effect of light on neuroendocrine processes; none have proven definitive.

Second, cultures characterized as individualist, such as North America and Western Europe, with their greater emphasis on the rights of individuals generally endorse more interpersonal touch than collectivist cultures, notably Asian, which put family and honor ahead of personal fulfillment. The philosophies of Buddhism and Confucianism also encourage attention to proper behavior. In collectivist cultures, touch may be perceived as disrespectful and intrusive.

Gender also plays a significant role in how touch is interpreted. For example, same-sex touching is more common between females than males; between genders, males are more likely to touch females than the reverse in a variety of contexts (Hall, 1990; Henley, 1986). A study observing heterosexual couples found that the length of the relationship tilts the asymmetry in the opposite direction. In couples married less than a year, or engaged or dating, males more often touched females, but in couples married more than a year, the wives touched their husbands more often (Willis & Briggs, 1992, cited in Hertenstein & Weiss, 2011).

Finally, religion plays a significant role in determining how touch is interpreted. Certain philosophies and religious traditions that are grounded in dualism give primacy of the soul (or mind) over the body, relegating touch to the "basest" of the senses (Harvey, 2003) and the source of the sins of carnality and lust. According to Montagu (1986), "Two of the great negative achievements of Christianity have been to make a sin of tactual pleasures, and by its repression to make of sex an obsession" (p. 312). His research also found that conservative Christians in the United States were more touch avoidant than Catholics or Jewish-Americans. Islamic tradition and beliefs also discourage touch except in the context of heterosexual marriage (Hertenstein & Weiss, 2011).

When various cultural messages have created an atmosphere of tactile taboos, intimate touch often becomes a goal-focused sexual activity that is restricted to stimulation of the genital organs with the aim of producing orgasm. This very narrow focus bypasses sensual touch and often leads to sexual difficulties through performance pressures, spectatoring, lack of arousal, and even boredom.

Helping couples experience sensuality, sexuality, and pleasure

In our consumerist, goal-focused culture that encourages us to "earn more money," "have a lavish wedding," and "buy another car," obsessive attention often puts us in an inattentive, nearly "senseless" state that does not allow us to "stop and smell the roses." This is true whether the goal is an object, an experience, or an orgasm. Therefore, helping clients make a distinction between sensuality and sexuality is often useful.

Sensuality is characterized by full absorption in the moment-to-moment experience of the senses, whether it is a wonderful meal or the sensations produced by a lover's tender, caring touch. As the Phantom of the Opera beautifully sang in *Music of the Night*, it involves "*. . .floating, falling, sweet intoxication; touch me, trust me, savor each sensation. . .*" (Hart, 1986).

To help bring couples "to their senses" regarding their sexual expression, invite them to be open to experiencing the pleasures of non-goal-focused, sensual touching. Women may need to be assured that sensual touch is not simply a ploy to prime them for sex; if they think of themselves as nurturers, they may also feel it is selfish to receive pleasure. Men often need to be assured that feeling uncomfortable with the suspension of a sexual goal is perfectly normal. When it comes to touch, most men have been raised to be givers, which may make them less comfortable being a passive receiver. Both partners need to be assured that taking the time to indulge in sensual touching in both roles, as receiver and as giver, often leads to deeper levels of connection and pleasure.

Some clients may not be ready for sensual touch activities, for example, those with a history of physical or sexual abuse. Helping clients to overcome the profound ambivalence or negative affect surrounding touch as a result of abuse goes beyond the scope of this article. The reader is encouraged to consult the excellent works of Maltz (2012) and Haines (2007) for interventions that help abuse survivors gradually discover positive, intimate touch.

Distinguishing "sensate focus" exercises from caressing exercises

Sensate focus

Masters and Johnson (1970) coined the term "sensate focus" to describe a series of non-demand pleasuring exercises for a couple to carry out to facilitate the resolution of sexual problems such as erectile difficulties, rapid ejaculation, and orgasmic problems. The couple in treatment was usually instructed to refrain from having intercourse, focusing instead on the range of physical sensations that could be elicited by touch. By removing the "goal" of sexual encounters, namely genital stimulation leading to orgasm, the couple learned to heighten their awareness of the pleasures of tactile stimulation on all parts of their body. Masters and Johnson (1970) also proposed that placing a "ban" on intercourse or other forms of genital stimulation would alleviate the performance anxiety and cognitive distractions characteristic of many sexual difficulties. The ban was also seen as a means of reducing "spectatoring," another term they coined to describe a person's tendency to see himself or herself in the third person during sexual activity – becoming an outside observer and evaluator of the sexual encounter, rather than focusing on the body's sensations (Masters, Johnson, & Kolodny, 1986).

In Masters and Johnson's clinical practice, completion of a series of sensate focus exercises often led to the resolution of sexual difficulties. A more recent study of 365 couples treated in an outpatient clinic for a range of sexual problems has also supported their effectiveness; the researchers found that the number of sensate focus exercises completed in the last week of treatment was the best predictor of success (Sarwer & Durlak, 1997).

Caressing exercises

Replacing the phrase "sensate focus exercises" with "caressing exercises" has several advantages. "Sensate focus" is a less familiar, clinical term. The phrase "caressing exercises" offers a more inviting, accessible, and descriptive way to capture both the sensual and the relational spirit of touching exercises that are focused on moment-to-moment touching for pleasure (De Villers, 1997, 2012; Kennedy & Dean, 1988).

As part of an integrated sex therapy program to resolve sexual difficulties, introducing touching exercises as caressing exercises offers another advantage. It carries a sex-positive connotation. From a client perspective, the term helps to shift the focus from overcoming dysfunction to sensual discovery. Similarly, therapists with a humanistic, spiritual or other positive psychology orientation are likely to prefer these phrases because they emphasize positive, relational experiencing.

Finally, the absence of a narrow association with treatment settings (as is true of sensate focus exercises) expands the use of caressing exercises in non-clinical settings. Some therapists specializing in sexuality offer sexual enrichment workshops to non-sexually distressed couples seeking to maintain or expand their current sexual connection. Such workshops are held in various settings, from private venues to well-known growth centers such as The Esalen Institute in California.

In either setting, clinical or non-clinical, several features of caressing exercises account for their effectiveness in bringing greater sexual fulfillment to couples. They are introduced gradually, in a "baby step" approach that most couples find reassuring and less anxiety provoking. Caressing exercises also break set; they invite couples to alter their beliefs and assumptions about rewarding sexual interaction. In more theoretical terms, Fraser and Solovey (2004) suggest that sensual touching exercises provide an opportunity to bring about "second-order change." The exercises, with their emphasis on experiencing pleasure throughout the body, literally from head to toe, enable many couples to acquire a new mindset that significantly expands their capacity to experience erotic pleasure.

Limitations and benefits of caressing exercises

Most often, the risks of caressing exercises are related to their use in "cookbook fashion." As a therapist, it is important to adapt them and introduce them at appropriate times that meet the specific needs of couples and invite the couple to participate in the decision-making process (Wincze & Carey, 1991). Any touching exercise must be described in detail; various resources provide clearly written directions (De Villers, 2012; Foley, Kope, & Sugrue, 2011; McCarthy & McCarthy, 2012).

In a clinical setting, it is also important as a therapist to recognize that caressing exercises are not a stand-alone approach to resolving sexual difficulties, and sometimes serve primarily as "an elegant diagnostic and exploratory device" (Apfelbaum, 1995, p. 39).

It is essential to work with couples after they have privately carried out an exercise to help them process the thoughts, emotions, and behaviors that arose during and after carrying it out. What images did the exercise evoke? What memories did it trigger? How did it feel to be the giver? The receiver? Working with this kind of information and addressing the underlying issues brought out by caressing exercises can be the most powerful part of treatment (Levine, 1992).

Therapists should feel reassured that the successful use of caressing exercises is not restricted to heterosexual couples. Both McWhirter and Mattison (1980), in their sex therapy with gay couples, and Hall (2001), in her work with lesbian couples, endorse their merits. Dodson (1996) extends their use to individuals and provides a number of sensual exercises that are auto-erotic.

In non-clinical settings, fewer published studies on the limitations and benefits of caressing exercises exist; however, this author has read hundreds of graduate and undergraduate student descriptions of their optional experiences carrying out diverse caressing exercises of their choosing. They have ranged widely in age, relationship status, sexual orientation, gender identity, and ethnic background. The response has been overwhelmingly positive. Only minor disappointments have ever been reported.

Introducing caressing exercises

As a therapist, before introducing a caressing exercise to a couple (or individual), it behooves him or her to be familiar with various caressing exercise options and the various resources that describe them. Only that way can appropriate options be suggested. Although an exercise can be verbally described to a couple, odds are that some key details will be overlooked; for that reason, a written description is preferable.

Presenting couples with a verbal overview of general guidelines for caressing exercises is appropriate. Here are five basic guidelines to follow when verbally introducing caressing exercises, subject to tailoring them for your clients:

(1) Emphasize to couples that caressing exercises are not intended to elicit a sexual response and that to help ensure that, breasts and genitalia are off limits in early caressing exercises. Even when they may be included in later caressing exercises, attending to the sensual experience remains paramount. The couple can also be assured that despite avoidance of these primary erotic areas, a sexual response (e.g., erection, lubrication, or, in women, even orgasm) may occur, and that if so, this is perfectly normal.

(2) Encourage couples to set aside an agreed-upon prearranged time, typically 60 minutes or so, to carry out a caressing exercise. This way, they can be assured that it will be leisurely paced and in a private setting that is comfortable and free

from distractions. This means turning off cell phones, televisions, etc. (See directions for the first caressing exercise below for more details).

(3) Tell couples to refrain from any verbal interaction during the exercise. This creates a deeper non-verbal sense of intimacy, harmony, and communication. Unless a receiver is experiencing pain or significant discomfort, in which case speaking up is appropriate, advise the couple to talk after the exercise has been completed. Between turns is also a good time. Encourage them to use specific terms rather than vague terms to describe their experience. For example, they can replace "great" and "wonderful" with descriptions like "flowing," "ticklish," "warm, "relaxing," "hard," "soothing," or "uncomfortable."

Additionally, remind couples to follow other effective communication guidelines such as giving each other lots of positive feedback and providing any negative feedback in a loving, constructive way. If needed, before assigning any caressing exercises, introduce them to John Gottman's excellent distinction between legitimate complaints and inappropriate, global criticism (De Villers, 2012; Gottman, Gottman, & De Claire, 2006).

(4) Provide couples with suggestions for selecting an appropriate oil or lotion. Using an oil or lotion provides a more sensuous experience by eliminating the friction for the giver's hand onto the receiver's skin. Encourage them to select an oil or lotion that is not heavy, is alcohol-free, and appeals to them both. Light vegetable or nut oils such as avocado, almond, apricot, soy, sunflower, or olive are good choices to suggest. To each ounce of oil, they may add five drops of a highly concentrated essential oil such as cedarwood, cinnamon, cloves, jasmine, neroli, patchouli, rose, sandalwood, or ylang-ylang, all said to enhance sensuality. Fragrant lotions are a great alternative for those who do not like oils; or recommend baby powder, used by some professional masseuses, instead of fluids.

(5) Although it is traditional to shift the giver/receiver roles in one longer session, time constraints or one partner's particular fatigue may make it more appropriate to focus attention on letting only the fatigued partner receive during a specific caressing session. Introduce this idea to a couple and emphasize that they must decide this in advance of starting the exercise. In either role, encourage the clients to steep themselves in the pleasure of the role.

The following two caressing exercises have been excerpted from *Love Skills* (De Villers, 2012). They represent two introductory caressing exercises not included in the books of early sex therapy pioneers (Kaplan, 1974; Masters & Johnson, 1970). The author was introduced to the first exercise below during her sex therapy training nearly 30 years ago. Variants of the "face–hands–feet" exercise below were first published in a book by a well-known and highly regarded surrogate partner, Adele Kennedy (Kennedy & Dean, 1988).

Caressing exercise: creatively exploring tactile sensations alone and with a partner

This exercise keeps the focus on heightening sensual awareness and pleasure and offers a gentle, creative introduction to later caressing exercises. The therapist can assign it as a solo exercise to an individual client, to each partner of a couple, or to a couple to carry out together.

Directions: Here is an exercise to do that helps you to heighten awareness of tactile sensations all over your body. Allow about 30–45 minutes. Create a sensual, warm environment in your bedroom or other private area. Choose your bed, a futon, a plush throw placed on your carpet, whatever is comfortable for you. Set the thermostat at a comfortable temperature. Add soft lighting, a scented candle or aroma lamp diffuser, appealing background music, and anything else that contributes to a sensuous atmosphere.

(1) Before beginning your exploration, select 10 different objects, each of which can be readily held in your hand. Select everyday objects that vary in their texture, firmness, shape, size, and temperature. For example, you might select a pen, a scarf, a fork, a comb, or a feather. Use your imagination until you have gathered together 10 objects. Some couples have creatively chosen the following: velvet jewelry holder, bracelet, wig, various brushes (artist's brush, hairbrush, toothbrush, eye shadow brush), fur mitt, piece of sandpaper, ice cube, backscratcher, piece of satin ribbon, wet washcloth, index or credit card, activated hand warmer, emery board, raw carrot with its feathery top, large leaf, flower, etc.
(2) On the far left of a lined 8.5″ by 11″ sheet of paper, list each of these 10 objects on a separate line. Leave space between each listing so you will have room to write your impressions of each.
(3) Undress and lie down on a comfortable surface. Select one of the objects, close your eyes, and slowly run the object the entire length of one side of your body. Do not forget to use it on the top and bottom of your arms and legs, and between your fingers and toes. Next, do the top of your head, face, neck, torso, abdomen, and genitals. Finish by using the object on the other side of your body.
(4) Record what you liked (or disliked) about the first object, being as specific as possible about the tactile sensations it evoked. Indicate where you liked it more, where you liked it less, what kind of pressure was appealing/unappealing, and what kind of speed created the most pleasurable sensation. Use specific words like "ticklish," "rough," "arousing," "slippery," or "delicate" rather than "great" or "did not like." Be especially aware that you may have liked the object on one part of your body, but not on another.
(5) Repeat steps 3 and 4 for each of the remaining nine objects.
(6) After recording and reviewing all of the 10 objects, reflect on what you enjoyed the most about the exercise and what new awareness you are taking away from it. Were you surprised to experience very pleasurable sensations in certain parts of your body? What new insights would you like to share with your lover? What, if anything, made you uncomfortable?

Variation: You and your lover might like to do this exercise with each other. Be sure to first review the guidelines for all partnered caressing exercises. When carrying this out together, the giver can also serve as the scribe by writing down the receiver's responses to each object (adapted from De Villers, 2012).

The following case history highlights the value of the above exercise with a married couple:

Case history: "Michelle," a 28-year old married woman entered sex therapy with a presenting concern that she did not reach orgasm during traditional penile-vaginal lovemaking. She also reported that she engaged in sexual activity largely to placate her husband of two years. They both shared very conservative Christian backgrounds and were both virgins when they met in their mid-twenties. She was encouraged to invite her husband to join her in therapy sessions, but they resisted, preferring that she work on "her" sexual difficulties. After completing a thorough sex history, which revealed both significant negative messages about sex and a touch-avoidant family background, she resonated with the idea that a very gradual introduction to touching was appropriate. This included a ban on intercourse during this stage of therapy. When the caressing exercise above was described to her, she was surprisingly open to carrying it out. When she returned the next week, she described in great detail the objects she'd selected, and which she had enjoyed most (e.g., a make-up brush). She was able to indicate which ones tickled, which one made her feel aroused, and where she felt the sensations. She was so enthusiastic that she expressed a desire to repeat the exercise with her husband, "Jake." They followed the suggestion to select objects out of sight of the partner, and to keep their eyes closed when receiving touch, in order to be open to all of the sensations without expectation. Their ensuing conversation opened them up to candid dialog about negative sexual messages they had received while growing up and their willingness to reevaluate them, including how refreshing the non-pressured sensual experience had been. They found the exercise fun.

The positive experience with the objects exercise led Jake to have a change of heart. He agreed to join her for conjoint sessions. During weekly sessions, Jake's concerns about his limited sex knowledge and performance, such as ejaculating sooner than they both wished, came to the fore. The small steps they conscientiously took each week both in talk sessions in my office and their at-home, between-session caressing exercises (as well as "lovetalk" and body image exercises) became motivation to continue in a positive direction. After four months, their sexual complaints had lifted, and they were delighted with their newfound confidence in experiencing sexual intimacy and pleasure.

Exercise: caressing the feet

The following exercise is an example of a caressing exercise that the therapist can suggest as a first partnered exercise. It is typically presented as a "face–hands–feet" caressing exercise that allows the receiving partner to select which of the three body parts he or she would like to have caressed. Space requirements do not allow for presenting all three options here; the interested reader is invited to consult *Love Skills* for face and hands directions (De Villers, 2012).

Directions: For this caressing exercise, if you have arranged to switch roles, set aside a total of about 70–80 minutes, spending 35–40 minutes in each role. For the first half of the session, one of you should be the giver and the other the receiver. As the giver, you will want to caress each foot for about 15 minutes, followed by about 5–10 minutes for feedback afterwards before repeating in different roles. If you will be switching roles, you will need six bath towels and enough soap, oil, lotion, or powder for both of you. Next, fill two small tubs with warm (not hot), softened water. The addition of a softener provides a wonderful fragrance and sensuously enhances the texture of the water. You will use one tub for washing and the other for rinsing. Gather all these supplies together in advance so you will not have to interrupt the session once you have begun.

As the giver, keep in mind that sensual touch requires a light touch – it is caressing, not massage. The pressure of deep tissue massage can actually numb the skin. Light stroking produces a far greater richness of sensation because it activates nerve tissue, not muscle tissue. Caressing is a special kind of intimate sharing, communicating your desire to give pleasure.

If you need to replenish oil or change position from time to time, make it a point to maintain body contact throughout the exercise. If you are using oil, simply turn one hand over, palm up, continuing to touch your lover. Use the other to pour oil into your palm.

The feet caress

(1) As the giver, arrange for both you and your partner to sit in comfortable chairs facing each other, about 24″ apart. Place one small tub for washing between your legs, and the other tub for rinsing nearby. Gently place one of your partner's feet into the tub of water between your legs. Slowly wash the foot with soap. Leave it in the water as you move on to the next foot, repeating the process.

(2) After you have given each foot an initial washing, place a towel over one of your thighs. Lift the first foot from the water and place it on the towel. Re-lather the foot generously and then place it in the rinsing tub. Repeat this procedure with the second foot. Remove each foot from the rinse water and wrap each completely in a dry towel.

(3) Push both tubs of water aside, unwrap one of the feet and slowly and thoroughly dry it. Be sure you dry carefully between the toes. Do the same thing with the other foot. Next, oil or powder both feet.

(4) Place the heel of one foot on your thigh so that you can easily touch both the sole and upper surface. Cradle the foot between your hands for a few moments to warm it, lightly oil it, and then begin stroking. Beginning with the lower leg area, use both hands to stroke downward onto the upper and lower surfaces of the foot to relax it. Then move from the base of the toes toward the ankle, making circular motions with your thumb. Repeat several times. Try using the heels of your hands, or several fingers together. Stroke every toe over its entire length, using your thumb and finger, and run your little finger slowly between each toe. Pay particular attention to the pad on the bottom of the big toe. Vary the speed of your stroking.

(5) If your partner can accept the touching without being ticklish, try light feathery strokes and use your fingernails as well as part of your caress. If your partner is ticklish anywhere, try using a slightly firmer touching in that area initially, and see if you can later return to it with a softer touch. If the feet (or anywhere else) are ticklish, it is often a sign of tension; it may be your psyche's defense against their potential as a source of enormous sensual pleasure. Being ticklish allows you to avoid being touched and inhibits sensations that might become sexual.

Consider going deeply into the feelings as they are evoked by the foot caress. These feelings might run the gamut from pleasure, or fear of pleasure, to a profound sense of connection and love, to deeply buried, and perhaps unmet, longing to be held and nurtured. You may be surprised by the intensity of these feelings, so allow ample time to process them.

Beyond this exercise, you can sensitize the soles of your feet. Go barefoot as often as you can. Walk on a variety of surfaces: cool tile, hardwood floors, grass, carpeting, sand, concrete, fabrics, etc. This will also be a form of sensual awareness for your feet. Your feet are richly endowed with nerve endings which, when stimulated, can produce extraordinary levels of pleasure.

(6) After 10 or 15 minutes, conclude by cupping your partner's foot between your hands for a moment; then gently remove your hands. Proceed to caress your partner's other foot in the same manner. If you arranged to switch roles, with the receiver becoming the giver and vice versa, take about 5 minutes to share your feelings and reactions before starting the second session (adapted from De Villers, 2012).

Many sex therapy clients have especially appreciated this gentle introduction to a caressing exercise that allowed them to be dressed, partly dressed, or nude, and in its actual "hands, feet, or face" format allowed them to choose which body part they wanted the focus on. In a non-clinical context, many of the author's human sexuality students have also selected this exercise, with very positive results.

The following student comment highlights its potential to enrich sexual experience in the absence of any sexual difficulty. He wrote:

> My favorite exercise was the "hands-feet-face," because it made me feel closer to my girlfriend. I was really surprised how good it felt to get my feet washed and stroked. At first my feet were very ticklish, but as soon as I started to focus on the feeling that this was producing, I was amazed at the pleasure I was experiencing. When it was her turn to receive, she requested her face. While I was caressing her, I lost track of time. It was so relating and enjoyable for both of us. I loved running my fingers through her hair, too. This was an excellent exercise, because both my girlfriend and I felt we experienced a great wealth of pleasure without having sexual intercourse.

Conclusion

Our sense of touch is essential to our survival. It is the most basic and profound language for communicating comfort, care, affection, pleasure, and passion. Many in our culture need assistance in moving beyond both tactile taboos and restrictive, goal-focused, sexual touch. Caressing exercises open a door to new dimensions of erotic pleasure and connection with their partner.

This final quote from the author's files sums it up:

> The (caressing exercises) are my favorites. I will be doing these exercises in the future. I think they are favorites because they involve no sex. It is all about light caresses and getting to know one another's bodies. You get to experience with different types of touches throughout all the body, and knowing what causes the most pleasure to your loved one. These exercises are wonderful for people who are not yet ready for sex. . .I think affectionate and sensual touch are among the most important things to have in a relationship. The sensual (caressing exercises) section reminded me of the scene in the movie "40 Days and 40 Nights" where the guy swore off sex for 40 days and then met this girl he started to fall for and wanted to be with, but couldn't because of the 40 day oath, so since he couldn't kiss or touch her with his own hands, he used a flower to touch her whole body. It was such a beautiful part in the film. That's what sensual touch is all about.

References

Apfelbaum, B. (1995). Masters and Johnson revisited: A case of desire disparity. In S. Leiblum & R. Rosen (Eds.), *Case studies in sex therapy* (pp. 23–45). New York, NY: Guilford.

Bowlby, J. (1969). *Attachment and loss. Vol. 1: Attachment*. New York, NY: Basic Books.

Brynie, F. (2001). *The amazing brain: Perception*. Woodbridge, CT: Blackbirch Press.

Carlson, R. (2010). *Physiology of behavior*. New York: Allyn & Bacon.

De Villers, L. (1997). *Love skills: More fun than you've ever had with sex, intimacy and communication*. San Luis Obispo, CA: Impact Publishers.
De Villers, L. (2012). *Love skills: A fun, upbeat guide to sex-cessful relationships* (5th ed.). Marina del Rey, CA: Aphrodite Media (originally published by Impact Publishers, San Luis Obispo, 1997).
Dodson, B. (1996). *Sex for one: The joy of selfloving*. New York, NY: Three Rivers Press.
Floyd, K. (2006). *Communicating affection: Interpersonal behavior and social context*. Cambridge: Cambridge University Press.
Foley, S., Kope, S., & Sugrue, D. (2011). *Sex matters for women: A complete guide to taking care of your sexual self* (2nd ed.). New York, NY: Guilford.
Fraser, J.S., & Solovey, A. (2004). A catalytic approach to brief sex therapy. In S. Green & D. Flemons (Eds.), *Quickies: The handbook of brief sex therapy* (pp. 189–212). New York, NY: Norton.
Gottman, J., Gottman, J., & De Claire, J. (2006). *10 lessons to transform your marriage: America's love lab experts share their strategies for strengthening your relationships*. New York, NY: Crown.
Haines, S. (2007). *Healing sex: A mind–body approach to healing sexual trauma*. San Francisco, CA: Cleis Press.
Hall, J. (1990). *Nonverbal sex differences: Accuracy of communication and expressive style*. Baltimore, MD: Johns Hopkins University Press.
Hall, M. (2001). Beyond forever after: Narrative therapy with lesbian couples. In P.J. Kleinplatz (Ed.), *New directions in sex therapy: Innovations and alternatives* (pp. 379–301). New York, NY: Brunner/Mazel.
Harlow, H., & Harlow, M. (1962). The effect of rearing conditions on behavior. *Bulletin of the Menninger Clinic*, *28*, 213–214.
Hart, C. (1986). Music of the night (lyrics). *Phantom of the Opera*. London: West End (performance).
Harvey, E. (Ed.). (2003). *Sensible flesh: On touch in early modern culture*. Philadelphia: University of Pennsylvania Press.
Henley, N. (1986). *Body politics: Power, sex and nonverbal communication*. New York, NY: Prentice-Hall.
Hertenstein, M., & Weiss, S. (Eds.). (2011). *The handbook of touch: Neuroscience, behavior, and health perspectives*. New York, NY: Springer.
Kaplan, H.S. (1974). *The new sex therapy*. New York, NY: Brunner/Mazel.
Kennedy, A.P., & Dean, S. (1988). *Touching for pleasure: A 12 step program for sexual enhancement*. Chatsworth, CA: Chatsworth Press.
Levine, S.B. (1992). *Sexual life: A clinician's guide*. New York, NY: Plenum Press.
Maltz, W. (2012). *The sexual healing journey: A guide for survivors of sexual abuse* (3rd ed.). New York, NY: HarperCollins & Harper Perennial.
Masters, W.H., & Johnson, V.E. (1970). *Human sexual inadequacy*. Boston, MA: Little, Brown and Company.
Masters, W.H., Johnson, V.E., & Kolodny, R.C. (1986). *Masters and Johnson on sex and human loving*. Boston, MA: Little, Brown and Company.
McCarthy, B., & McCarthy, E. (2012). *Sexual awareness: Your guide to healthy couple sexuality* (5th ed.). New York, NY: Routledge.
McWhirter, D.P., & Mattison, A. (1980). Treatment of sexual dysfunction in homosexual male couples. In S. Leiblum & L. Pervin (Eds.), *Principles and practice of sex therapy* (pp. 321–345). New York, NY: Guilford.
Montagu, A. (1986). *The human significance of the skin* (3rd ed.). New York, NY: Harper & Row.
Patterson, M. (2007). *The senses of touch: Haptics, affects and technologies*. New York, NY: Berg.
Sarwer, D., & Durlak, J. (1997). A field trial of the effectiveness of behavioral treatment for sexual dysfunctions. *Journal of Sex & Marital Therapy*, *23*(2), 87–97.
Spitz, R. (1946). Anaclitic depression: An inquiry into the genesis of psychiatric conditions in early childhood. *The Psychoanalytic Study of the Child*, *20*, 213–342.
Willis, F.N., & Briggs, L.F. (1992). Relationship and touch in public settings. *Journal of Nonverbal Behavior*, *16*, 55–63.
Wincze, J.P., & Carey, M.P. (1991). *Sexual dysfunction: A guide for assessment and treatment*. New York, NY: Guilford Press.

"Extraordinary" sex coaching: an inside look

Patti Britton[a,b] and Sarah Rose Bright[c]

[a]*Sexology Department, Institute for Advanced Study of Human Sexuality, San Francisco, CA, USA;* [b]*Somatic Psychology Department, The Chicago School of Professional Psychology/Somatic Psychology, CA, USA;* [c]*Suite 3, Quadrant House, Hoylake, Wirral, UK*

The emergence of sex coaching as a phenomenon within the landscape of treatment of sexual concerns is a growing force today. This "inside look" illustrates the client–sex coach relationship, discusses the origins of sex coaching, the scope of practices, use of the MEBES© model, distinctions between sex coaching and traditional sex therapies, and provides examples from among the "extraordinary" ways in which sex coaching can transform sexual wounding and limitations into healing for clients. Sex coaching is a broad-spectrum approach, allowing for the creativity and dynamic freedom that clients deserve.

Introduction

The emergence of sex coaching as a phenomenon within the landscape of treatment of sexual concerns is a growing force today. This article discusses the origins of sex coaching to give a perspective of how it evolved, the scope of practice among sex coaches today, a glance at the primary MEBES© model (Britton, 2005), and makes distinctions between sex coaching and traditional sex therapies. Further, it provides examples from among the "extraordinary" ways in which sex coaching can transform sexual wounding and limitations into healing for clients to illuminate the client–sex coach relationship and brings examples of what we consider to be "extraordinary" within the profession of sex coaching. Sex coaching is a broad-spectrum approach, allowing for the creativity and dynamic freedom that clients deserve.

Prevalence of sex coaching

In 2010, a Google search engine report yielded fewer than 87 responses, when searching "Sex Coach(ing)" as key terms. In 2013 that number exceeds 443,000. Although neither professional criteria nor licensure exists for those calling themselves sex coaches, people worldwide are using such terminology to describe their services to clients. Sex coach training and certification currently is being offered in 23 countries by Sex Coach University (co-owned by author Britton) at (www.SexCoachU.com), delivering Internet-based curricula with high-quality requirements and promulgating a universal code of ethical standards.

The appearance of sex coaches is becoming ubiquitous. For example, at *Cosmo UK* magazine, the resident sexuality expert and advice columnist is Irma the Sex Coach, not a licensed therapist (Cosmopolitan UK, 2013). Within the past six months, British magazine journalists have conducted interviews about what sex coaching is, how it is conducted, and whether touch is involved, creating a media buzz of interest. These inquiries further show the mainstreaming effect that the concept and practice of sex coaching is having on the consumer world.

> For me, sex coaching is not a profession that can be pigeon-holed. Each and every one of us will be unique in our own coaching styles and bring something different and enriching to our clients. Sex coaching involves elements of sex therapy but is very different in that it focuses on personal sexuality goals rather than the past. Sex coaches heal, empower, and guide. (Respondent of 2012 Sex Coaching Survey)

Evolution of sex coaching

Sex coaching originated as an aspect of the medical patient visit for men, with the urologist speaking with the patient about sexual behaviors or performance concerns. The five-minute sex status conversation by the physician explored the causation of sexual dysfunction and was labeled sex coaching. This label implied that the physician was moving away from classical physical examination or medical treatment to the more psychosocial aspect of asking for, then providing, information as it is related to the patient's sexual concerns. This was first documented in the literature of sexual medicine by sex therapist, Michael Perelman (Perelman, 2003).

In the early 1990s Britton and sexologist Betty Dodson began to utilize the term "orgasm-directed sex coaching," building upon Dodson's legacy of orgasm-enhancement "BodySex" workshops for women, as a means for describing their one-on-one client work with pre-orgasmic women. During that time they also advertised their services through new age publications, defining their work as Sexual Health And Fitness Training or SHAFT. This may have been the genesis of a new ideology in targeted sessions for men, women, and couples using a sex-positive, integrative, behavioral, body-based approach that evolved into sex coaching. Britton first publicized the term in 1993 while addressing a sexual health conference in Vermont, presenting as a professional sex coach and demonstrating the creation of her MEBES© model with its focus on integration of mind/emotions/body/energy/spirit. In 1996 one of the first websites (SexClinic.com) was launched by Britton to provide online sex coaching services, garnering press and media attention. (Sexclinic.com became YourSexCoach.com in 1998, then drpattibritton.com).

What is sex coaching?

Sex coaching is built upon the methodologies of effective sex therapy (Leiblum, 2006; Kleinplatz, 2012) with personalized sex education as its foundation. Sex coaching approaches the client relationship from the methodologies derived from the popular new field of life or personal coaching (Kimsey-House et al., 2011). Coaching emphasizes a wellness focused, empowerment-based, client-centered, results-oriented style of working toward client goals (Stoltzfus, 2008); this departs from a "medical" or "mental health" model of assessment that relies on diagnoses and treatment of sexual issues as pathology.

As one researcher writes:

> Sex coaching is well-adapted to the bio-psychosocial directives of the World Health Organization, which mandates a holistic account of sexual health (specifically accounting for the

> physical, psychologically and social needs of the individual). In this respect, sex coaching's adaptive and holistic program offers an advantage that modular and manualized therapies cannot: the nature of the interaction between client and coach is dictated by the client's unique, and holistically-considered identity. (Berry, 2012)

Range of sex coaching services

Sex coaching addresses over 46 clinical concerns of men, women, and couples of all sexual orientations and backgrounds, emphasizing a combination of talking and doing, particularly emphasizing home assignments for clients to develop on their own and between coaching sessions. Sex coaching covers a range of typical male sexual dysfunctions (Castleman, 2004; Zilbergeld, 1999; Metz & McCarthy, 2003), from erectile or ejaculatory problems to the occurrence of low sexual desire to negative body image issues and recovery from sexual trauma. It covers an equally broad range of female sexual dysfunctions (Foley, Kope, & Sugrue, 2012; Komisaruk, Beyer-Flores, & Whipple, 2006), from lack of orgasmic response to painful sexual intercourse, from low sexual desire to arousal difficulties and includes body image and social/dating skills enhancement. For couples, sex coaching focuses on helping those who suffer from uneven sexual desire to the "sexless marriage" phenomenon, coping with the implications of aging on sexual function and sexual self-image, to survival from an affair (McCarthy & McCarthy, 2003; Resnick, 2012; Schnarch, 2009) to those seeking to open up a traditional relationship and actively explore a lifestyle that includes polyamory, Bondage and Discipline/Dominance and Submission/Sado-Masochism (BDSM), spiritual pathways for sexual expression, or coping with medical, prescription drugs, or pregnancy-related challenges:

> Sex coaching is a practical, goal oriented short term sex positive approach to helping people of all ages lead healthy, fulfilling and pleasurable sex lives by guiding and supporting them in resolving any challenges and/or concerns they may have within this arena. This pertains to sexual health, intimacy, relationship challenges/communication and body image. (Respondent of 2012 Sex Coaching Survey)

Critiques of sex coaching focus on sensational aspects of the profession, and sometimes conflate sex coaching with sexual surrogacy, its own profession that demonstrates intimacy, arousal, anatomy, sensuality and touch that often involves full sexual engagement, as beautifully portrayed in the film "The Sessions" (imdb.com). However, rarely in our work as sex coaches do we escort a couple to a BDSM dungeon, accompany them to a sex or strip club, get naked or have them show us their genitals.

Most sex coaches begin in other professions, as shown in the First International Sex Coaching Survey (Bright & Britton, 2013; $n = 80$), including: sex educator (39% of all respondents), relationship coach, sexuality counselor, psychotherapist, life coach, body worker, tantric practitioner, clinical sexologist, love coach, sex therapist, marriage and family therapist, and healer. Sex coaches often focus on a specific population or "niche", such as aging clients, newlyweds, Gay/Lesbian/Bisexual (GLB) or trans clients, or even the kinky set. One coach, for example is the "Coming Out Coach" (Clemons, 2013). Others are nurses, seeking to add sex coaching dynamics within the spectrum of patient care.

Sex coaches may employ bodywork or touch in their practice. This practice may evoke a controversial response in therapists trained to use only talk therapy. The selected and therapeutic use of touch in conjunction with talk may serve as a component of successful sex coaching. As a sex therapist Jack Morin insightfully observed, "Some of my clients' issue would take years or might never be resolved by standard non-touching therapy" (Morin, 2006).

In sex coaching, the client may be invited to show as well as tell. For instance, a coach may hold a mirror for a client to view her own clitoris for the first time or help a male-to-female trans client walk gracefully in her new stilettos. Most use a talk-only approach, although some utilize body-based or somatic methods as a component of their range of services. The Sex Coaching Survey illustrates a growing trend toward an integrated practice, offering sexological bodywork or other forms of appropriate healing touch as part of the sex coaching relationship. Among the respondents who worked as paid sex coaches (39), over two-thirds offer a combination of talk and bodywork services, including observational bodywork (e.g. live observation of a client's sexual pattern for masturbation) that is one of the hallmarks of "extraordinary" sex coaching today:

CASE: JOHN

Patti writes:

John was an unusual client. It was the mid 1990s, the pre-Viagra era. Aged 64, he had suffered from surgical removal of his cancerous prostate, leaving him with erectile difficulties, a grave sense of loss of his manhood, no ejaculate, and embarrassment that left him lonely and afraid to date. Our sex coaching involved helping him reframe his sense of masculinity by eliciting from him where he truly was a man in other ways. It included one "extraordinary" session early on, when John felt it would be helpful to bring in his new erection pump. John removed his trousers, and revealed his slightly erect penis to stuff it into the long plastic vacuum tube. Once he sufficiently pumped up an erection, he slipped the fitting ring over the base of his penis, showing me with great pride how it produced the desired result. "Voila!" he shouted with joy. But the issues surrounding his no longer producing ejaculate troubled him. Over the next few weeks we constructed a plan of action steps that included self-soothing techniques for his anxious self-talk. I taught him to catch himself when he was using self-judging thinking, to refute his inner voice and use positive affirmations, such as "I John am a strong, complete sexual man!" I normalized his feelings then sent him home to conduct a grief ritual for the loss of his ejaculate. In a sacred ceremony he buried his feelings of grief in hand-painted wooden boxes under a grove of elms, while dancing naked on his private property in the moonlight.

Just weeks later, John had morphed into a dynamic, confident and playful dater, one who never would ejaculate again but felt happy with his sense of self. At the end of our coaching together, John had met a younger woman and they were both becoming comfortable with his pump as a bedside friend during sex, with lasting erections that gave him and his partner pleasure together. This was one "extraordinary" man!

Sex coaching personalizes sexuality education or information-directed sessions, eliciting goals for the highest good of the client, and co-creating a set of steps or pathways for the client to move forward on his/her own continuum of growth toward these goals. Sex coaches provide a container of caring and safety, based on knowledge, competency-based skills, and a supportive context that guides the client toward successful outcomes. The primary modalities for working with sex coaching clients are one-on-one sessions, webinars, and workshops. Other modalities include trainings, groups, blogs, podcasts, radio shows, hosting DVDs, and bodywork.

Distinctions: sex coaches vs. therapists

Distinctions vary between sex coaching and sex therapy; however, the four main characteristics of sex coaching are as follows:

(1) *Use of non-medical approach and non-pathologizing language*: Rather than the diagnosis/treatment model, sex coaching focuses on assessments and actions plans. Sex coaching embraces a sex-positive and de-pathologizing frame of speaking about clients' sexuality, sexual expression, body parts or specific sexual activities. Sex coaching emphasizes terms that are stripped of judgment, for instance using "early" or "rapid" rather than "premature" ejaculation. Coaches are trained to be comfortable with clients' explicit language, and move away from terms like "dysfunction". Using neutral or empowering language about sexual concerns shifts away from disease-based messages and is at the foundation of sex coaching.

(2) *Education not counseling is the foundation of sex coaching work*: Most good sex coaching begins with thorough training in comprehensive sexuality information and personally directed sex education. That basic groundwork may include: (1) reviewing sexual anatomy with realistic models of genitalia in the session, such as teaching her how to locate her G-Spot or him to locate the frenulum on his penis; (2) conducting bodywork sessions in which the client is shown directly how to find her pubococcygeal (PC) muscles or view her own clitoris; (3) assisting clients about specific sexual positions for enhancing pleasure and minimizing sexual discomfort by showing explicit DVDs; and (4) offering specialized sex education ranging from Tantric or Taoist sexual practices to kink and BDSM. Encouraging clients to reframe normal to what is instead natural is a pivotal part of the content of sex coaching.

CASE: JESS

Sarah writes:

Jess, (age 32) had always believed her genitals were ugly and this greatly impacted her sexual confidence. She did not like her partners looking at them and felt very uncomfortable when receiving oral sex. She shared how her labia were different shapes and looked "unsightly". Talking with her I uncovered that she was comparing her genitals to images she had seen in pornography. I showed her pictures of a range of different women's genitals yet, she was adamant that hers were unusually different or "distorted". Together we looked at her genitals in a mirror. While describing what she saw, it was clear that she viewed her genitals extremely critically. I showed her how her genitals looked like many of those in the pictures, and she began to see herself in a new light. Because of this simple exercise that so directly addressed Jess's anxiety, she felt great relief. After only three sessions of sex coaching she left our work a vastly different person.

(1) *Present vs. past focus*: Traditional therapy often focuses on the client's past, especially family of origin issues, whereas coaching focuses on the person in the here and now, spending time and energy to facilitate a client's accomplishments toward a positive future. The emphasis on the present is a cornerstone of sex coaching; a person's past informs the present and an intake of the sexual history is conducted over time, but the client does not find the coach spending significant amounts of time in talking about the past. Of course some noted sex therapies have emphasized a short-term, behavioral treatment approach, such as Masters and Johnson.

(2) *Settings*: In sex therapy, typically, the client meets privately in the therapist's office. Sex coaching can also be conducted in physical settings, such as a clinic, home-based office, the client's home, or virtually via the Internet or telephone.

Geographical and technological restrictions govern much of therapy, yet coaches may work from their car, a mountaintop cabin, or one's kitchen. Session times and length vary case by case. Sex coaches often meet in public settings, for example: a cafe for talk-only sessions to work on relevant issues such as social/dating skills; a sex toy boutique to be a guide and to allay embarrassment; or shopping together for size 13 heels for the cross-dressing client just beginning to discover her new gender expression.

CASE: FRED

Patti writes:

I recall one such meeting with a wonderful older male client who seemed to grow up in front of me during our three years of coaching. We met initially in person then transferred our sessions to telephone. Occasionally I would visit his city and share coffee with him, hearing about his progress in person during a complimentary sex coaching session. His primary work with me as his sex coach involved debunking the myths he thought were truths from watching Hollywood films about dating, love and sex. He was stuck in an adolescent view of women and dating, which some basic Sex & Relationship Ed 101 fixed quickly. His lack of assertiveness skills left him behind in the dust about approaching prospective women to date. We worked on methods he could use to boost his assertiveness in social situations, overcome social awkwardness, and find outlets for self-expression through referral sources that he could explore on his own and report back on during our sessions. One of those fruitful outlets was improvisational theater classes. There he gained confidence, found his "inner comic" as he put it, and discovered a love of performance on stage that could easily translate into confidence in the bedroom.

Our last "spot coaching" follow-up session, four years after terminating our ongoing work, took place at a huge mall atrium over lattes in the middle of the cacophony of a busy public gathering place. Often the role of being "incognito in public" liberates inhibitions for a client to talk openly with a coach about the client's needs and progress on the sex coaching journey. This was one "extraordinary" client in an "extraordinary" setting!

Another distinction with most sex therapy is that the sex coaching role is primarily collaborative and cooperative, without trying to fix clients. The coach witnesses the person, elicits the best for the client, listens deeply on many levels, especially using some of the most popular methodologies taught by leading life coach trainers (Kimsey-House et al., 2011). Those levels of witnessing and listening permit the coaching process to evolve from simply listening to intuiting and suggesting interpretations from the energetics or felt sense of the session. Sex Coaching can parallel the work of sex therapy, by encouraging the clients' growth, seeing clients as whole and not broken, and enhancing their growth while walking beside them as an advocate and ally.

CASE: MARILYN

Patti writes:

Another one of my favorite clients was a CD (or cross-dressing) male who was an avid contestant each year at the local "Drag Queen Night of All-Stars". He had been questioning his gender identity and was beginning to show up as a "she" in our sessions together. At one of our coaching sessions, "she" leaned over and sheepishly asked, "Dr. Patti, you know I am a well known Diva, right? Will you come with me to the ball this weekend? I'd love to have you there at my table while I walk in stilettos 'in drag' for the last time. Would you? Please say YES!"

"Of course", I cried out.

I showed up in person (and in a tuxedo) to show support and understanding of this client's experience in public. Being a part of her outside world was one of the high points for her in our sex coaching relationship. I'll never forget seeing her crowned the "Queen of the Ball" that night and rushing back to our table for the click-click of flashing lights from photographers. That was one "extraordinary" night!

Life coaching vs. sex coaching

Making distinctions between sex coaching and life coaching is also important. Life coaching traditionally uses a Wheel of Life framework as its foundation (Williams & Davis, 2002). Sex coaching uses models such as MEBES© to address what is/is not working and define goals for clients' sexuality or sexual expression that the sex coach can assist the client in attaining. Life coaching emphasizes clients' finding their life purpose, life balance, and rarely considers their sexual fulfillment. Therefore, sex coaching today is not a derivative of life coaching; rather it is a derivative of sexology: "The study of what people do sexually and how they think and feel about it" (McIlvenna, 2012). Sexology is the "what" of sex coaching; and coaching as a skills base for working with the client is the "how".

Dearth of training in sexuality among therapists

Most psychology or therapist-training graduate programs shun the requirement for learning about sexuality, not to mention the skills to elicit the delicate information and know which nuanced questions to ask a client about his/her most intimate details of a sexual life. Even in the liberal state of California the requirement for sexuality training is for 10 hours in an entire pre-licensure graduate therapy program. No wonder so few psychotherapists, have little comfort or skill with sexual concerns of their clients. Lacking training, they feel discomfort in discussing sexual issues or hearing or using sexually charged language and are unaware of the direction to take a therapeutic conversation about sexuality without causing shame, discomfort or fear for themselves. These professionals tend to refer out to a sexologist, sex coach, or other type of sexuality practitioner or simply avert discussions of the sexual aspects of a client's history or situation. This resembles the "donut hole" approach found in practices of licensed massage therapists who are untrained in sexual issues and who avoid touching the breasts, lower pelvic region, and anything that may be construed as sexual touch.

Despite lack of sexuality training, some mental health practitioners step in to the therapeutic sexual arena to attempt to provide services that a sex coach may be more suited to offer the client. The approach is often to define the client's issues as disease-based, relying on DSM5 distinctions to determine billing for insurance purposes (DSM5.org).

CASE: LUISA

Patti writes:

Luisa was a highly educated, wealthy married businesswoman, mother of young child, ready to birth her 2nd, and had just discovered that her husband was having an affair with a co-worker. She presented herself in her first session as unkempt, stressed and low energy, lacking self-confidence and asexual in her interests. She blamed herself for his breach of their bond. "I let myself go, no wonder he strayed. My hair is a mess, I'm going to bed in my sweats to hide my fat body that I hate, and I've avoided him for sex during the whole pregnancy…" she confessed as we began to work. Our work for the first three months revolved at first around her confronting her unhappiness in this marriage, the discovery of his cheating, her desire to return to working full time after baby, a fitness program we designed together, her dedication to changing her diet and exercise habits (the lifestyle switch that often changes everything in a sex coaching client's life) and her disclosure as an afterthought that she had never experienced an orgasm. Eight weeks after the new baby, a newfound determination set in for Luisa to work out, lose weight, get a make over, find a fashion stylist, and resume her career. She began to transform into a sexy woman, with hair extensions, full professional make up, a fitness trainer who motivated her, and a shift in focus away from not being good enough to becoming a better woman. She was determined to find her orgasm whatever it would take. One of the extraordinary parts of our work was my meeting her at a local sex toy boutique to guide her for the best options to buy. That included lubes, lotions, a glass dildo and a set of vibrators for clitoral stimulation, G-spot, vaginal and anal pleasures. She dedicated herself to weeks of solo practice based on our orgasm-directed sex coaching sessions despite being the mom of two demanding children who thrived under the care of her nannies. We went over (1) photography books of female anatomy, (2) self-viewing of her own genitalia, (3) techniques for self-touch with a bodymap to illustrate her erogenous zones, (4) PC exercise guidelines, (5) strategies for discovery of clitoral-vs.-G-spot, vaginal and anal sensitivity, (6) erotic DVDs, and (7) discussions about continual stimulation of the clitoral region with vaginal barbells for the sensations of containment. She boasted in our final few sessions about her orgasms with" Miss Lelo" (her chic vibrator) as she joked about it, and the anticipation to share her newly eroticized body and mind-blowing orgasmic responsiveness with her husband who was making progress in their marital counseling. This was another "extraordinary" coaching client.

The MEBES© model

Traditional therapies and other pathways inspired creation of the MEBES© model: (1) Masters and Johnson's process of sensate focus; (2) common therapeutic approaches including cognitive behavioral therapy (CBT); (3) mindfulness practices, that promoted self-soothing, shifting internal narrative, or other means for assisting clients with negative internal dialogue ("I'm going to lose my erection" or "I'm never going to have an orgasm"); Eastern philosophical influences on this author's own spiritual paths; and increasing knowledge of the role that energies play in the sexual experience. All helped to form the new holistic MEBES© model.

The MEBES© model can be considered as five elements of the sexual self and/or five components of a sexual relationship. It assesses what blocks the person and/or couple in each realm, and then creates specific action steps for each of the five elements, trackable over time. In any or all of the five elements, there may be a blockage for the client or for the client's relationship. Action steps help free those blockages allowing for the person and/or the sexual relationship to find flow. Flow is the inherent goal for the individual and the relationship that MEBES© ferrets out.

Defining the five realms:

M: Mind or mental realm (your thinking about sex/uality)
E: Emotions or feelings realm (your feelings or emotional states about sex/uality)
B: Body or physical realm/body image and behaviors (what you do sexually)
E: Energy (how your sexual or life force energies move, are stuck or blocked within and between you and others)

S: Spirit or spiritual realm (your sense of authentic sexual self; potential spiritual pathways toward sexual self realization and/or sexual ecstasy)
(Britton, 2005).

The MEBES© model is comparable to other holistic models, including the ISIS model of Sexual Experience (Ogden, 2013). It can be conceptualized as a wheel, with E for Energy as the integrative center.

CASE: MARTY AND ZELDA

Patti writes:

Marty and Zelda were an older couple (58/72 years) and professionals working together at a therapy clinic. Married for seven years, they came to sex coaching because they suffered from uneven desire and lack of energy for sex. She never initiated sex, instead waited for him by "playing possum" (as she called it) in bed at night, when the flame of desire lay dormant. He claimed he had "no clue how to read women" and didn't know when or if his wife wanted sex. He had given up on sex, due to a fear of rejection and fatigue from his pace of 24/7 work demands. They were both recovering alcoholics, dedicated to 12-steps, who took regular mini-vacations to decompress and reboot themselves.

MEBES Assessment:

M (Mental assessment): Marty thought that being rejected was not worth the risk of asking. Zelda thought that being older meant that sex was gone and that she was no longer desirable to him. They both believed that asking for sex might rock the marital boat.

E (Emotional assessment): He felt stuck and fearful; he felt slightly resentful and worried that sex might not continue as part of their marriage. She felt too embarrassed to ask for sex and guilty that she didn't have the libido or intensity of orgasm she once had, along with body shame.

B (Body assessment): She hated her body now with sagging breasts, nipple sensitivity, back pain, overwork fatigue. He was exhausted from overworking; he liked his body despite its aging. They loved to cuddle, sex was good when it occurred, and lacked time or energy to begin it.

E (Energy assessment): They both lacked energy for sex; both of them invested energy into work rather than play, with the exception of Sunday mornings that they reserved for relaxation together.

S: (Spiritual assessment) As recovering alcoholics in regular 12-step programs, they believed in Higher Power. They felt strongly about their spiritual connection; they celebrated a divine spark between them. They were dedicated to a spiritual life of serving others.

MEBES Action Plan: (designed over several sessions)

M (Mental action steps): Help them learn how to reframe the "I can't/I'm not desirable enough" thinking for both of them by teaching them mindfulness exercises; encourage him to risk asking her if she's in the mood by being direct; shift the self-deprecating self-talk about her aging body by replacement with self-empowerment, self-soothing messages she can say and write daily; reverse her cognitive resistance to ask to be touched; teach her verbal/non-verbal skills to show him of her sexual interest or receptivity to his sexual invitations.

E (Emotional action steps) Help them both release fear, shame or guilt by providing sample dialogues they can rehearse using a worksheet on processing emotions that is effective in letting the couple exorcise negative emotions while leading back to a loving spirit of connection; help her feel empowered to let go of her childlike attitude of not wanting to ask for sex; teach her a code word she can use without feeling embarrassed :("Quality Time" felt natural to her); engage her in activities that elicit her adult womanly self, such as a make-over at a nearby beauty salon, a wardrobe excursion, and showing her in our session specific ways to walk or talk seductively that invite his response; encourage him to move past his resentment about the sex he is missing with her by journaling about it and sharing his feelings as they change, when they meet in the hot tub on Sundays for their weekly check-in that they initiated.

B (Body action steps) Encourage her to find ways to relax and sensually pamper her physical self, especially having her get manicures and full body nurturing massages weekly at the local spa; help him find rejuvenation to alleviate his fatigue such as joining a Tai Chi group, adding morning meditation to his daily regime and consciously breathing in fresh air each day; encourage more "down" time and less workaholism; show them ways to share affectionate, playful, erotic and/or sexual touch using the Touch Continuum (Britton, 2005) and encouraging them to take classes in sensual massage or join a Tantra massage group; and develop signals for sexual engagement, such as texting, phone messages, coffee dates where they flirt, going to bed in lingerie, selecting romantic tunes for evenings, having them go on regular vacations.

E (Energy action steps): Get them out of the work mode into relaxation; offer energizing strategies, such as exercise, less caffeine, better diet, time to rest and play.

S (Spiritual action steps): Encourage rituals on Sunday mornings for reconnecting; affirm their connection through Higher Power and prayer; show them optional spiritual/sexual pathways, such as exploring Tantric offerings in their own community, starting a singing prayer group (his idea), and finding new means for connection and spiritual exploration, even shamanic training.

After our initial session they coyly reported that this was the first-and-only time in seven years of marriage that they had spoken about sex. They agreed that she could text him the code word "Quality Time" to show her desire for sex with him; they decided to expand their coffee dates and "Getaway Time" each month. They told me after three sessions, that things were working so well they felt like newlyweds and couldn't keep their hands off each other. They were lingering in the car after work to make-out passionately in the driveway. That was an "extraordinary" couple!

The future of sex coaching as a profession:

Sex coaching is in its infancy today. Research studies and promotion to other professionals and to the public are necessary to develop the evolution of this profession. These opinions were echoed by almost every respondent of the survey by Bright and Britton (2013).

Ethical guidelines and standards for the practice of sex coaching are developing worldwide. Initial criteria exist through the World Association of Sex Coaches and the Sex Coaching Certificate Program at the San Francisco-based Institute for the Advanced Study of Human Sexuality. Refinement of standards and ethics for the practice of sex coaching are needed universally to assure that consumers receive competent, proficient, compassionate and qualified care.

Although sex coaching is in its developing stages, it is proving itself as a unique pathway and a complementary option for clients seeking sexual help. Among its signature contributions are the spirit of celebration and the go-ahead for a coach to accompany the client on the journey toward sexual self-realization.

Acknowledgments

We salute the many sex coaches in the world and we are grateful for this opportunity to share our stories.

References

Berry, M. (2012). *Developing the foundations for a multi-modal, psychodynamically-informed biopsychosocial treatment model for male sexual dysfunction* (Unpublished doctoral dissertation). University College London, London, UK.

Bright, S., & Britton, P. (2013). *First international sex coaching survey* (Unpublished paper).

Britton, P. (2005). *The art of sex coaching: Expanding your practice*. New York, NY: W.W. Norton.

Castleman, M. (2004). *Great sex: A man's guide to the secret principles of total body sex*. Emmaus, PA: Rodale Press.

Clemons, R. (2013). Retrieved from www.thecomingoutcoach.com.

Cosmopolitan UK. (2013). Retrieved from http://www.cosmopolitan.co.uk/love-sex/help/.

Foley, S., Kope, S.A., & Sugrue, D.P. (2012). *Sex matters for women, Second Edition: A complete guide to taking care of your sexual self*. New York, NY: Guilford Publications.

Imdb.com. The Sessions. Retrieved from http://www.imdb.com/title/tt1866249/?ref_=sr_1.

Kimsey-House, K. et al. (2011). *Co-active coaching: Changing business, transforming lives* (3rd ed.). Boston, MA: Nicholas Brealey Publishing.

Kleinplatz, P. (2012). *New directions in sex therapy: Innovations and alternatives* (2nd ed.). New York, NY: Taylor & Francis.

Komisaruk, B., Beyer-Flores, C., & Whipple, B. (2006) *The science of orgasm*. Baltimore, MD: Johns Hopkins University Press.

Leiblum, S. (Ed). (2006). *Principles and practice of sex therapy* (4th Ed.). New York, NY: Guilford Press.

McCarthy, B., & McCarthy, E. (2003). *Rekindling desire: A step-by-step program to help low-sex and no-sex marriages*. New York, NY: Brunner-Routledge.

McIlvenna, T. (2012). Lecture at the Erotic Heritage Museum. Las Vegas, NV.

Metz, M., & McCarthy, B. (2003). *Coping with premature ejaculation: How to overcome PE, please your partner & have great sex*. Oakland, CA: New Harbinger Publications.

Morin, J. (2006). Paper presentation. *Therapist—sexological bodyworker collaboration: Considerations and suggestions*.

Ogden, G. (2013). *Expanding the practice of sex therapy: An integrative model for exploring desire and intimacy*. New York, NY: Routledge/Taylor & Francis Group.

Perelman, M. (2003). Sex coaching for physicians: Combination treatment for patient and partner. *International Journal of Impotence Research: The Journal of Sexual Medicine, 15*, S67–S74.

Resnick, S. (2012). *The heart of desire: Keys to the pleasures of love*. Hoboken, NJ: Wiley & Sons.

Schnarch, D. (2009). *Intimacy & desire: Awaken the passion in your marriage*. New York, NY: Beaufort Books.

Stoltzfus, T. (2008). *Coaching questions: A coach's guide to powerful asking skills*. Charleston, SC: BookSurge, LLC.

Williams, P., & Davis, D. (2002). *Therapist as life coach: Transforming your practice*. New York, NY: W.W. Norton.

Zilbergeld, B. (1999). *The new male sexuality: The truth about men, sex, and pleasure*. New York, NY: Random House Publishing.

Sexual healing with Amazonian plant teachers: a heuristic inquiry of women's spiritual–erotic awakenings

Yalila Espinoza

East West Psychology, California Institute of Integral Studies, San Francisco, CA

This article explores how women's sexual/spiritual lives were transformed with sacred Amazonian plant teachers (i.e. plants believed to have spirits that communicate with humans). The research was guided by the belief that the practice of vegetalismo (a South American healing tradition that uses plant teachers for healing) holds important lessons for guiding women's sexual/spiritual lives and possibly for future plant-facilitated psychotherapy for women who have experienced sexual trauma. A heuristic research methodology was utilized involving interviews with seven North American women who participated in ayahuasca ceremonies and plant diets within the Shipibo vegetalista tradition of Peru. The findings highlighted that sexual trauma was healed through energetic purification and openings on the physical, emotional, mental, and spiritual levels. The core themes identified from the data analysis were: purification and support for reproductive health, increased sensory awareness, transforming relationship with self, empowered decision-making, enhanced intimacy with others, increased cognitive awareness, connecting with subtle energies, and connecting with God.

Definition of key terms

The following definitions of key terms were used in this research: shamanism, vegetalismo, plant teachers, plant diets, and eroticism.

Shamanism: In the context of this study, shamanism is defined as an ancient tradition utilizing altered states of consciousness (ASC) to contact spirits and journey between worlds and dimensions of reality (Narby & Huxley, 2001). Shamanic practices involve diagnosing and curing illnesses, communicating with spirits and animals, soul retrieval, transforming positive and negative energies, and divination (Eliade, 1972). Shamans are healers in service of their community who seek to open, balance, and translate energy channels between individuals, groups, and the cosmic source (Halifax, 1979).

Vegetalismo: This term refers to the shamanic mestizo tradition in the Peruvian Amazon where traditional healers, or vegetalistas, ingest plants and enter ASC with the intention of exploring heightened perceptions of nature, animals, and the spiritual world (Luna, 1984). Ayahuasqueros, a type of vegetalista, specialize in the ritual use of ayahuasca as a means for channeling information from the spirit world. There are other vegetalista specialists such as tabaqueros, who use tobacco, and perfumeros, who use various fragrant plants such as agua de florida (flower water) (Beyer, 2009). The Shipibo-Conibo is an indigenous group in the Amazon rainforest in Peru who use plant teachers within the vegetalismo tradition for healing individuals (Arevalo, personal communication, July 1, 2009).

Plant teachers: Believed to possess spirits that communicate with humans, plant teachers can be used to heal physical, emotional, and spiritual imbalances (Dobkin de Rios, 2005). One plant teacher venerated as the grandmother of the Amazonian plant world is ayahuasca, a traditional brew comprising two plants: a vine (*Banisteriopsis caapi*) and a leaf (*Psychotria viridis*). A number of other plants can be added to the brew to complement the effect of ayahuasca, such as mapacho or tobacco (*Nicotiana tabacum*), toe or angel's trumpet (*Brugmansia suaveolens*), and coca (*Erythroxylum coca*) (Castner, Timme, & Duke, 1998). There are dozens of plant teachers used in the practice of vegetalismo that communicate in different ways with the plant drinker depending on the physical, emotional, and mental state of the person and what type of healing they require (Campos, 2011). Each plant has a feminine and a masculine energy; however, the perception of the dominant energy can vary depending on the particular plant drinker. In addition, each plant can take on a motherly or fatherly role to balance the healing energy of the shaman (Arevelo, personal communication, July 1, 2009).

Examples of non-hallucinogenic native plants in Peru are ajo sacha (*Mansoa alliacea*), boahuasca, coca (Erythroxylaceae), and oje (*Ficus anthelmintica*) (Castner et al., 1998). Ajo sacha contains several of the main sulfur compounds that garlic has and is well known and used all over Peru for medicinal purposes. It is used for inflammation and pain of arthritis and for treating colds as well as to ward off evil spirits and to bring good luck. Boahuasca is used for inflammation and to heal cancer of the stomach, intestines, and ovaries. Coca is a mild stimulant that suppresses hunger and fatigue and is a widely used medicinal plant for digestive problems and altitude sickness in many countries in South America. Oje is used for deep purification and curing intestinal parasites and bacteria, and can be used to cleanse someone before they ingest ayahuasca. All of these plant teachers can be ingested alone and some are mixed into an ayahuasca brew.

Plant diet: Within the vegetalismo tradition, the plant diet comprises daily ingestion of plant teachers (as described above), the elimination of salt, sugar, alcohol, and red meat (plus other particular foods), and abstinence from sexual stimulation (Arevalo, personal communication, July 1, 2009). When people are dieting with plants they are drinking the leaves and/or roots and/or flowers of plants that have been brewed into a liquid form. The plants are ingested either in the morning, in the late afternoon before an ayahuasca ceremony, or in the evening before bedtime. The amount of liquid may vary from one tablespoon to one cup depending on the strength of the concoction and the reason for the diet.

The plant diet assists in achieving an ASC that fosters one's receptivity to plant teachings and transmission of power (Luna & Amaringo, 1991). The particular plant chosen by the vegetalista for a diet is one that is best suited to the needs of the individual. Each plant teacher works on many levels and is effective for certain issues. For instance, ajo sacha and pino blanco are known as excellent cleansers on the physical and spiritual levels. Marosa can be very effective with the emotional aspects of the heart, i.e. releasing grief and evoking compassion. Boahuasca can heal physical issues in the area of reproduction. Coca can be used to enhance psychic vision and as an aphrodisiac.

A healing diet is for alleviating physical, mental, and spiritual ailments, and the more rigorous apprenticeship diet is for vegetalista training. Plant drinkers on both types of diets are supervised by a vegetalista, and the diets can range in duration from several days to several years. Traditional diets take place in isolation in the Amazonian jungle; however, a contemporary social diet created by a Shipibo vegetalista allows North Americans to diet in their home environment, so they can continue fulfilling their familial and work obligations. The study focused on women who participated in social diets with both healing and apprenticeship intentions.

Eroticism: The literature includes anecdotes suggesting a connection between plants in the areas of love, sex, and reproduction (Beyer, 2009; Perruchon, 2003; Razam, 2009; Tedlock, 2005). Although some authors allude to the erotic nature of Amazonian plants, there has been no rigorous research conducted on this phenomenon. I was compelled to explore the belief that some plant teachers have sexual personalities and can experience sexual playgrounds within human bodies.

Amazonian plants are used in South America in the areas of sex, love, and reproduction. The various plants available for sale in Peruvian markets to enhance male sexual potency include Levántate Pájaro Muerto (Arise Dead Bird), Siete Veces Sin Sacar (Seven Times Without Pulling Out), and Tumba Hembra (Knock Her Over). A pusanguera, one type of vegetalista who uses plants for love potions, rubs a buceta potion onto a woman's vagina to cause intense pleasure for the male partner during intercourse (Beyer, 2009). Also, annual maca festivals, honoring maca as an aphrodisiac food, take place in towns such as Churin, Peru. The plant piri piri is used for reproductive health to assist women with menstruation, infertility, miscarriages, pregnancy, and pain-free labor and deliveries (Chuquimbalqui, personal communication, June 1, 2009). The plant boa-huasca is used to heal female reproductive organs, and coca leaves – known to be an aphrodisiac – are chewed for calcium by mothers who are nursing their babies.

The energy of ayahuasca has been reported as having an erotic quality. The metaphor of sex has been used to describe ayahuasca as "juices and hormones of plant chemicals and essential essences. It's the sex of the world and its being milked to connect with the cosmic orgasm of the spirit world" (Razam, 2009, p. 91). The metaphor of birth has also been utilized explaining that:

> when we are in the womb of our mothers, we are connected to the placenta, which is for us the universe. When we are born, the umbilical cord is cut. Yage is a new umbilical cord connecting us to the universe. (Luna as cited in Strassman, 2008, p. 101)

Eroticism is defined in this study as the experience of a sexual/spiritual energetic opening or union that is experienced through bodily sensations, emotions, and visions. This may be experienced as a spiritual rebirth that could include an erotic connection between the plant drinker and physical beings such humans, animals, plants, trees, lakes, mountains, moon, planet, and stars, or an erotic connection between the plant drinker and nonphysical beings such as ancestors, deceased spirits, mythic and future beings, elves, giants, and Gods and Goddesses. For example, an erotic experience could be a sexual union with a mythic being during an ayahuasca ceremony or a spiritual union with an animal in dreamtime during a plant diet.

Personal involvement

I began my academic studies inspired to integrate transpersonal experiences and transformational healing with plant teachers into my work as a counselor in reproductive health education and maternity care. I had been immersed in the medical model and it seemed that there were many pitfalls in this system that did not serve the needs of women. My intention was to explore vegetalismo as a healing modality that could enable women with a history of sexual trauma to reclaim their sexuality as a sacred connection with themselves, nature, and the cosmos.

As I went deeper into my own emotional healing and needed to find a research question, I decided to diet in isolation for three months in the Peruvian jungle. A master Shipibo-Conibo ayahuascero opened a diet for me with pino blanco, tobacco, and ayahuasca. On the first day of this diet I asked the plants for guidance for a research topic and in dreamtime I received a clear message to explore sexual perspectives and practices. I realized that the research topic found me once I offered my body as a conduit for the voice of the plants.

Methodology

A qualitative approach that uncovers the meaning of a particular phenomenon, heuristic research "is a way of engaging in scientific search through methods and processes aimed at discovery; a way of self-inquiry and dialogue with others aimed at finding the underlying meanings of important human experiences" (Moustakas, 1990, p. 15). The purpose of this heuristic study was to investigate how erotic experiences with Amazonian plant teachers transformed the quality of women's sexual/spiritual lives. The focus was on female plant drinkers who had erotic experiences during ayahuasca ceremonies or plant diets, two practices within the vegetalismo tradition. In particular, this study focused on the vegetalismo practices of the Shipibo, an indigenous group in the Peruvian Amazon. This investigation was qualitative, used a heuristic methodology, and data were collected through semi-structured, open-ended interviews with seven North American women aged 35–55. This methodology recognizes the participants as equally valuable contributors to the research and therefore refers to the women as coresearchers. Each of the coresearchers was given pseudo names (the seven Pleiadian sisters) to protect their identity.

In heuristic research individual depictions highlight the central themes of each coresearcher's experience. These depictions give the essence of the phenomenon experienced and the meaning ascribed to these experiences by individual coresearchers. Each depiction embodies the key elements using verbatim quotes of each coresearcher's experience of the phenomenon explored in the research study. The individual depictions are not shared in this article; however, an exemplary portrait based on the individual depictions highlighting the essential features of the coresearchers' experience is included.

Results

To explore how erotic experiences with Amazonian plant teachers can transform the quality of the women's sexual/spiritual lives, the individual themes in each of the coresearcher's reported experiences were identified. Once the individual themes were determined, the following eight core themes emerged: purification and support for reproductive health; increased sensory awareness; transforming relationship with self; empowered decision-making; enhanced intimacy with others; enhanced cognitive awareness; connecting with subtle energies; and connecting with God. A core theme was identified if it was a central element for at least 50% of the entire group. These eight core themes represented the experiences of at least four coresearchers and often six or seven of the coresearchers (Table 1).

The findings expressed how physical and emotional purification as well as cognitive and behavioral realignments were necessary for sexual/spiritual healing. The importance of setting boundaries, protecting their energetic space, and exercising assertiveness and discernment in their relationships was highlighted. Once the plant teachers purified the coresearchers' bodies, there was a greater determination to protect this cleansed space

Table 1. Eight core themes.

Core theme	Individual themes included
Purification and support for reproductive health	• Recovering from ovarian cyst • Receiving support during pregnancy and childbirth • Cleansing reproductive system • Reversing the need for a hysterectomy • Transitioning into menopause • Recovering from endometriosis • Purging energy for perpetrator • Clearing the cellular memory of sexual trauma
Increased sensory awareness	• Opening the energy channels • Reprogramming the nervous system • Listening to gut communication • Increasing olfactory awareness • Increasing sexual energy
Transformation of relationship with self	• Honoring self needs • Realizing one's sexual nature • Enhancing trust in self • Increasing creativity • Releasing aggression • Correlating physical pain with emotional mindset • Honoring feminine sexual identity • Recognizing one's own power • Experiencing wholeness of being
Empowered decision-making	• Becoming one's gatekeeper • Developing boundaries with sexual energy • Enhanced discipline • Protecting one's energetic space • Protecting healed parts of self • Listening to intuition • Learning assertiveness and discernment • Releasing identification with sexual trauma
Enhanced intimacy with others	• Recognizing the wounds of others • Feeling love for ceremonial plant drinkers • Healing relationships with men and family members • Abstaining from sexual relations • Enhanced awareness in romantic relationships • Feeling love for husband • Opening heart to a romantic relationship • Using plants as an aphrodisiac
Increased cognitive awareness	• Recognizing sexual behavioral patterns • Calming the mind • Focusing energy with clear intention • Perceiving reality with clarity • Increasing awareness of energy exchange • Learning from challenges • Liberating self-confidence • Expanding capacity to receive plant teachings

(continued)

Table 1. (*Continued*).

Core theme	Individual themes included
Connecting with subtle energies	• Discerning between positive and negative energies • Experiencing sexual unions with animal and plant spirits • Recognizing challenges of transference with subtle energies • Interpreting spirit attacks as sexual seduction • Experiencing a symbiotic marriage with plant spirits • Perceiving dark visions • Experimenting with sexual fantasies
Connecting with God	• Learning how all life is interconnected • Discovering life force as sexual energy • Strengthening communication between one's soul and God

Note: Author's table.

and to be mindful of how they replenished it. I will now describe in more detail how women experienced transformation in the physical, emotional, mental, and spiritual categories.

Physical

Several of the women drank plant teachers with the intention of curing physical reproductive ailments and found that their journey transformed into a spiritual one. The Western medical system had diagnosed three women with ovarian cysts (one of them requiring a hysterectomy) and one woman with infertility. These women reported that they recovered from all of their physical imbalances (confirmed by medical tests) after drinking ayahuasca and other Amazonian plants. The coresearchers stated that they felt physically supported through reproductive phases such as menstruation, fertility, pregnancy, and menopause. One coresearcher shared how dieting plants taught her to be at her edge and thrive in the midst of challenging physical experiences. For instance, she called on the plant spirits for confidence and perseverance during the final labor push as she delivered her baby.

All of the coresearchers emphasized how plant teachers assisted with re-establishing a connection with their bodies. The plant teachers were able to reprogram the nervous system that enabled energy to flow freely throughout the whole body. This recalibration heightened the capacity to receive external information through their five senses. The women commented that because plant teachers cleansed their physical bodies and enhanced their sensitivity, they were more inspired to listen to bodily communication. They also experienced an expansion of sexual energy that felt different from their previous orgasm-centered pleasure. During a diet they raised their vital force through abstaining from all sexual activity that enabled more energy to be circulated and channeled in creative ways.

Emotional

Five of the seven coresearchers were deeply grateful that they were able to release blocked emotions in their bodies stemming from sexual trauma. The coresearchers had visions in ayahuasca ceremonies of their own experience of sexual abuse as well as scenes of sexual trauma within their ancestral lineage. These disturbing sexual visions involved themselves, family members, strangers, and other-than-human entities. Two of the coresearchers described having similar visions involving sex slaves in dungeons. Some of the coresearchers reported being able to witness the sexual trauma energetically being extracted out of their physical body. One coresearcher heard spirit doctors say that they took out the negative energy of her grandfather who sexually molested her as well as several other children.

The quality of the coresearchers' sexual/spiritual lives was interdependent with the emotional quality of all their relationships. They felt that they were shown the truth about their relationships in a revelatory way that inspired them to make significant life changes. An empowered way of choosing healthy relationships required embracing a heightened level of responsibility for their lives. They shared how an aspect of reconnecting with their power included trusting their intuition and acting from this intelligence. Healing familial relationships with mothers, grandmothers, spouses, and children occurred for several of the coresearchers. Women expressed how the plants taught them how to honestly communicate their needs in relationships. One woman left a physically abusive marriage, another divorced her spouse, and another chose to accept a marriage proposal.

Mental

The plant teachers helped most of the coresearchers to see how disempowering decisions, such as choosing to have sexual intercourse with particular partners, lead to a bleeding of their vital energy. There was a greater understanding of how in the past they attempted to fill gaps of self-worth with romantic partners who they knew were inappropriate for them. A key shift in healing sexual trauma for one woman was the ability to accept the archetypes of victim and perpetrator within herself and have compassion for both. The majority of the coresearchers became more disciplined with their patience and discernment before entering into a sexual relationship. They realized how they were sexual beings regardless if they had sexual relations with other people or not. This awareness empowered them to be less dependent on others' judgment of their worthiness as sexual beings.

Spiritual

In the spiritual realm, coresearchers experienced sexual unions with other-than-human beings and plant spirit marriages during both ayahausca ceremonies and plant diets. One union was described as "plants growing out of my uterus and giving birth from my belly button". One coresearcher was able to experiment with her sexual fantasies. She realized that the transformation of her aggressive fantasies (i.e. rape) to erotic merges with subtle energies symbolized the progression of her healing. Coresearchers became more aware of their intimate relationship with God. Connecting with plant teachers became a spiritual practice that awakened a sense of the sacred and a discovery of their own spiritual identity. The necessity of devotion, gratitude, and humility was highlighted in order to be able to connect with the plant world and receive the teachings. They experienced a relaxation in surrendering to a greater creative force that reinforced the continual flow of energy within their bodies and energetic fields. When they learned how to listen to the subtlety of plant teachers they had greater communication with their soul as a portal to God.

Exemplary portrait

In heuristic research an exemplary portrait of a selected coresearcher is provided to represent all the coresearchers as a whole. This portrait is based on the individual depictions including the essential features of the coresearcher's experience as well as demographic and autobiographic information. I include an exemplary portrait of "Maia" to highlight the transformation of sexuality on the physical, emotional, mental, and spiritual levels.

Maia

Maia is a 41-year-old single woman with three children. She has been an elder home care nurse for over a decade. Maia decided to drink ayahuasca in traditional ceremonies in 2006 after witnessing a family member's deep healing process with this Amazonian plant. Over the next six years she participated in over 50 ayahuasca ceremonies, and dieted ajo sacha for six months and marosa for three months.

Maia recognized that her avoidance of healing past sexual trauma was manifesting as addictive self-destructive behavior and poor physical health:

> I knew that the sickness that ruled my life was a sexually oriented sickness. I had endometriosis and pelvic and uterine pain all the time. I was supposed to get my uterus removed and had menstrual cycles where I was bleeding constantly for six months at a time. I had physical sickness that I knew was a result of sexual abuse as a child. . . .Before I started dieting plants I had more partners than I want to mention. There was a ridiculous amount of lack of discretion in sexual partners; men, women, married, unmarried, someone I knew, someone I didn't know. It didn't matter because it was impulsive and the language of seeking. It's the same as seeking drugs and trying anything, LSD, mushrooms, ecstasy. I was seeking but in the wrong direction. I think my sexuality in the past was evidence of how deep my sickness was but also evidence of my desire to be healthy.

After years of marriage Maia realized she could no longer stay in an emotionally and physically abusive relationship with her husband. She left the marriage with the help of her family's emotional and financial support. Maia felt it took her a long time to leave because of an attachment to her victim identity. "There was an identity I had created around being sick with my sexuality that I wasn't ready to let go of yet. There was some victimization that I was hanging onto that took a lot to let go of."

She knew that she desperately needed physical, emotional, and spiritual healing in order to survive. During her first diet with ajo sacha Maia felt a deep spiritual cleaning:

> This particular plant is to clear up baggage and in a ceremony I was shown what I was going to be cleaning up. Some of the visions were extremely disturbing and erotic as well. The images were of vampires, sex slaves, abuse of power, and men and women chained to stone walls in dungeons where they were sex slaves born in this role and they found ways to enjoy the role and play with this power.

Maia clearly articulated how a diet with ajo sacha supported her process of healing sexual trauma in her past:

> There were the times I was molested, abused and raped when I was younger and the generational sickness around sexuality that I carry, that my family carries. It's a cellular memory. So the diet cleared this up and to know what's clean sexuality and what's a misuse of power sexuality. That was the purpose of the diet. There was an identity I had created around being sick with my sexuality that I wasn't ready to let go of yet. There was some victimization that I was hanging onto. Once I processed the shame of being the perpetrator and saw what I was capable of doing I had compassion for both sides. After recovering from what I saw in terms of how sick we can be as humans and I was willing to accept the whole picture the healing happened pretty quickly.

Maia realized how the lens through which she perceived her reality was skewed and how the diet made a significant impact in aligning her with a more harmonious perspective:

> Before the diet I saw everything through multiple layers of sickness. I couldn't tell what was reality, what was insecurity, what was my sickness or what was someone else's. You're looking at something through 15 different lenses and you don't know what's reality even through your intention is to be clear, but you don't know what's clouding what. And post diet it's so much clearer. You know what's yours and what's someone else and you know how to clean it off. You're not looking at past, present, future. You're only looking at the present. There's a huge difference. When you're reacting it's only in the present moment. When your reaction is disproportionate you're dealing with all kinds of cloudy issues. There's a huge difference in how you walk in the world. You're not walking as a damaged 1-year-old, 2-year-old, 6-year-old, and teenager.

After Maia's first diet she became aware of the importance of exchanging sexual energy in a "clean" way:

> I don't think I'll ever be able to be in a sexual relationship with anyone in a carefree way. I'm so much more aware of what it actually means to exchange energy. I won't want to expose myself to someone's energy if they're not clean or there are only a few times when I'm clean enough to expose my energy to someone else. I've abused sexual energy so much and for so long that I'm totally not interested until I know I'm going to be totally clean with it.

Maia found her healing process was a huge relief but that there was some fear in not knowing what to do next. She had to admit to herself that it was necessary to change behavior patterns in order to be healthy and balanced:

> The energetic spaces needed to be healed and I needed to take responsibility for what I was going to put back into those empty spaces. . .learning to not repeat the pattern of filling those spaces with more sickness and learning to guard those spaces and what to put there or how to leave them open.

Maia stated that it was difficult to learn to be her own gatekeeper in staying safe and living in integrity. "It's been a hard lesson, first how to trust, how to trust appropriately, and who to trust. I've learned the hard way to trust my own intuition over other people that I have high respect for."

Maia found that discovering a deeper bodily intelligence during her first diet was an ally in the process of navigating challenging experiences:

> The diet has helped me fine-tune it so when my intuition is talking to me and I'm not listening I will stop everything and figure out what I'm supposed to be listening to. When I have that kind of clarity and discipline it's easily dealt with. When I ignore the gut feeling and I'm busy being angry or distracted it can progress to sickness and more anger. The body ups the ante so the gut ache turns into double-over pain that can turn to into diarrhea and other things. The body will keep trying to get your attention and if you continue to not listen I think it turns into cancer and really deep diseases.

Enhancing her ability to listen to her intuition fostered an opening with spirit:

> The diets have helped me get clear communication between me and my soul. I think that intuition is the dialogue between my earthly self and my soul. . .that there's a dialogue that happens between my higher self and my humanness. My soul is connected to the Great Spirit

> or God so that's the umbilical cord between my humanness and God. There is an actual dialogue that sometimes is in symbols, language and dreams.

Overall Maia feels the plant diets highlighted her longing to be well and enabled her to have greater communication with her soul and God;

> The diet taught me discipline, out of sheer survival how to call for help. Through making the decision daily to stay on the diet it reinforced my decision to heal and be well. It helped me through all the parts that lead me to believe that I deserved to be well. I became stronger because that's the connection to being well, however you define well. What the diet is doing is clearing out space and putting in God, however you define it. So spiritually I had a much richer life because there was more space for God. Ultimately my goal in life is to be more connected with Spirit. All of these feelings of sickness are feelings of home-sickness for God.

Maia's journey with Amazonian plant teachers healed aspects of her sexual trauma that was expressed physically, emotionally, mentally, and spiritually. Maia recovered from endometriosis and her menstrual cycles became more regulated. She left an abusive marriage and energetically began healing sexual trauma in her ancestral linage. Maia learned how to protect her emotional and psychic space and strengthened her connection with God.

Summary

This article reports findings that plant teachers may have been a valuable component of women's healing journey. This was not a standardized quantitative study proving that plant teachers heal women. Some of the coresearchers integrated other healing modalities into their lives before and after dieting plants. Several of the coresearchers began dieting with plant teachers to address physical imbalances; however, they realized that emotional and spiritual aspects were intimately interwoven with their physical ailments stemming from past sexual trauma. Repressed feelings were excavated from their subconscious and shifted to conscious awareness during ayahuasca ceremonies and plant diets. There was recognition of how sexual trauma caused a disassociation from their body and how after drinking plants they had increased awareness of the multiple forms of bodily communication. Along with physical and emotional purification there were cognitive and behavioral realignments that occurred.

The practice of dieting plants was a key pathway to the coresearchers' feeling safe within their bodies and inspired them to honor this feeling in their intimate relationships. The coresearchers were offered the opportunity to see how their reactions were laced with several levels of sickness attached to sexual trauma. After dieting plants they were able to be more in the present and react from their adult consciousness. Body image, sexual identity, sexual behavior, and sexual perceptions were all transformed in a positive way. There was also a shift in releasing cultural taboos around sexuality and embracing a fun and loving perception of sexuality and creativity.

The work in vegetalismo with plant teachers involves energetic realignments and openings that inspire transformation on the physical, emotional, mental, and spiritual levels. The coresearchers shared how the wisdom of ayahuasca and other plant teachers emphasized the importance of the body as the foundation in becoming spiritually embodied. They reported that plant teachers reminded them that they are the embodiment of the divine feminine and that their body is a sacred temple. For these women ingesting plant teachers was an entheogenic-based spiritual practice as a pathway to God.

Women's liberation

Sex therapists may wonder what the applicability of this research study is to their clinical practice. I believe a common intention of all helping professionals is to nurture client empowerment. This study sheds light on how plant teachers can be sexual/spiritual guides and can provide wisdom for therapists about how to be intelligent healers. For example, the coresearchers experienced an opportunity to honor their feminine sexual identity and felt greater trust in knowing they embodied the divine; they learned how to respect this gift by being true to themselves. The unconditional love and subtleness of plant teachers model how human practitioners can nourish a feeling of wholeness for clients. The plant teachers can also show how to assist clients in connecting with deep internal resonances of what it means to be a woman, a mother, a daughter, and a lover.

The coresearchers emphasized the importance of women's power and hopefully therapists hold similar beliefs as they work with their clients:

> Women have been abused and misused for centuries and now we're in a time when women are finding their power. It may not be pretty as women learn how to say "no" and not be connected to victimhood which is the same with all oppressed groups in society. As people find their power they find their intuition and don't allow the victimization to begin. Maia

> If we are empowered sexually, spiritually, mystically, emotionally, and intellectually we have the means to not only protect ourselves and safeguard ourselves from acts of violence, but actually be empowered in power. Until we embrace the feminine principle we'll be entrapped in the cycle of violence. We actually get to develop ourselves as human beings and bring back to life the many parts that have been suppressed by male dominance. It's not power over, it's being empowered – in power. Electra

Closing thoughts

It is with eloquent mastery and mystery that these plant teachers continue to guide spiritual seekers through an enchanting sexual/spiritual transformation. Through a process of purification, heart opening, and remembrance of how one is connected to the spiritual whole, a person can learn to live with integrity and compassion for both human and other-than-human beings. The guidance of plant teachers fosters enhanced self-awareness of one's energetic body and provides deeper insight into one's perception of their health and wholeness. An integration of plant wisdom into daily life can support the sexual/spiritual aspects of individual and community healing. It would behoove healing professionals to contemplate the value of complementary allies such as plant teachers at this particular time in human evolution. I am eternally grateful for the love and spiritual–erotic awakenings I and many other women have experienced with sacred plant teachers.

References

Beyer, S.V. (2009). *Singing to the plants: A guide to mestizo shamanism in the upper Amazon.* Albuquerque: University of New Mexico Press.

Campos, D.J. (2011). *The shaman and ayahuasca: Journeys to sacred realms*. Studio City, CA: Divine Arts.
Castner, J.L., Timme, S.L., & Duke, J.A. (1998). *A field guide to medicinal and useful plants of the upper Amazon*. Gainesville, FL: Feline Press.
Dobkin de Rios, M. (2005). Interview with Guillermo Arrevalo, a Shipibo urban shaman, by Roger Rumrrill. *Journal of Psychoactive Drugs, 37*(2), 203–207.
Eliade, M. (1972). *Shamanism: Archaic techniques of ecstasy*. (W.R. Trask, Trans.). Princeton, NJ: Princeton University Press.
Halifax, J. (1979). *Shamanic voices: A survey of visionary narratives*. New York, NY: Dutton.
Luna, L.E. (1984). The concept of plants as teachers among four mestizo shamans of Iquitos, northeastern Peru. *Journal of Ethnopharmacology, 11*(2), 135–156.
Luna, L.E., & Amaringo, P.C. (1991). *Ayahuasca visions: The religious iconography of a Peruvian shaman*. Berkeley, CA: North Atlantic Books.
Moustakas, C. (1990). *Heuristic research: Design, methodology, and applications*. Newbury Park, CA: Sage.
Narby, J., & Huxley, F. (Eds.). (2001). *Shamans through time: 500 years of the path to knowledge*. New York, NY: J.P. Tarcher/Putnam.
Perruchon, M. (2003). *I am Tsunki: Gender and shamanism among the Shuar of western Amazonia*. Uppsala: Uppsala University Press.
Razam, R. (2009). *Aya: A shamanic odyssey*. Mullumbimby: First Icaro.
Strassman, R. (Ed.). (2008). *Inner paths to outer space: Journeys to alien worlds through psychedelics and other spiritual technologies*. Rochester, VT: Park Street Press.
Tedlock, B. (2005). *The woman in the shaman's body: Reclaiming the feminine in religion and medicine*. New York, NY: Bantam Dell.

Reclaiming women's sexuality: the intersection of Shamanic practices and sex therapy

Linda E. Savage

Private Practice, Vista, CA, USA

This paper delineates a treatment model for healing and empowering women's sexuality co-created by a psychologist and sex therapist and an elder in Shamanic work. The interweaving of perspectives and experience using yoga breathing patterns, movement, guided meditation, Mesa work, and Shamanic ceremony offers new pathways for awakening feminine sexual energy, creativity, and personal power.

Introduction

I have been a practicing psychologist and sex therapist for nearly three decades and some years ago, I began to do Shamanic work which brought new awareness to my therapeutic practice. I was immediately attracted to the deep psychological shifts that I observed by those who participated. Shamanic journey work has the ability to develop awareness of self and the world beyond the limited western model of psychology. Because of this much broader perspective, I recognized the unique potential for healing and empowering women from this expanded awareness since the prevailing culture has portrayed limiting views of women for millennia which has significantly restricted female sexual development (Savage, 2004). As a clinician working with women for many years, I welcome methods that allow women to experience themselves outside "the box" of sexuality as it is defined in our culture.

My creative juices surged when the opportunity arose to co-facilitate a Women's Intensive Weekend with an elder in Shamanic work. I saw a unique opportunity to combine my knowledge about sexuality with experiential Shamanic practices. My co-facilitator, Ro, had 30 years of training and experience in nonlinear awareness practices but had no formal training in my field of human sexuality. I had marginal skills in her world. It was a perfect interweaving of perspectives and experience. Her written comments will be noted throughout this paper in italics.

The participants for this weekend were all women who were part of the extensive Shamanic community to which I belonged. The theme for the weekend was "Energy, Power and Sexuality" and the flyer for the retreat stated:

> Energy, power and sexuality in women are inextricably woven streams. Yet our cultural formatting defines sexuality, even when liberated, as something to be contained until an acceptable act of sex. In such a context, no wonder women struggle with energy and power. Back

> when God was a woman and women were sacred vessels, girls would be sent to the temple to be initiated as a part of their coming of age.* Through breath, movement and story, they would learn to build the inner vessel in order to support the awakening life-streams. Once a girl had opened to and tamed the natural currents that flowed through her body as her own... only then would she be ready to love and experience sexual initiation with a partner. *(Gadon, 1989; Gimbutas, 1981; Redmond, 1997)

Our 10 participants for this weekend had an age range of 34–67. Each woman who enrolled was asked to bring two items: one which represented a part of her sexual story she wanted to let go of or transform and the other which represented a part of her sexual story she would like to keep or expand. This process comes from Gina Ogden's ISIS work and I have found it a powerful way to create a community at the outset as women share their sexual stories (Ogden, 2006, 2013). The following is both a template for on-going workshops and a description of the extraordinary experiences of the event.

The Elements of the Weekend

The Mesa

In Shamanic work, the Mesa, or altar is understood as a dynamic, multidimensional energetic portal that builds power as the participants interact with it. Using the Mesa as a map for organizing areas of experience is a guiding principle for exploring the complexities of sexual stories (Ogden, 2008). Sacred objects are placed on the floor or table which has been covered with woven cloth; it looks similar to a Native American Medicine Wheel. It has separated quadrants for the four directions (North, South, East, and West) with the boundaries of the quadrants delineated in some way. The four elements (Fire, Water, Air, and Earth) are represented by symbols such as a shell for water, a clay pot for earth, etc. Psychological meaning is associated with each element and in this Shamanic tradition, Earth is Body, Fire is Mind, Water is Heart (emotions), and Air is Spirit. The center of the Mesa is known as the place of transformation. As the women place their objects, the Mesa becomes a complex and lovely tableau. Many choose to set their objects across boundaries. Throughout the weekend the array of objects were moved as women shared their insights and their objects developed deeper meaning.

Chaotic Meditation

This involves movements and sounds that literally shake the person free of tension, thoughts, and holding patterns in the body, and prepare the self for quiet meditation. Ro was trained in this form of meditation by various sources (Psychokhemia Institute (http://www.psychokhemia.com/essays/chaotic-or-natural-meditation.html)).

Transformational Movement

This is a healing practice with two parts: one that opens up the chakras (energy centers in the body) and another that clears out stuck energy. Specific breathing patterns, called keys, are blended with freeform movement and sounds for each chakra. As the woman discovers herself in the movement, she becomes aware of the body "speaking," which allows her to listen to herself intuitively and develop trust in her body. Karen Troxell was our guest presenter and the originator of Chakra-based Transformational Movement which grew from Kundalini Shakti Dance (Lilien).

Kundalini Yoga

Kundalini is a Sanskrit term meaning "coiled one" which is a reference to the life force energy that coils at the base of the spine and when awakened, becomes a powerful force for sexuality, creativity, and personal empowerment. One of the main branches of yoga, Kundalini Yoga focuses on the expansion of sensory awareness and intuition in order to raise individual consciousness. For this weekend we used primarily Kundalini breathing and simple stretching in order to open the energy of the body.

Dream Circle

Ro writes:

> This is a women-only ceremony designed to build skills in "Second Attention" or nonlinear awareness. A dream is shared and then the dream stone is passed counterclockwise to the next woman in the circle. The recipient shares what she saw, felt, or intuited while standing in the Teller's dream, then the stone is passed. Each woman explores her experience of the first person's dream until the sharing comes full circle and a round is completed. Then the next dream is shared and we each in turn report. It is not uncommon to have women reporting details of the dream that the teller had forgotten. Dream analysis is counterproductive to the function of Dream Circle; in traditional dream gatherings the old ones hiss should anyone digress. It is a process gifted to me years ago by a family friend, Heather Valencia. A legendary Dreamer, Heather is author of Queen of Dreams (Valencia & Kent, 1993), and the former wife of Yaqui leader Anselmo Valencia.
>
> Some women judge their dreams as nonsense but through the intimacy and presence that the others bring to those dreams, many women find new value intrinsic to those cast off bits of dream. Women learn to use their non-linear awareness which is the same skill that is used to guide in journey space and to track the energetics connecting all things.

Integration

This is a term used in the Shamanic community to refer to a deep sharing the next day after a journey experience. The co-facilitators may choose to work with the person, similar to a "hot seat" approach, or allow the participants to build on each other's experience. Typically, advice giving is discouraged. Our intention for the weekend was to honor the weaving together that occurred with minimal interpretation or advice. The immeasurable trust that developed made it remarkably safe for women to share.

Journey

Journey work is a path of discovery through direct experience with the self in altered states. There are many ways to induce a journey state which can be likened to waking dreaming or an altered state of consciousness. Drumming, humming, chanting, toning with Chakra Bowls made of quartz crystal or bronze, dancing all night and day (such as the Native American Sundance), and ingesting sacred plant medicines are all part of indigenous traditions. The women gathered for the weekend were members of a Shamanic community and they were experienced in sacred plant medicines. The work is supported by clear maps of consciousness and a safe community with shared values of support and acceptance.

Many describe their journeys as heart opening, finding harmony with self, feeling a part of something larger, and redefining the self through a deep encounter with the mystery of life. There is a tendency for journey work to teach at profound levels and it has been described many times as more than a year's worth of therapy in one evening.

The following is Ro's perspective on journey work and plant spirits:

> Nature has provided us many plants offering diverse teachings (Narby, 1999). There are plants that open the heart, peel back memories, and or awaken the spirit, body, or emotional fields (Passie, 2012). Many of these have been studied and tested, they are known to be non-addictive, and produce generally positive human interactions (Hancock, 2013). The Native American church has their Peyote Road-Men, who can administer Peyote. Ayahuasca has been made legal for use in several traditional South American Churches: Santo Daime is one. As an elder in my church (defined as a widespread community of participants sharing a similar philosophy and desire for personal growth), I am trained in the use of these plants. This training is available to those who are interested in learning more about the specific plants and their uses but I cannot be specific in this article. I will say that all women in attendance at our weekend were seasoned in journey work; each woman was included in the plant selection along with considering her intention, her journey history, and any medical factors.

The Setting

The 360-degree views at Ro's property and the gently cultivated grounds allowed a connection to nature; this type of natural setting is extremely helpful in order for women to experience their affinity to the Earth. We created three distinct areas in the home: one was a large area for movement, dance, and journey work. Another area was a ring of cushions and couches with the Mesa set in the middle. The third was the kitchen and patio where we prepared soups, made fresh organic juices, and enjoyed breakfast together on the last morning.

The Energetic Field

When you enter into working with multidimensions, the heart of Shamanic practices, there is an energetic field set in motion that allows for many things to occur outside ordinary experience. As we prepared the space, we began to get messages from the women and realized that strange delays were taking their toll. The plan was to open with the Mesa but because of the importance of everyone participating, Ro offered to lead the Dream Circle Friday night with the seven women who were there.

Ro writes:

> We gathered women in a snugly relaxed nest by the fire and asked them to choose a dream from any time in their lives that had the themes of energy, power, and/or sexuality. Unconscious night musings become resonant empowered reflections by the circle's end. Often with Dream Circle, common themes emerge. This time it was birthing the self and personal potency, both of which were to become major processes in the journey-work the next evening.

The women settled into sleep by 11:00 pm but in the middle of the night, all of us were awakened by a loud tapping sound – some heard three taps, one woman heard five. When we talked about it in circle the next day, a woman we shall call Esther told us that she knew it had to be her mother who had gotten her daughter's attention in similar ways after she had died. When we were discussing the sound each one heard, Esther felt it was an owl's beak tapping loudly on the window, owls being sacred to her mother. Our late arriving participant, whom we will call Saman, was able to tell us it had happened very close to 2:22 in the morning as she had arrived at 2:15 and was just settling in when she heard the noise. Esther's mother had been born on 2 February 1922 and the tapping sound came in the early hours of 2 February. This extraordinary shared experience was one of many community building moments of the weekend.

Saturday

We started the day with Kundalini yoga as a way to begin to energize the life force energy that coils at the base of the spine. The purpose was to help awaken this energy that becomes available for sexuality, creativity, and personal empowerment.

Ro writes:

> This was followed by *Chaotic Meditation*. We began with fast-paced primal drum music, encouraging participants to move and shake their bodies free of tension, thoughts, and no longer needed patterns. After six minutes the music then shifted, melody added to the beat, inviting dancers to articulate feelings, energies, and ideals into movement. As we moved into a third and final track the group settled into stillness and quiet meditation. Even those who had traditionally struggled with meditation were able to slide gracefully into deep quiet of self.
>
> In traditional Shamanic journey work, participants fast or eat lightly on the day of a session, so organic fruits, veggies, and protein powder were available for custom juice blends. The women each chose to add what best supported her own body. With glasses of juice in hand we gathered for Mesa.

Each woman blew her name into the Mesa and lit her candle (Ogden, 2008, 2013); she began her story with the items she brought from home. As the women placed their objects, they told the group how they chose their objects and what each meant. It is always fascinating to see what women bring and how they weave its meaning into their sexual stories. These included loveless marriages, a husband permanently disabled from a brain aneurism, a woman recovering from vulva cancer and multiple surgeries, and many other body image issues as well as rape and incest trauma. The process revealed the incredible courage of these women who chose to join together in the process of healing their sexual energy.

The items continued to take on meaning as they were added to the Mesa. For example, one woman brought a statue of St. Francis to represent the vow of poverty she wanted to release and her monk statue ended up facing a statue of Isis with her baby, Horus, which represented another woman's desire to relinquish mothering so many people. Isis is a goddess of pleasure and St. Francis was the ultimate ascetic, so we decided that they were in conversation with one another about sexuality.

As we shared our stories, the mutual honor and respect was palpable; we knew that the individual experiences represented universal themes for all women. We closed the Mesa session with honoring the Divine Feminine in all her forms and welcoming the life force energy flowing through our bodies.

Ro writes:

> We chose to build the energy on Saturday with breath, yoga, dance, meditation, and juice fasting because these are paths to self that women can duplicate by themselves. Our intent was for the women to access their power and aliveness before taking plant medicine. Taking into consideration that for most women, the path to "opening" is linked with sex which may have been combined with drugs and/or alcohol, we sought to avoid confusion or transference with the ceremonial plants which also open. I know the teacher plants being used Saturday

evening and I trusted them to open the women to a deeper connection with their bodies and their personal power.

The next offering was *Transformational Movement*. Building on knowledge from the Far East, the movement makes use of specific sounds and breathing patterns blended with free-form dance for each chakra. The seven chakras (root – groin, sacral – below navel, solar plexus – high belly, heart, throat, third eye – between the eyes, and crown) have long been considered centers of conscious awareness. Transformational movement opens and clears these centers and allows for a free flow of energy up the spine linking the centers into a cohesive field of awareness. Just about everyone present settled comfortably into a greater field of self.

We had just taken a break following Transformational Movement when a Cooper's hawk flew with a thunderous bang into the eastern glass door of the great room. The hawk lay limply with neck tweaked; by all appearances it was broken. Esther raced to slide the door open and grab the bird before Chester, the cat who had been outside to hear the sound, claimed his prize.

One woman in our group was an avian biologist and came out to examine the bird. As she turned over the hawk, it came to, dug in her talons to get perched upright and flew away. The two women who had had the speed and courage to help this magnificent bird shared a powerful process later that evening in journey space.

After the break, we gathered for Q&A on feminine sexuality and how it connects to our energy and power. For 2 hours we discussed whatever the women wanted. We framed the meaning of sexuality as our life force energy rather than as a genital act and emphasized the importance of this energy for creative expression (Wolf, 2012). The women asked questions that ranged from the basic mechanics of passion and orgasms to abstracts like perception of self as a sexual being. The factual information about women's physiology, neural pathways, and sexual anatomy and functioning is an essential component to empowering women. The participants became increasingly aware of the disempowerment that comes from being cut off from their sexual energy and of their desire to follow pathways to reconnection.

It is challenging to create the sense of safety for women to express what is in their hearts: to talk about their secrets and deepest yearnings. Perhaps it was the mysterious events that bonded the group or the exercises that relaxed them but the women were able to move very deep into feeling. Their stories became more revealing, self-disclosure more vulnerable, and the energetic mapping with Mind/Heart and Body/Spirit more embedded. Many universal themes were explored, helpful information provided, and tears were shed. It was an excellent entry for the journey night ahead.

Setting *intention* is traditional among the Shamans in the USA and the Peruvian and Brazilian Rainforest and may come in the form of a prayer, or in simply stated words, as was our way for that evening. When the women spoke their words of power around the Mesa, additional layers of meaning emerged and our collective intention was to support each woman's intent.

Ro passed out the spirit plants (prepared in gel capsules) that had been individually chosen with regard to each woman's intention and journey history. We said a prayer for a good journey and the women swallowed the capsules with a drink of water. Water bottles are essential and were at each woman's side. Throughout the night, the facilitators made sure each participant was well hydrated.

The women settled into their pads and blankets on the main floor as they waited for the expanded state to gently wash over them. With music in the background, I led the group in a guided meditation created to help women further awaken the Kundalini energy. The combination of breathing, pelvic rocking, and imagery allowed their bodies to access this deeper awareness. The script for this meditation is available upon request from lindasavagephd@goddesstherapy.com. Spiritual music maintained the uplifted feeling in the room as they waited for the journey to deepen.

Within half an hour, I went to check on one of our women, whom we shall call Amy, who was experiencing intense discomfort and tension in her body. I motioned Ro over and she sensed that Amy's energetic pattern appeared similar to labor contractions. The metaphor felt right so Ro tested her theory by having Amy bear down as if pushing in the act of birthing. Sure enough she stopped writhing and then, even though she had never given birth to a child, Amy settled into the work of birthing with fairly rhythmic contractions.

Amy was encouraged to breathe and push and several other women surrounded her to help her lift her shoulders and bend her knees in order to push. From an angel on the ceiling it would have looked and sounded for all the world like a birthing scene. The helping women, whom we dubbed "the Doulas," pushed and roared with her – deep guttural sounds – that truly moved her energy. They continued to help her make sounds and movements until she finally felt she had birthed herself.

Here is Amy's description of her experience, written a few days later:

> First, I want to thank all of you for holding such a gentle safe space for my birthing. For the first time in my life I feel my life is actually my own. Your love and support for me physically, emotionally and energetically was exquisite. I really don't think I could have done it without all of your love to hold and envelop me. Thank you for loving me through my messy needy process. It was a little strange to be a 51 year old infant, but better now than never & I am now emotionally maturing at a pretty fast clip. Each of you offered gifts from your heart that I will always treasure. Thank you for enriching my heart with your love!

Although Amy was worried that too much time was centered on her process, during the integration on Sunday, each of the "Doulas" described how powerful the experience was for her own expanded awareness. After this birthing and throughout the night women continued to go within or to move about, relating to other women, sharing stories, experimenting with playful movement, and holding space for each one in her turn. One woman whom we shall call Miriam wrote:

> For me the experience reminded me of the importance of bonding with the feminine energy. I have not bonded well with the feminine, in myself or in others. I came away with a huge desire to connect with the feminine. If I could paint the picture of what that looks like for me:, it would be women coming together in a puppy pile just sharing in laughter and tears.

Ro writes:

> Years ago, while pregnant with my son, my mind freaked when it realized that I did not know how to make a baby but the body did it anyway. Guiding is a lot like that. A guide must be comfortable in not knowing and in holding space. Much like standing in the dream of another without pretext or agenda, to guide is to be so present with another that the world becomes translucent and only the energetic web that connects everything is left. Once in the field, one can look around and "see" or "feel" the wholeness of a person and map her backwards. This usually looks like just the right question popping in that once asked and answered from the client's journey self can form new ground and enhance the woman's ability to shape her experience.

As the journey energy was cooling, I checked on everyone: all was well in journey land. A couple of women called me over, as they were not in as deep as they would like to be and thought they should take another capsule. Rather than add more, I helped them to go deeper since the point with a journey is to find new paths to self. I lay down between them, taking each by the hand. I knew that Miriam had been shadowed in loss and sadness for some time. The other, whom we shall call Chloe, was a brainiac research biochemist in need of a holiday from mind. I asked if they wanted to visit the land of Fairie (which is a dimension of Earth spirits). They both said yes and were hopeful.

Dimension-hopping is easier when journeyers are in deep. I explained to them that in order to shift dimensions, one must energetically dial it in, like the tuner on a radio. I told them that to dial in the dimension of Fairie, the price of admission is pure joy. Chloe had a fabulous toddler son at home and was quickly able to dial in her joy by thinking of him. Miriam had to work to find the feeling of joy, eventually going back to before her father was killed in Vietnam when she was three. Once Miriam accessed this earlier innocence, she had a big smile. From the look on her face I'd say it was her first return to joy since she lost her father and was subsequently molested by her stepfather. Miriam had told this part of her sexual story during the Mesa process and had described the shadow of depression that followed her throughout her life. If nothing else happened I knew that Chloe and Miriam already felt joy… which is its own point of arrival!

I found the dimension of Fairie as a kid and never lost the trail in, so I began to generate the doorway that lives in me, hoping that Chloe and Miriam were still enough "in" to track. I opened my eyes and checked to see if they were following. Chloe had her eyes closed and had the biggest grin I've ever seen on her. She later shared her visions of fabulous adventures in sprouting wings, becoming a butterfly, and sipping dew from flowers. It interested me that she had no doubt that she could find her way back. The spirit plants are good that way; they make sure you mark the trail and can return to places of value. Looking at Miriam, I saw a little girl with the sweetest smile of pure enchantment!

Esther's journey took her into the dimension of her very anxious one-and-a-half year-old self with the temperament of a wounded animal. Not trusting to be in the big, noisy room, she retired to her own bedroom in the house. Both Ro and I checked on her from time to time, knowing that she was an experienced journeyer who had safely navigated this dimension many times. Towards the last half of the evening, the avian biologist, whom we shall call Sally, came to tell us Esther needed her sparkly bracelet. Sally remembered that her hawk rescue compatriot had placed it on the Mesa to signify that she wanted to expand her "Sassy Self." We immediately sent Sally to bring the bracelet to Esther. We did not hear the story until integration the next day but Sally, who had extensive experience in the field working with wild animals, was able to meet Esther in her one-and-a-half-year-old dimension and slowly but surely win her trust, just as she would a frightened animal. It was a profound experience for both women and their mutual sharing at integration was filled with laughter as they told the story from each one's vantage point. Sally wrote:

[The weekend] created this amazing feeling of connection to everyone else, and that feeling of connection is something that is frequently missing or difficult for me to tangibly feel. It helped me to trust myself enough to reach out to Esther during her process, something that was so completely out of my comfort zone because a) I didn't know her and b) she was already in what appeared to be a very fragile and fearful place that I didn't want to hurt her in any way. Yet, in just relaxing and going with the process, we created this awesome bond together and really connected, even though we were both (I think) scared out of our wits about what we were doing and didn't know what came next. It was a chance for me to not get scared and just run away, but to hang in there with another person, to honor and respect

> where she was and yet find a way to be with her simply because I was feeling so much love and compassion for her and wanted to be there for her so she wasn't alone in her fearful place. In the process, it had nothing to do with me, and yet everything to do with me. It created this really cool cycle of energy and I was able to completely let go and have some fun with it. I am so thankful for our time together. In doing this in the safety of the space we created, it has helped me to bring this into my relationship with [my fiancé].

After midnight, most of the women were ready for the chicken soup we had prepared the day before and many wandered out to the dining patio, wrapped in blankets and ready to share or just to enjoy the beautiful surroundings, lighted by the stars and a last quarter moon. By then Saman, whom we fondly referred to as "the teenager of the group" (though she was 34) came out of her room and shared her most remarkable story. Having emigrated as a girl from Iran, her previously privileged family had made its way through different countries until finally being granted asylum in the USA to start over again. Saman had left home at the age of 15 and after many harrowing experiences with her rebellious nature, managed to finish high school and go to community college while holding down two jobs.

That night was the first time during this weekend that she had revealed anything about herself below the surface and Saman told us the next day that it always took a great deal for her to trust anyone. As it turned out, she was very intuitive. After this powerful entrance into our weekend Saturday night, she was able to speak to each woman during the integration the next day and accurately read each one's energy.

Sunday

We practiced Kundalini breathing once more in the morning and after a sumptuous breakfast, gathered for the final time at the Mesa for *Integration*.

By now, there were many bonds and all had found a sense of inclusion. Amy, the one who had given birth to herself, was emotionally tender and raw. She was hesitant to give her emotions free reign yet everyone extended love to her. It was the universal mother energy finding expression as each woman found a special time to hold Amy. Because of the group's collective experience with journey work, women were not trying to fix her. They instinctively knew that gentle loving and acceptance were the powerful healing agents she needed.

Amy apologized for not sitting up and talking at the Integration. She said, "It isn't easy being a baby, we are so needy." Yet as I told her "it's okay to be needy," it was a message for all of us: that in a safe place of open-hearted women, we can let down the burden and be held by one another.

By midday Sunday, as the women reclaimed their Mesa items during Integration, they were not just telling individual stories, they were weaving themselves into new patterns that would continue to activate within them as the days, weeks, and even months would unfold. As it happened, the birthing journey paved the way for Amy to be with her previously estranged mother a few weeks later as she breathed her last breath. In response to an email Amy sent to all the women, telling this story, a woman we shall call Diana wrote:

> For all of us who made the decision – heeded the invitation that came to many – to gather that amazing weekend, this was a life-giving time together. [Amy's] experience may be the most dramatic, while at the same time; it is a manifestation of changes that occurred for all of us. We have to wonder how her experience of her mother's death might have been, had she not

> experienced the death of what had not served her or her mother, and her own rebirth. I have to believe that the loving, courageous work you have allowed had to be very healing for your mother as well.
>
> This is coming to you from [Hawaii], the place that has meant so much to so many of us. You and all of us have been on my mind and in my heart this entire time, actually since we were together, but especially here. The healing that I experienced with you has flowed into an unparalleled time with [my husband] these past few days. All of the experiences we shared seem to be at the cellular level – my body is cell-abrating. OK, lousy pun, but I hope you can feel my gratitude and love.

At the very end of integration, I made a circle with my arms, encompassing the energetic field that we had opened and played in, deepening our connection with one another. I said, "This is the Divine Feminine and we are not only healing ourselves but we are helping heal the masculine as well." I told the group that reconnecting to our energy, power, and sexuality accesses both our strength and vulnerability, allowing us to express our creative energy in new ways.

In summary, the intersection of Shamanic practices and right brain sex therapy techniques such as movement, breath-work, pelvic rocking, guided imagery, and meditation offered an extraordinary opportunity to raise awareness of energy pathways for sexuality, trauma release, feminine creativity, and personal power. Working with multiple dimensions set the field for the participants of this weekend to enter into deep experiences of Kundalini energy and also set the field for optimal experiences with expanded states of consciousness. Although this weekend was unique in terms of the natural setting, an established community of participants, and collaboration with my co-facilitator Ro, it holds lessons for therapists working on their own in other settings, with different clients and using alternate forms of journey induction such as drumming, chakra bowls, or dance.

Framing sexuality as energy, rather than a set of behaviors, removes the performance-based definitions that have held women accountable to live up to cultural images focused on pleasing the partner. In shifting the attention away from the "other" as reference and using "self" as reference, the context in which women judge themselves dissolves. This model allowed participants to experience their energy through breath, work, movement and guided imagery, reconfiguring pathways that connect to sexuality. Journey opportunities can be accomplished through simple rhythmic drumming (Ingerman, 2004) and can unite these experiences into holistic knowing.

The use of symbolic representations, such as the objects placed by each woman on the Mesa greatly can enhance self-understanding (Ogden, 2013). Offering the framework of Mind/Heart, Body/Spirit adds many layers to women's narratives and may interrupt stories that are stuck. For example, the meaning of the St. Francis statue evolved over the time and multiple spaces in the Mesa, creating surprising sharing opportunities. The combination of symbolic representations and an expanded framework can help participants "feel into meaning" or sense a change rather than simply reporting a story in linear fashion.

Sharing in groups where emotional safety is developed over several days creates a sustained momentum. The presentation of a beginning story can be likened to dipping one's toes into water. Practicing exercises to enhance the participant's awareness of her energy centers can be likened to feeling the water, breathing, and becoming comfortable with the temperature, and then entering deeper into the water as the feeling of comfort grows. Finally, releasing blocks and allowing energy to move freely can be likened to swimming, fully aware of senses, emotions, and expanded connections to self. This sustained momentum can set the stage for profound and instant shifts.

Experiential learning has great power and once the woman's story is explored, it is the experience with her own energy that allows her to move into wholeness; the body fully alive to sensing, the mind noting and recording the experience, the emotions becoming more freely expressed, and the spirit felt as connection to expanded inner joy or whatever else needs to be explored, released, and embraced.

References

Gadon, E. (1989). *The once & future goddess*. San Francisco, CA: HarperOne.
Gimbutas, M. (1974). *The goddesses and gods of Old Europe*. Berkeley, CA: University of California Press.
Hancock, G. (2013). TEDx talk "The War on Consciousness". Retrieved from http://vimeo.com/61941401
Ingerman, S. (2004). *Shamanic journeying*. Boulder, CO: Sounds True.
Narby, J. (1999). *The cosmic serpent*. New York, NY: Jeremy P Tarcher/Putnam.
Ogden, G. (2006). *The heart and soul of sex*. Boston, MA: Trumpeter Books.
Ogden, G. (2008). *The return of desire*. Boston, MA: Trumpeter Books.
Ogden, G. (2013). *Expanding the practice of sex therapy*. New York, NY: Routledge.
Passie, T. (2012). *Healing with entactogens*. Santa Cruz, CA: Multidisciplinary Association for Psychedelic Studies.
Redmond, L. (1997). *When the drummers were women*. New York, NY: Three Rivers Press.
Savage, L. (2004). *Reclaiming goddess sexuality* (Revised ed.). Encinitas, CA: Divine Feminine Publications.
Valencia, H., & Kent, R. (1993). *Queen of dreams*. New York, NY: Fireside Press.
Wolf, N. *Vagina: A new biography*. New York, NY: HarperCollins.

OPINION PIECE

In praise of "ordinary" sex therapy

Pam Henderson

Private Practice, Cambridge, Cambridgeshire, United Kingdom

Introduction

I was struck by the call for contributions for this special issue that asserted that most sex therapy models focus on diagnosing and treating dysfunctions, rather than exploring sexual health and pleasure. It requested "innovative" approaches and models that "expand the conversation about sex beyond measurable outcomes" and labelled such sex therapy "extraordinary". In this opinion piece, I would like to make the case for "ordinary" sex therapy, practised by hundreds of my colleagues in the UK; a way of working that regards exploring pleasure and treating dysfunctions as fundamentally compatible rather than mutually exclusive; a model that is not "innovative" by any means, but is grounded primarily in cognitive behavioural therapy (CBT) theory and encourages flexibility and creativity from all parties. Clients can find this process useful, satisfying, productive, rewarding, transformative and sometimes "extraordinary".

Exploring pleasure and treating dysfunctions

In my experience, clients do not arrive with a goal of "I'd like to explore sexual and erotic intimacy with my partner" or "I want to discover pleasure and optimal sexuality". They say things like "I want firm, reliable erections", "I want pain-free sex" or "I have to start wanting sex or he'll leave me". They have frequently made a diagnosis that makes sense to them before they come to see us. They (or someone else) may even have named it. Their goal is usually symptom reversal. They perceive themselves as having a dysfunction, and they want it treated. To ignore this client goal ("let's not bother with erections, let's focus on pleasure and erotic intimacy") would be unethical – we have a basic duty to respect the autonomy of clients and their right to self-determination (College of Sexual and Relationship Therapists [COSRT], 2012) – and it would make the building of any meaningful therapeutic relationship close to impossible. The problems with using diagnostic labelling with clients has been well documented (Barker, 2011; Tiefer, 2004). Fortunately, sex therapy offers a potential resolution to this tension, namely, a process in which client goals can shift as their understanding of themselves, their relationship(s) and the impact of their cultural contexts evolves. The history taking process, seeing a client individually for one or two sessions, is an opportunity for guided discovery (Padesky, 1993) where the client can explore and respond to ideas around pleasure, intimacy and eroticism. If we accept that sexuality is a social construct (Tiefer, 2004), then sex therapy can be an invitation to explore a different meaning for sex. Thus when goals are revisited at the formulation stage, it becomes possible to hold onto the original goal of "I want firm, reliable erections", and introduce other goals linked to optimising sexuality (Kleinplatz, 2012) such as "I'd like to feel closer to my partner, and for sex to be more fun and pleasurable". Indeed, in my own practice clients may reach the end of therapy with a sexual relationship they might joyfully describe as "intimate, erotic and pleasurable", yet according to DSM guidelines one or both of them still has a "sexual disorder".

There is an important caveat here: as therapists, it is vital that we acknowledge that we are not working from a neutral position. Like our clients, we are a product of our own cultural contexts and are in the powerful position of using language to shape a new narrative with our clients (Shotter, 1993). Acknowledging and respecting difference is at the heart of working ethically, and for some clients the idea of sex for pleasure may be viewed as immoral (Hall & Graham, 2013), or just not a priority. In such cases, goals may remain focused on symptom reversal throughout therapy.

A theoretical framework

In my introduction I stated that I am making the case for "ordinary" sex therapy that is grounded primarily in CBT theory. Despite its behavioural origins, sex therapy is often criticised for its lack of theory and apparent eclecticism (Hertlein & Weeks, 2009). This may not matter. Meta-analyses by Norcross and Wampold (2011) into evidence-based therapy relationships shows that it is the therapeutic relationship itself that makes the most substantial and consistent contribution to the outcome of therapy, rather than the specific type of treatment. However, the criticism about lack of theory in sex therapy may not be accurate either. Like many of my UK psychosexual colleagues, I was trained by the Relate Institute to use the CBT model as my primary theory in sex therapy. Building on the work of Beck (1976), the theory is that what we do has a powerful influence on our thoughts, emotions and somatic responses, and vice versa (Padesky & Mooney, 1990). When possible and appropriate, I will work with both partners together not just because there is no such thing as an "uninvolved partner" (Masters & Johnson, 1970), but because sex is frequently another way in to the couple relationship – sexual and couple difficulties are often inter-twined and inter-related. The resolution of one can be dependent on, or sometimes exacerbated by, the resolution of the other and will often benefit from incorporating systemic and psychodynamic approaches

Norcross and Wampold (2011) identified four other effective aspects of therapy: collecting client feedback, goal consensus, collaboration and positive regard. These are all core elements of a CBT approach to sex therapy. CBT is a transparent process where the clients and therapist go on a collaborative voyage of discovery; where the clients become their own therapists: they become curious about their thoughts and feelings and become motivated to change. In treatment, clients can experience relational and individual change. These changes encourage clients to ask more of their sexual and couple relationship, to hope for more than mediocre sex. Their increased confidence means that they assume these changes can be achieved; and the more the clients become their own therapists, the more likely this becomes. This can be a powerful, transformative and even extraordinary process.

We have an ethical responsibility to remain clinically competent and fit to practise (COSRT, 2012), regardless of the way in which we choose to work with clients. I suggest that this includes a moral responsibility to be able to explain the theories that inform our work using everyday language. We need to be able to explain why we choose to work this way, and what evidence there is to support it. CBT is a modality for which the evidence base is strong (Butler, Chapman, Forman, & Beck, 2006), although I realise that the research methodologies used will assume everyone with the same diagnosis is the same as each other and that all therapists are the same.

Conclusion

In this opinion piece, I have sought to demonstrate that the foundations of "ordinary" sex therapy are a strong ethical stance underpinned by a clear theoretical framework. As such, "ordinary" sex therapy can explore sexual pleasure and treat dysfunctions simultaneously; it can explore relationship dynamics and at the same time aspire to measure performance outcomes. It is the clients themselves who make the work extraordinary.

References

Barker, M. (2011). Existential sex therapy. *Sexual and Relationship Therapy, 26*(1), 33–47.

Beck, A. (1976). *Cognitive therapy and the emotional disorders*. New York, NY: International Universities Press.

Butler, A.C., Chapman, J.E., Forman, E.M., & Beck, A.T. (2006). The empirical status of cognitive-behavioral therapy: A review of meta-analyses. *Clinical Psychology Review, 26*, 17–31.

College of Sexual and Relationship Therapists. (2012). Code of ethics and practice for general and accredited members [Online]. Retrieved from http://www.cosrt.org.uk/documents.asp

Hall, K., & Graham, C. (2013). *The cultural context of sexual pleasure and problems*. New York, NY: Routledge.

Hertlein, K.M., & Weeks, G.R. (2009). Towards a new paradigm in sex therapy. In K.M. Hertlein, G.R. Weeks, & N. Gambesica (Eds.), *Systemic sex therapy*. New York, NY: Taylor and Francis.

Kleinplatz, P.J. (2012). *New directions in sex therapy: Innovations and alternatives*. New York, NY: Routledge.

Masters, W., & Johnson, V. (1970). *Human sexual inadequacy*. London: Churchill.

Norcross, J.C., & Wampold, B.E. (2011). Evidence-based therapy relationships: Research conclusions and clinical practices. *Psychotherapy, 48*(1), 98–102.

Padesky, C. (1993, September). *Socratic questioning: Changing minds or guiding discovery?* Invited keynote address delivered at the 1993 European Congress of Behavioural and Cognitive Therapies, London. Retrieved from http://padesky.com/newpad/wp-content/uploads/2012/11/socquest.pdf

Padesky, C.A., & Mooney, K. (1990). Clinical tip: Presenting the cognitive model to clients. *International Cognitive Therapy Newsletter, 6*, 13–14.

Shotter, J. (1993). *Conversational realities: Constructing life through language*. London: Sage.

Tiefer, L. (2004). *Sex is not a natural act and other essays*. Boulder, CO: Westview Press.

Index

For Product Safety Concerns and Information please contact our EU representative GPSR@taylorandfrancis.com Taylor & Francis Verlag GmbH, Kaufingerstraße 24, 80331 München, Germany

Batch number: 10726294

Printed by Printforce, the Netherlands